Ageing and Income

FINANCIAL RESOURCES AND RETIREMENT IN 9 OECD COUNTRIES

ORGANISATION FOR ECONOMIC CO-OPERATION AND DEVELOPMENT

ORGANISATION FOR ECONOMIC CO-OPERATION AND DEVELOPMENT

Pursuant to Article 1 of the Convention signed in Paris on 14th December 1960, and which came into force on 30th September 1961, the Organisation for Economic Co-operation and Development (OECD) shall promote policies designed:

- to achieve the highest sustainable economic growth and employment and a rising standard of living in Member countries, while maintaining financial stability, and thus to contribute to the development of the world economy;
- to contribute to sound economic expansion in Member as well as non-member countries in the process of economic development; and
- to contribute to the expansion of world trade on a multilateral, non-discriminatory basis in accordance with international obligations.

The original Member countries of the OECD are Austria, Belgium, Canada, Denmark, France, Germany, Greece, Iceland, Ireland, Italy, Luxembourg, the Netherlands, Norway, Portugal, Spain, Sweden, Switzerland, Turkey, the United Kingdom and the United States. The following countries became Members subsequently through accession at the dates indicated hereafter: Japan (28th April 1964), Finland (28th January 1969), Australia (7th June 1971), New Zealand (29th May 1973), Mexico (18th May 1994), the Czech Republic (21st December 1995), Hungary (7th May 1996), Poland (22nd November 1996), Korea (12th December 1996) and the Slovak Republic (14th December 2000). The Commission of the European Communities takes part in the work of the OECD (Article 13 of the OECD Convention).

Publié en français sous le titre :
Vieillissement et revenus
Les ressources des retraités dans 9 pays de l'OCDE

© OECD 2001
Permission to reproduce a portion of this work for non-commercial purposes or classroom use should be obtained through the Centre français d'exploitation du droit de copie (CFC), 20, rue des Grands-Augustins, 75006 Paris, France, tel. (33-1) 44 07 47 70, fax (33-1) 46 34 67 19, for every country except the United States. In the United States permission should be obtained through the Copyright Clearance Center, Customer Service, (508)750-8400, 222 Rosewood Drive, Danvers, MA 01923 USA, or CCC Online: *www.copyright.com*. All other applications for permission to reproduce or translate all or part of this book should be made to OECD Publications, 2, rue André-Pascal, 75775 Paris Cedex 16, France.

FOREWORD

This report provides, for the first time, a comparable picture of the material well-being of older people in Japan and in a range of European and North American countries – and of the significant but often indirect ways in which those living standards are influenced by public policy. The findings are often surprising and, at least on the surface, paradoxical. For example, the real level of well-being among older people in all the countries is quite similar, despite large differences in the size of public and private pensions.

New data paint a picture of retirement income systems that are more complex, and resilient, than is usually taken into account in policy analysis. The figures illustrate the importance of household living arrangements and the income of other family members in addition to the income of older people themselves. They point to the importance of disability and unemployment benefits as well as pensions as part of the system of resources available to the "younger" old. Taxation and assets must also be taken into account to understand the relative economic position of older people.

The analysis points to a convergence of outcomes among the nine countries in terms of the material living standards of older people, but also much diversity – possibly growing diversity – in institutional arrangements and approaches to policy. It shows that policies have, on most counts, been successful in meeting their fundamental goals. When people retire today, they typically enjoy material living standards that are at least as high as when they were working. That very success, however, makes new reform difficult. And further reform is needed.

The analysis confirms earlier OECD findings that the key challenge for policy is a growing imbalance between the time people spend in work and the time they spend in retirement, imbalance that will become worse as a result of population ageing and the coming retirement of the baby-boom generation. Labour force and demographic trends compound to heighten the challenge. Although there has been a recent stabilisation, and even a reversal, of long-standing trends towards early retirement, policy action is still needed. The major incentives to early retirement in pensions and other income support programmes need to be modified. Even quite modest reform could have large effects. By exploring and contrasting the experience of nine diverse systems, the report explores how this could be done without undermining income security.

A report of this richness could not have been prepared without the active assistance of officials in the nine countries. Japan played a major role in initiating the project and in its funding. All countries contributed by providing information, often including new data and by reviewing successive drafts of this paper. A number of participating countries were also able to make important additional financial contributions to the project. The work was undertaken by a team in the Social Policy Division, headed by Peter Scherer, of the Directorate for Education, Employment, Labour and Social Affairs. The team was led by Peter Hicks and included Monika Queisser, Bernard Casey, Atsuhiro Yamada, Bettina Kashefi, Maxime Ladaique and Victoria Braithwaite. Juan Yermo, of the Directorate for Fiscal, Financial and Enterprise Affairs, contributed the work on the operation of private pensions. The work of Atsuhiro Yamada in analysing the income data and of Edward Whitehouse in modelling pension and tax rules was critical to the success of the project. Independent work by the Economics Department on age-related fiscal projections, led by Howard Oxley and Pablo Antolin, has also been integrated into the report. This book is published on the responsibility of the Secretary-General of the OECD.

© OECD 2001

TABLE OF CONTENTS

Chapter 1. **Summary and Key Points** ... 9

1.1. Structure of the report ... 9
1.2. The economic well-being of older people: a success story ... 10
1.3. The three challenges ... 10
1.4. Country-specific conclusions ... 15

Part I
CONVERGENT OUTCOMES, DIVERGENT MEANS

Chapter 2. **The Resources of Older People: Complex Systems and Successful Outcomes** ... 21

2.1. Introduction ... 21
2.2. Success in meeting earnings-replacement objectives ... 22
2.3. Success in meeting the goal of preventing low incomes in old age ... 24
2.4. Why older people can have similar incomes in all countries, despite widely differing levels of public support ... 27
2.5. How income streams get converted into economic well-being ... 30
2.6. Combinations of work, public pensions and private pensions ... 35
2.7. The relation between income sources, levels and distributions ... 38
2.8. The role of consumption and wealth, especially housing assets ... 40

Notes ... 45

Chapter 3. **The Determining Role of Public Policy** ... 47

3.1. Introduction ... 47
3.2. Modelling pension and tax rules – a better approach to cross-country comparisons ... 48
3.3. Statutory entitlements vary considerably ... 50
3.4. Non-statutory occupational pension benefits ... 54
3.5. Tax treatment and net replacement rates ... 55
3.6. The experience of the individual countries ... 58

Notes ... 64

Chapter 4. **The Need for Reform** ... 67

4.1. Introduction ... 67
4.2. The projected results of recent reforms ... 67
4.3. Potential effects of further reform ... 69
4.4. The scale of the challenges in the nine countries ... 70

Notes ... 73

Part II
A COMPARISON OF POLICY RESPONSES TO KEY RETIREMENT INCOME CHALLENGES

Chapter 5. **Reforms to Re-balance Work and Retirement** ... 77

5.1. Introduction ... 77
5.2. The potential for major increases in effective retirement ages ... 78

© OECD 2001

5.3. What can countries do?	83
5.4. Pension ages	85
5.5. Repairing work incentives in pensions – linking benefits and contributions	86
5.6. Closing or restricting pathways to early retirement	88
5.7. Gradual pathways to retirement	91
5.8. Promoting a workforce for all ages	95
Notes	100

Chapter 6. **Responses to the Challenge of Balanced Resources in Retirement**	105
6.1. Introduction	105
6.2. A changing balance: its rationale and likely public reaction to change	105
6.3. What can countries do?	111
6.4. Diversifying financing mechanisms	112
6.5. Encouraging more occupational and personal provision	113
6.6. Job changing, vesting and portability	115
6.7. Increasing the financial security of private arrangements	118
6.8. Raising awareness of retirement income needs and opportunities	121
Notes	123

Chapter 7. **Maintaining Economic Well-being and Protecting the Vulnerable**	125
7.1. Introduction	125
7.2. Key vulnerable groups	125
7.3. What can countries do?	130
7.4. Protecting people with gaps in their working history	131
7.5. Providing for survivors	132
7.6. Other action aimed at low-income groups	133
7.7. Adequacy of annuitised benefits	134
7.8. Protection of pension benefits against inflation	134
7.9. Setting target replacement rates in diversified systems	136
Notes	137

Chapter 8. **Conclusion – Lessons about Reform Strategies**	139
8.1. Introduction	139
8.2. Strategic frameworks for policy development and consensus-building	139
8.3. Information to sustain effective reform	142
Notes	145
Bibliography	147

ANNEXES

I. **Main features of the retirement income systems in the nine countries**	153
II. **Retirement incentives**	155
III. **Statistical annex**	163

LIST OF BOXES

2.1. Uses and limitations of the comparative income analysis	23
2.2. The case of Canada – the importance of the changing relative size of income sources	25
5.1. The situation of older workers in Japan is quite different	94
6.1. Risks and risk diversification	109
6.2. The Maxwell case and its consequences	119
6.3. The pension mis-selling scandal in the United Kingdom	120

LIST OF TABLES

2.1.	Quasi-replacement rates	22
2.2.	Disposable income of the population aged 65 and over by income decile	24
2.3.	Pseudo-simulation: countries assumed to have the living arrangements of Japan and of Finland	34
2.4.	Real income growth, retirement age, by income quintile	38
2.5.	Contribution of taxes and transfers to income distribution	41
2.6.	Ratios of market wealth to gross income	42
4.1.	Old-age pension spending	68
4.2.	Average effects of making different assumptions on old-age pension spending	69
4.3.	Work-retirement challenge	71
4.4.	The challenge of balanced resources in retirement	71
4.5.	The challenge of economic well-being	71
5.1.	Age of withdrawal from labour force and retirement duration	82
5.2.	Public views on own preferred labour force status, 1997	83
5.3.	Public perceptions on ease of finding a job, 1997	83
5.4.	Employees working part-time	92
5.5.	Younger and older workers, and older people not at work, by educational level	97
6.1.	Financial assets of pension funds	108
6.2.	Coverage of occupational pension plans	113
7.1.	Percentage of the oldest old that are in the lowest income quintile	126
7.2.	Disposable income of widows living alone compared with that of couples	127
7.3.	Percentage of men aged 60 to 64 in the lowest income quintile	128

Annexes

A.	Retirement age and "actuarial" reduction and enhancement	156
B.	Parts of the pension system considered	156
A.1.	Selected demographic estimates and projections, 2000 and 2030	163
A.2.	Life expectancy at ages 60 and 65, 1998	164
A.3.	Selected employment indicators, 2000 and three scenarios in 2030	165
A.4.	Employment/population ratios for older men	166
A.5.	Employment/population ratios for older women	167
A.6.	Self-employed, older age groups	168
A.7.	Disposable income of older age groups	169
A.8.	Recipients of means-tested benefits, private pension beneficiaries and amount of benefits, older age groups	170
A.9.	Percentage of individuals by household type	171
A.10.	Combination of private and public pension of early retirees and normal retirees	172
A.11.	Views on role of government in providing a decent standard of living for the old	173
A.12.	Views on more public retirement spending	173
A.13.	Preferences for spending more time in a paid job, 1997	174
A.14.	Proportion of households reporting market wealth, mid-90s	174
A.15.	Earnings of the average production worker, 1998	175
A.16.	Maximum pensionable earnings and maximum pension benefits	175
A.17.	Concessions to the elderly in personal income tax systems	176
A.18.	Defined-benefit occupational pensions in Canada, the United Kingdom and the United States	176
A.19.	Data sources and definitions for Tables 4.3, 4.4 and 4.5	177

LIST OF CHARTS

2.1.	Mean disposable income of the lowest income quintile of people aged 65 and over	25
2.2.	Percentage of population that is below the low-income cut-off line	26
2.3.	Ratio of disposable incomes of people aged 65 to 74 to people aged 18 and over	27
2.4.	Social security transfers, people aged 65 to 74	28
2.5.	Disposable income by source of income, age 65 and over	28
2.6.	Trends in income sources, by income group, age 65 and over	29
2.7.	Disposable income by main components	30
2.8.	Disposable income by "own" income components	32
2.9.	Household size by age of individuals	33
2.10.	Work and benefit status of men, older age groups	36
2.11.	Real income growth, by income component and income quintile	39
2.12.	Market wealth-to-gross income ratio by household type	43
2.13.	Difference in financial and housing wealth: top and bottom quintiles	44

© OECD 2001

3.1. Pension values for illustrative workers earning between half and twice the economy-wide average 51
3.2. Mandatory pension benefits by earnings in nine countries as a proportion of economy-wide average earnings 52
3.3. Mandatory pension benefits by earnings in nine countries as a proportion of individual earnings 53
3.4. Value of public and private pension benefits in Canada and the United Kingdom 54
3.5. Taxes paid by pensioners and workers 56
3.6. Gross and net replacement rates 57
5.1. Ratio of retirees to employees, trends and scenarios 79
5.2. Average ages of withdrawal from the labour force: trends 81
5.3. Trends in beneficiaries, for persons aged 55-64, 1975-1999 89
5.4. Percentage of the workforce aged 55 and over 96
5.5. Participation in adult education and training 98
6.1. Public social expenditure related to the retirement-age population 107
6.2. Categories of public social expenditure 108
6.3. Pension replacement rates by number of schemes joined and rate of individual earnings growth 116

Annexes

A. Replacement rate and changes in pension wealth 157
B. Replacement rates and changes in pension wealth for working an extra year 159
A.1. Retirees/employees ratio and social expenditure as a percentage of GDP 178
A.2. Percentage of young adults living with parents 178
A.3. Percentage of workers (without a pension) and early retirees (not at work, with a pension), by income quintile 179
A.4. Income composition by quintile 180
A.5. Pensioners who work and who do not work by income quintile, age 60 to 64 183
A.6. Recipients of private and public pensions, by income quintile 184
A.7. Percentage of population that is above the middle-upper income cut-off line 185
A.8. Workers per retiree, 1970, 2000 and three scenarios in 2030 186
A.9. Percentage of total population that is employed 187

Chapter 1
SUMMARY AND KEY POINTS

1.1. Structure of the report

In all nine countries studied here – Canada, Finland, Germany, Italy, Japan, the Netherlands, Sweden, the United Kingdom and the United States – retirement income systems are coming under increasing pressure as fertility rates drop and longevity increases. The very success of past retirement policy is at the heart of the dilemma facing policy makers today. For perhaps the first time in history most people can look forward to old age without trepidation about their economic circumstances. Yet the consequent numbers of people retiring early, greater longevity, the possibility of future labour shortages and, especially, the coming retirement of the large baby-boom generation mean that however successful the retirement income system has been to date, and however reluctant people are to see it change, change it must. How can retirement income systems continue to provide high replacement rates in the light of demographic and labour-market pressures? Or, phrased differently, how can retirement income systems be made sustainable for the future without jeopardising the income security they have achieved?

In Part I, new tools are used to make a comparison of the income situation of older people in the nine countries and of the complex role of public policy. A perhaps surprising finding is that older people maintain similar income positions in all nine countries despite large differences in the sources of that income, including major differences in the generosity of public pensions.

This finding reflects the high level of substitutability among income sources among middle and upper-income older people. Newly developed data show how living arrangements and multi-generational households also must be taken into account to provide a consistent picture of the economic well-being of older people, particularly in Italy and Japan. Assets should be taken into account as well, both because of their potential for conversion into income and because of the effects of imputed rents of owner-occupied housing. The role of various benefit streams, in addition to pensions, is also essential to understanding the differences between countries, particularly for people in the transition to retirement.

The retirement income systems are then compared from an institutional, public policy perspective. Here the replacement incomes of hypothetical individuals at various income levels are examined in light of the pension and tax rules of the nine countries. The strategies that underlie the systems in the different countries are fundamentally different in the role they assign to public pension schemes, the space they leave for additional occupational or personal pension provision, the incentives they provide for early retirement and in approaches to taxation. Nevertheless, the outcomes are similar, at least in terms of replacement income of older people and, in all cases, public policy plays a determining, if sometimes indirect role. Part I closes with a summary of the likely future fiscal effects of reforms implemented to date and of avenues for future reform that are likely to have the largest fiscal payoff.

Part II describes the large numbers of recent reforms in the nine countries as they have responded and continue to respond to three main challenges to the existing retirement income system, which are outlined below. Emphasis is placed on the range of possible reform options and the way they have been selected by the nine countries. A major theme is that reforms that are directed to a single objective, such as encouraging people to work longer, can have adverse consequences on other goals, such as meeting basic income support goals for some vulnerable groups. Much care is needed to ensure that reform packages are designed to take into account the complex balances and interactions among the many resources on which older people depend. Part II closes with a conclusion that emphasises the importance of strategic approaches to future reform, the need for significantly better data to sustain effective reform and some lessons that have been learned from the experience of the nine countries examined here concerning the process of reform.

Annex I contains a short description of existing arrangements in each of the nine countries. A more extended discussion of these arrangements can be found in the final section of Chapter 3.

1.2. The economic well-being of older people: a success story

All countries reviewed in this study have formal retirement income arrangements, public and/or private, through which people of working age make provision for their old age. These systems provide a retirement income package that consists of far more than just a minimum floor; they replace a large share of previous incomes. But they have chosen to do so through very different combinations of public, occupational and personal pension schemes, tax-financed benefits, earnings and other sources of retirement income.

In all nine countries, pensioners (at all points in the income distribution) have disposable incomes that, on average, correspond to about 70 to 80% of the income of comparable groups of people during later working life – despite the wide variety of retirement income systems. Bearing in mind that some work-related expenditure are no longer necessary in retirement, and taking account of greater home ownership, this means that in most countries people experience almost no or only a minor reduction of their standard of living when moving from later working life to retirement. In some countries, the consumption of older couples equals or exceeds that of younger couples. In general, older people do not have to work to survive and, unsurprisingly, a large majority do not, although the situation varies by country: in Japan, in fact, older people largely continue in employment.

The success of the systems cannot be explained by the levels of public pensions alone, or by any one component of retirement income in itself. The study finds that the importance of working income for people aged 65 and older has declined over past decades. In several countries, capital incomes have risen over time with the growth of private and occupational pensions; in other countries, the reduction of working income has been compensated by an increase in net social transfers.

The analysis also shows that systems in the nine countries have been largely successful in preventing very low incomes in old age. In all the countries surveyed, public transfers constitute the overwhelming share of income for elderly people in the lower deciles of the income distribution. "Own" contributions from low-income groups during working life are rarely sufficient to prevent low income in retirement. The ways in which low income in old age is avoided vary. Some countries use a flat-rate pension scheme based on residency, regardless of individual contributions, which is called the "basic pension" here. To the extent that such schemes are financed by pension contributions levied in proportion to income, they thus involve a transfer from higher to lower-income earners. Other countries rely on combinations of a minimum pension guarantee within the public pension system, tax-financed social assistance benefits and other means-tested minimum income guarantees to help the low-income older population. In these cases, redistribution takes place through the tax system.

1.3. The three challenges

This report examines in depth three major challenges facing retirement income systems: *i)* the growing imbalance of time spent in work and in retirement, *ii)* the changing mix of different forms of retirement income provision, and *iii)* the need to maintain adequate replacement income and tackle any persisting problems of low income in old age – while avoiding unintended harm to vulnerable groups as a result of reform.

First challenge: rebalancing time spent in and out of work – delaying access to retirement income benefits

Fiscal pressure on retirement income systems resulting from demographic change is aggravated by the fact that, in many countries, workers are leaving the labour force at much earlier ages than the standard retirement age. But this trend is reversible. The analysis of Chapter 5 shows that there is nothing inevitable about the effects of demography. Indeed, the trend towards earlier retirement has been arrested in most of the nine countries; during the past ten years there has been no decline in the net age of withdrawal from the labour force. However, this will not be sufficient to sustain benefit levels in the future as birth-rates fall and those in retirement live longer. Particularly in light of increasing life expectancies, the success of retirement income systems can be most easily maintained in the long term if access to the stream of income available from public and private systems is delayed beyond current effective retirement ages. Simulations found in Chapter 4 show that even quite moderate increases in the effective age of retirement could have large effects.

There is widespread recognition in the nine countries of the multiple benefits that could result from reforms that increase effective retirement ages. Yet there is an asymmetry between the general acceptance of re-balancing work and retirement in the public statements of governments, employers' associations and individuals' responses to opinion polls, on the one hand, and what people actually do. Individual employers still shed older workers, and governments do the same with their own older employees. Individuals often say they want to work in retirement, but few do.

The reasons for this discrepancy include easy access to generous public and private early-retirement benefits, which are attractive to employers and workers; the availability of alternative pathways such as disability and unemployment pensions; a lack of suitable employment opportunities for older workers; skills gaps among older workers; health considerations; and, in some countries, a general culture of early retirement.

In many countries, the way that pensions are calculated – when taken in conjunction with other factors such as labour-market or health factors – discourages work at older ages. Expected pension wealth – the discounted value of pension benefits less the cost of obtaining them – usually falls with continued work after a certain age. This can be corrected by moving towards actuarial neutrality. In such a system, the expected pension wealth would remain constant and independent of when labour force participation ends. Benefit levels would be fully adjusted to take into account the period of contributions made and the period during which pensions will be received. However, factors outside the pension system that influence the retirement decision need to be taken into account in introducing such reforms. These include the existence of alternative means of supporting early retirement, such as disability benefits, special pensions for unemployed older workers, or other benefit programmes that serve as quasi-retirement programmes in many countries, bridging the gap until the workers reach the minimum retirement age. If such benefits allow labour-market and age factors to influence eligibility (in addition to health-related incapacity), then actuarial neutrality in pensions could result in workers "choosing" disability or other benefits to finance early withdrawal from the labour force. The importance of these alternative pathways varies widely across the nine countries.

Moving to a pension system that applies actuarially correct adjustments for early and late retirement will help, but this would not be sufficient. It would be difficult to remove all incentives for early retirement from the existing systems, in particular in those schemes that offer a flat-rate benefit or a minimum pension directed to those with low incomes. Actuarial reductions for early retirement would push early retirees below low-income thresholds and transfer the problem to the means-tested social assistance scheme. Means-tested benefit also discourages workers from making any savings for retirement. Most countries with flat-rate benefit schemes therefore do not allow early retirement in their public systems.

An alternative, which some countries have chosen, would be to allow early retirement only for those workers who will receive a pension above the social assistance threshold. This, however, raises equity issues, since low-income workers may have at least as much need to retire earlier. They are likely to have physically more demanding jobs and fewer employment opportunities in older age, and they also have a shorter life expectancy than higher-income people.

© OECD 2001

Policy action will also be necessary in the area of private pensions, particularly in those countries where public pensions are relatively small and targeted to low-income groups. Here the design of private pensions may well have more impact on the retirement decision than does the design of public systems. Indeed, as discussed in Chapter 5, private pension systems are an important avenue to early retirement. In many countries, occupational schemes provide earlier benefits and bridge financing until the worker is eligible for the standard retirement benefit. Individual retirement savings can also serve as a source of early-retirement income if they are accessible before the standard retirement age. This would not be an issue if occupational and personal retirement plans were given the same tax treatment as other forms of savings. But most countries offer preferential treatment to retirement arrangements by exempting contributions and capital gains from taxation and taxing only distributions from such plans. This means that there can be a contradiction between public policies that try to reduce access to publicly financed early retirement and policies which allow tax-advantaged plans to act as bridges for unemployed older workers.

It follows that there is no single panacea to the problem of early withdrawal from the labour market. The solution will consist of a package of different policy measures addressed at the different dimensions of the problem and adapted to the specific circumstances of each country. Elements of this package would include:

- Moving toward greater actuarial neutrality of pension benefit formulas while preserving those elements of the retirement income system that are directed to eliminating very low incomes and encouraging those who do want to work longer by rewarding longer life-time work through higher benefits.
- Removing the systems' most obvious distortions promoting early retirement, for example, retirement schemes that are based only on seniority regardless of age, or schemes that move older workers quasi-automatically from unemployment to early retirement.
- Raising the age at which benefits first become available and, in the longer run, raising the standard retirement age.
- Adjusting benefit formulas to reflect the cost to the system of taking early retirement.
- Possibly moving to regulate retirement ages in tax-advantaged occupational and personal pension arrangements.
- More clearly distinguishing between retirement income systems and other schemes of social protection applicable to all age groups, such as disability programmes and unemployment benefit schemes which, in some countries, have evolved into alternative means of financing early retirement. Older people need access to such programmes, but not on grounds of age alone.
- Promoting employment opportunities for older workers, including through upgrading skills, training and lifelong learning.
- Filling major information gaps that now impede policy-making and consensus-building through investments in data collection, applied research and information dissemination related to the determinants of retirement, the interactions among the many elements of the retirement income system and the likely effectiveness of various policy levers.

All nine countries have adopted some or all of the above measures. The policy focus has rightly been on reducing the number of people retiring before the standard retirement age (usually 65 years); due to increasing longevity, future attention will likely turn to ways of making the work-retirement transition more gradual after this age. Most current interest has been in reforming existing incentives to retire in public pension systems and in restricting access to alternative pathways to early retirement. Tackling these is not straightforward, however, and it is still too early to measure whether these changes have succeeded in changing retirement behaviour. Policies were introduced mostly during the past decade and are being phased in gradually. It is certain that individuals will react to these signals differently; some workers will decide to delay retirement if this would result in a sizeable increase of their pension entitlements, whereas others will value leisure higher and opt to retire at the earliest possible moment, even if this implies a substantial reduction of benefits. There is unquestionably more that can be done. The fiscal simulations in Chapter 4 suggest that past reforms in this direction have usually not been deep enough to offset the effects of an increasing number of older people becoming eligible for pensions (which results from, for example, the greater employment of women and maturing pension systems).

Policy attention has focused mostly on the supply side of the labour market for older workers. The demand side, however, needs more research to identify the barriers to employment of older workers as perceived by employers. The importance of this issue and, in particular, of collecting more empirical evidence has been recognised by many countries. (The OECD will commence shortly a thematic review of the obstacles facing older workers in Member countries that will analyse the determinants of demand for older workers in more depth.)

The basic message, despite the many qualifications, is clear and reasonably optimistic. If concerted action is taken on a number of policy fronts, and if economies remain healthy, then it should be possible to make significant progress in achieving a better balance of work and retirement. Even modest success is likely to have a high payoff – certainly in fiscal terms, but also for the broader operation of the economy. If the work-retirement process is flexible and offers individuals a wider choice in the way work and leisure can be allocated, then the social benefits will also be large.

Second challenge: the mix among different forms of retirement income provision

Public pension systems, especially those financed according to pay-as-you-go principles, are faced with a diminishing number of contributors per pensioner and will have to increase contribution rates substantially if they are to continue guaranteeing current benefit levels (OECD, 2001a). Many countries have reacted to this increasing demographic and fiscal pressure by changing the mix of sources of retirement income and, in particular, the balance between public and private provision, and between defined-benefit and defined-contribution arrangements, in their retirement income systems. Public pension schemes are being scaled down to reduce fiscal pressure and to increase space for contributions to occupational and personal pension arrangements.

A retirement income system based on different components and different financing mechanisms (i.e. the combination of pay-as-you-go financing and capitalised schemes) enables a better balancing of risks. It can also facilitate burden-sharing between different generations, provide more flexibility to individual workers in making retirement decisions and offer more flexibility in adjusting systems to changing economic and demographic conditions. A pay-as-you-go system suffers from the risks associated with uncertain demographic and labour-market trends. A fully capitalised system where each cohort saves for its own retirement is less vulnerable to demographic developments, but it is inevitably subject to investment and rate-of-return risks. As future benefit expenditure are certain to rise due to ageing pressures, more and more countries are trying to contain future contribution rate increases by raising the degree of advance-funding in their pension systems. Several countries have increased capitalisation of their public pension systems, but the strongest policy emphasis has been on the promotion of funded private arrangements, i.e. occupational and personal pension schemes.

In almost all of the nine countries, coverage by occupational pensions (that is, employer-provided pensions) is much higher than personal pension coverage, although occupational plans cover less than half the workforce in most countries. The exceptions to this are countries that have made occupational pension provision statutory or quasi-mandatory by extending collective agreements to the majority of the workforce. In those countries, occupational pensions have become an important component of the retirement income package and their benefits are generally integrated with the benefits provided by the public systems, i.e. pension policy targets a combined replacement rate from the public and occupational systems. In most countries, occupational plans are provided predominantly as defined-benefit plans (where the amount of benefit is determined in advance, often linked to final salary levels), but newly established schemes are often in the form of defined-contribution plans (where the benefit is determined by the contributions made).

Individual defined-contribution plans are, in the main, personal voluntary supplementary retirement arrangements. The evidence in several of the nine countries shows that the administrative

© OECD 2001

cost of personal pension arrangements can be quite high, which substantially reduces the net returns on accumulated balances. Further cost is added when the balance of a defined-contribution plan is converted to a guaranteed lifelong monthly stream of pension payments through an annuity contract.

The experience of the nine countries shows that collective management and annuitisation of defined-contribution plans, either at a centralised or occupational level, can help to reduce the operational costs of defined-contribution plans. This is an important finding for occupational and mandatory personal defined-contribution plans,* but voluntary personal pension arrangements need to remain individualised almost by definition.

Thus, more diversified retirement income systems are desirable, although it is not clear whether the cost of ageing and pension provision can be substantially reduced through private sector involvement. Moving to more private pension provision does not mean that government involvement in pensions is reduced. On the contrary, demands and responsibilities increase as the public sector reduces its role in the direct provision of benefits and takes on the additional tasks of regulation and supervision of private pension schemes; the experience of some countries in this study shows that this area requires considerable policy attention. Finally, encouraging private provision will come at a cost to government. Here too the experience of several of the countries shows that tax incentives are necessary to ensure take-up of private pensions.

An important precondition for effective policy-making is the availability of reliable and comprehensive data. The nine-country study shows that only very few countries collect data on occupational and personal pension arrangements on a systematic basis. Available information is mostly based on surveys among workers, which provide only spotlights and fail to give a complete picture of coverage, benefit levels and other important characteristics of private retirement schemes. If private arrangements are to play a greater role and replace part of the publicly provided benefits, data collection efforts will have to be stepped up urgently. There are correspondingly large weaknesses in the empirical understanding of the role of retirement savings, consumption and assets over the course of an individual's life, including the role of bequests and gifts to other family members. Chapter 8 describes the longitudinal data and microsimulation models that need to be developed.

Third challenge: maintaining economic well-being and protecting vulnerable groups

Ensuring economic well-being in retirement has been a policy success story, but maintaining that success remains a challenge. In most of the nine countries, future generations will receive a significant part of private pension benefits from defined-contribution plans. This is likely to come either as a result of the substitution of some public and occupational pension plans by personal pension plans, or by the transformation of existing occupational defined-benefit plans into defined-contribution plans. As well, if current reforms are successful, more of the income of older people will come from earnings as a result of higher effective retirement ages. How will the economic well-being of future retirees be affected by such trends?

In public pension plans, a close link between benefits and contributions is desirable to reduce incentives to retire early, and such a link is inherent to defined-contribution plans. But an increased reliance on defined-contribution mechanisms also entails a higher risk of inadequate retirement income for some groups of the population, *e.g.* workers with broken contribution careers, the long-term unemployed and (depending on the rules of the public scheme) people moving in and out of self-employment. It also raises the problem of combining better work incentives with a programme addressed to eliminating low incomes, as discussed above. There is a risk that this problem worsens as the share of defined-contribution plans increases. The newly evolving arrangements are, in the absence of remedial measures, likely to lead to more skewed income distributions and, possibly, newly vulnerable groups.

---

* Including "personal" plans that can be administered jointly, such as Registered Retirement Savings Plans (RRSPs) in Canada or 401Ks in the United States.

The challenge is not only about new vulnerable groups. There remain some long-standing vulnerable groups among the retired. As shown in Chapter 7, there is a higher risk in all nine countries for older women who have had no or very weak labour-market attachment over their lives and are living alone. Within this group, single older women are the most likely to be poor. Widows are usually better protected through survivors' benefits, although in this group, too, there are cases of very low pensions when the deceased husband's income was low and the wife spent her life at home raising children.

Most countries regard this problem as a legacy of the past, which can be solved through anti-low-income benefits targeted to the affected persons, without structural reforms. Women are now spending increasing time in the labour force and earning their own pension rights, especially if they are not married. The main focus has been more on measures that improve pension credits for time spent bringing up children and which help women to acquire their own pension rights, even if they are temporarily or permanently outside the labour force.

1.4. Country-specific conclusions

Canada

The Canadian system is well diversified, as it makes use of many different elements of retirement income provision, including a major role for tax policies. Basic retirement income goals are successfully met at moderate public cost: for most citizens, these goals have been attained in recent years as the earnings-related public pension system has matured. Effective retirement ages are about average. A large increase in the ratio of retirees to workers can be expected in the absence of changes in retirement behaviour. Also, the workforce will age at an above-average rate in the future, which could pose a challenge for maintaining employment rates for older workers. Since public pensions are, relatively, small and concentrated on lower-income Canadians, there may be somewhat less room to use public pension reform to encourage later retirement – and hence more need to take concerted action on several policy fronts. Occupational pension coverage is still partial, but Canada has been more successful than other countries in promoting personal pensions (through informing individuals of their entitlements and industrial advertising) and consistent tax privileges. In fiscal terms, public pension spending will grow more than in other countries over the next half century, doubling in size from its present relatively low base. In the nine-country comparison, Canada is the country with the least problems in ensuring pensioners' economic well-being and protecting vulnerable groups, but is only average in its success in balancing time spent in work and in retirement.

Finland

Finland, like Germany and Italy, faces large challenges in the work-retirement transition and the continued employment of older workers. Action here is of top policy priority, as is well recognised in Finland. Finland still has a wide range of early retirement and other special pension programmes for older workers, who continue to use these extensively to exit from the labour market, although access has been restricted in recent years. Finland has been particularly active in research on the labour-market situation of older workers. The pension system seems diversified at first sight, with its basic pension for all and its complete coverage by occupational schemes. However, the situation differs from other countries in that these plans are part of the public statutory pension scheme and are only partly funded, but with the funded amount gradually increasing. In fiscal terms, public pension spending is likely to increase by about 5 percentage points of GDP over the next 50 years, starting from a base that is near the nine-country average.

Germany

The retirement income system in Germany is dominated by the public pension system, which along with the disability scheme, has made access to early retirement relatively easy. Public pension expenditure and contribution rates are high; in addition, the pension system receives substantial transfers from the government. The country faces a serious policy challenge in delaying the work-retirement transition. The rules for access to benefits are gradually being tightened, but more action will be needed to promote the continued employment of older workers. To stabilise contribution rates, the government is planning to gradually reduce the replacement rate of the public system while building up an initially small component of voluntary, tax-advantaged personal pension plans. Given the long time horizon involved, it is not clear, however, that the measures envisaged will suffice to stabilise contribution rates to the pay-as-you-go system at the targeted rates. There is a risk that the future evolution of employment and labour force participation might turn out less favourable than officially assumed. The reduction in replacement rates appears mild in comparison to the projected dramatic increase in the old-age dependency ratio over the next 30 years. Hence, further action to consolidate the pension system may become necessary, and indeed the new legislation commits the government to take action if it appears likely that the targeted contribution rates will not be attained. This could be combined with widening the scope for voluntary pension arrangements. Such reform would be aided by explicitly linking future pensions to life expectancy, and increasing discounts for short contribution periods, thereby reducing incentives for early retirement. Making part of the funded layer mandatory, rather than giving tax preferences to contributions, would be preferable on fiscal grounds and is worth considering. Unifying taxation rules for different types of pension schemes would be important as well. Moreover, eligibility for invalidity pensions should be determined exclusively on health criteria, making them independent of labour-market conditions.

Italy

Italy, which had one of the largest problems in the work-retirement transition, has gone further than most other countries in changing the relevant parameters of its retirement income system. In a series of reforms, the most generous early-retirement and seniority pension programmes were closed down and benefits were shifted from a final salary basis to a basis of working-life contributions. Retirement will still be possible at age 57 under the new system, but benefits will be reduced considerably. New rules were established in 1995 that deeply modified the functioning of the public pension system. They will be phased in very slowly, however, and during the transition period a large fiscal burden will persist due to unique demographic factors. As in Germany, public pensions are by far the largest component of the retirement income system. Steps have been taken, however, to encourage more supplementary pension coverage. Italy, along with Japan, is one of the countries where living arrangements have the greatest effect on the incomes of pensioners, many of whom live with children. In many cases, the living standards of older people would be much lower if they were to live alone. But in some cases, the same living arrangements reduce the economic well-being of the elderly. As Italy does not have a comprehensive unemployment insurance or social assistance system, pension benefits constitute the only family income for households in which older parents live with their children. Special policy attention has to be given to these vulnerable groups. In fiscal terms, the recent reforms, if they are maintained, should keep public pension spending in 2050 at about today's level expressed as a percentage of GDP. Today's base is, however, the highest of the nine countries.

Japan

Japan stands out in the nine-country comparison as the country with the highest employment rates among the older population. Less action is thus required to delay the work-retirement transition in Japan than in the other countries (although Japan is the only one of the nine countries for which age of withdrawal from the labour force appears to be falling). Japan is already experiencing the dependency ratio pressures that other countries will face in several years. Retirement incomes are heavily dependent on earnings both from work by those aged 65 and over and from other adults in the same household. Japan is trying to diversify its pension system by expanding coverage through occupational and personal pension provision. However, this is difficult in the current financial climate, in which defined-benefit plans (which account for the vast majority of private plans in Japan) have been exposed to significant under-funding as a result of low bond yields and the collapse of the stock market. In order to bring the level of funding back in line with actuarial principles every five years, as required by regulations, employers will have to respond by increasing contributions. Living arrangements play an important role in social protection today as pensioners often live in the same household as their children. If this structure changes, however, and more pensioners live by themselves in the future, replacement rates could deteriorate substantially. Policy action would then be necessary to ensure adequate income replacement. In fiscal terms, public pensions spending in 2050 should be only slightly higher than today's level, assuming no changes in programming.

Netherlands

The Netherlands faces its largest challenge in the work-retirement transition. The use of special early-retirement and disability schemes as an exit from the labour market for older workers has been widespread. The rate of awards of disability programmes has been high for men at all ages. Female labour force participation has been low (though it is now rising). On the other hand, the labour market has been strong in recent years and employment ratios, while still not high, have been growing, both among those 55 to 59 and 60 to 64. The pension system in the Netherlands is the most diversified for the largest number of people in all of the nine countries, as occupational coverage extends to more than 90% of all employees. The occupational benefits are well integrated with the public pension benefit: by targeting a combined replacement from both systems a consistent pension package is provided. In fiscal terms, the Netherlands and Canada are similar. Both start from a relatively low base of public pension spending, but that figure could double over the coming half century.

Sweden

Sweden needs less policy action on the work-retirement transition than many of the other countries. Disability and part-time pension schemes were used as avenues to early retirement in the past. A major reform of the pension system has now adjusted the incentives and made the system financially sustainable, while still allowing for some flexibility in the retirement decision. Thus, the problem has been addressed, but it is still too early to tell whether the new system will alter retirement behaviour. Sweden is one of two countries in the study that have introduced a mechanism to adjust pension benefits to increasing life expectancy. But the pension system is less diversified than in many other countries. Again, first steps in this direction have been taken recently by introducing a small mandatory, funded and privately-managed component and through reforms of occupational pensions, but more action may be required in the future. The country compares well with others in the levels of pensioners' economic well-being and the protection of vulnerable groups. In fiscal terms, public pension spending is projected to increase by less than in most of the other countries over the coming fifty years, but today's spending is relatively high compared with the others.

United Kingdom

In the United Kingdom, a series of retirement income reforms have been instituted over past decades. Although successful on some fronts, they have resulted in major policy challenges for the future. The basic pension system is financially sustainable in the long term due to price indexation of benefits, though in the absence of the social assistance safety net there would be a serious low-income risk for older people. Past reforms have also led to strong diversification of the pension system, with extensive personal choice of retirement arrangements. But these arrangements do not extend to all pensioners, and policy action is required to increase coverage of supplementary pensions to a larger part of the population. Serious weaknesses have also been revealed in the functioning, regulation and supervision of private pension provision. These have led to the further changes and proposed changes in the regulatory regime, which are discussed in later chapters. In fiscal terms, the United Kingdom is in the best situation among the nine countries; public pension spending is low as a percentage of GDP and is not projected to increase by 2050, assuming existing arrangements continue.

United States

In the United States, more people are drawing pension while continuing to work than in the nine-country average. Occupational and personal pension arrangements play an important role, but occupational plans still cover only about half of all employees at any point in time, though a somewhat higher proportion of the labour force are covered over a lifetime. Moreover, the take-up of defined-contribution plans has been growing markedly amongst younger people. A comparatively high share of pensioners rely on means-tested benefits, and the poorest quintile is in a less favourable situation than in many of the other countries. The United States faces a special challenge in old-age income security due to incomplete health insurance coverage for older people; large pharmaceutical expenditure, which are excluded from the standard health insurance cover for older people, can be a major threat to the economic well-being of pensioners. In fiscal terms, public pension spending is among those lowest of the nine countries and, in the absence of change, is projected to grow only moderately over the next half century. Pension policy is in a state of evolution in the United States. In May 2001, a commission was established to make specific recommendations regarding social security reform, with one of its guiding principles being the inclusion of individually controlled, voluntary personal retirement accounts.

Part I
CONVERGENT OUTCOMES, DIVERGENT MEANS

Chapter 2

THE RESOURCES OF OLDER PEOPLE: COMPLEX SYSTEMS AND SUCCESSFUL OUTCOMES

2.1. Introduction

For reasons of simplicity, retirement income systems are often described in terms of their mix of public and private pensions. However, that characterisation misses the critical roles played by other elements in the system, including earnings, resources used in the transition to retirement, taxation and wealth. It also leaves aside the importance of household living arrangements in the retirement income system. This chapter examines the cumulative result of the different components of the system for the incomes of older people and explores how the various elements of the retirement income system interact at the level of individuals and households.

The new household data analysed here establish that retirement income policies have been highly successful in meeting their two fundamental objectives: preventing unacceptable declines in income when people retire and guarding against very low incomes among older people. The first objective has been met, at least for most retirees, across the nine countries. Replacement rates are high for people in all income ranges, with people with the lowest incomes often gaining most on retirement. Success in preventing low incomes among old people has, however, been somewhat less consistent than is the case for replacement income goals overall (Sections 2.2 and 2.3).

Section 2.4 points out that the disposable income of older people, at each income level, is reasonably similar in most of the countries when compared with the income of people of working age. This happens even though levels of public pension vary greatly. The basic reason for this is that, while pension systems in some countries provide higher-income people larger pensions than in others, higher-income people in the countries with lower public pension replacement rates fill the gap with private savings and working income. The fuller story behind this substitutability among working income, capital income and public transfers is quite complex, however. It is also necessary, for example, to take account of the effects of the sharing of income within households and household living arrangements, which are considered in Section 2.5.

Section 2.6 examines the interplay of the various components of the retirement income system as they affect and are affected by the work-to-retirement transition process. It underscores the need for retirement income policy to take account of the various pathways to retirement, including the role of unemployment insurance, disability benefits and early retirement schemes.

Success in meeting income-replacement objectives and preventing very low incomes among the elderly thus results from the interplay of the many elements of the system. Section 2.7 explores these interactions in more depth and shows how the overall improvement in the economic position of older people in recent years reflects changes in the size of each income source in each income group. A concluding discussion covers the role played by wealth, especially housing assets, and consumption. This additional information confirms the basic finding that many, perhaps most, older people enjoy a standard of material well-being and economic security that remains unchanged or even rises after they stop working (Section 2.8).

2.2. Success in meeting earnings-replacement objectives

A main objective of retirement income systems is to protect people against drops in their income when they retire. A true measure of success would require an examination of panel data to examine how the income (and wealth) of specific individuals rose, or fell, as they moved into retirement and into later life. Such data do not yet exist at the international level. However, the household income data in Table 2.1 provide some insight. The first three columns show a "quasi-replacement rate". The quasi-rates compare the disposable income of people in the 10 years after the normal retirement age of 65 with that of people in the 15 years prior to 65.[1] It can be assumed that the first group are mainly retired (a reasonable assumption) and that the second group are employed (a less reasonable assumption).

Table 2.1. **Quasi-replacement rates**[a]
Mid-70s, mid-80s and mid-90s

	\multicolumn{3}{c|}{Percentage of mean disposable income of people aged 51-64}	\multicolumn{3}{c}{Percentage of mean disposable income of people aged 41-50}
	Mid-70s	Mid-80s	Mid-90s	Mid-70s	Mid-80s	Mid-90s
Canada	69.1	82.4	86.9	51.1	78.2	86.6
Finland	79.9	77.6	75.5	67.5	69.2	71.6
Germany	..	78.1	84.4	..	75.5	78.2
Italy	..	76.4	78.7	..	77.8	78.1
Japan	..	82.3	79.6	..	84.8	81.8
Netherlands	81.2	83.1	80.7	85.8	85.2	78.9
Sweden	71.0	76.1	76.1	64.9	73.6	80.3
United Kingdom	66.9	70.4	74.1	61.5	59.9	65.0
United States	75.6	82.2	79.9	77.0	84.3	83.6

.. Data not available.
a) The quasi-replacement rates compare the mean disposable income of people aged 65 to 74 with that of those aged 51 to 64 and 41 to 50, respectively.
Source: Calculations from the OECD questionnaire on distribution of household incomes (1999).

Quasi-replacement rates: high on average

Table 2.1 shows that:

- In most countries, the quasi-replacement rate is, on average, close to 80%. It suggests that, when housing assets and work-related expenses are taken into account, material living standards are unlikely to fall when an average individual retires.[2]
- Quasi-replacement rates rose between the mid-1970s and the mid-1980s in Canada and to a lesser extent in the United States, the United Kingdom and Sweden. However, replacement rates remained largely unchanged between the mid-1980s and the mid-1990s.

Because so many people are retired before age 65, the final three columns of Table 2.1 also compare the situation of the older group with the population aged 41 to 50, when most people are certainly working. There is a big gap in years between people aged 41-50 and 65-74 – a problem since replacement rate comparisons should be for the periods just before and just after retirement. Nevertheless, the differences between the two sets of comparisons are not large except in the case of the United Kingdom, with aggregate replacement rates that are typically only a little lower in the comparison with the 41-50 age group (see Box 2.1 for a more general discussion on the uses and limitations of the household income data).

No sign of large gaps between the younger old and the older old, at least on average

Table A.7 in the Statistical Annex tests whether income levels deteriorate over the course of retirement. It provides a wide range of age comparisons of real disposable income, including

> Box 2.1. **Uses and limitations of the comparative income analysis**
>
> **Household income surveys**
>
> The data used in Chapter 2 are derived from two compilations of household income surveys. One is a data set developed by the OECD that has readings in the mid-1970s, mid-1980s and mid-1990s. The other is a more in-depth set of readings from the mid-1990s obtained from a comparable data source known as the Luxembourg Income Study (LIS). For further information see Yamada and Casey (2001) and Yamada (2001).
>
> Together these data sets constitute an exceptionally rich source of comparable data. They, however, share the usual limits of cross-sectional data. They provide snapshots of the population at a point in time, but cannot track individuals over time. Longitudinal data would be needed to fully explore the particular characteristic of groups whose economic position deteriorated (or improved) after retirement and the relationship between the timing of retirement and the resources available in retirement.
>
> Household income data have other limitations as well. They do not cover assets or services such as health insurance. They are out of date. The income of older people in the mid-1990s, for example, reflects the pension rules, retirement patterns and savings arrangements of the 1980s and early 1990s. Much has changed since then. Later chapters therefore provide supplementary information from other sources on gaps and trends. However, this additional information cannot be completely integrated with the household data.
>
> **The representativeness of the nine countries**
>
> This is a comparative analysis among nine of the most industrialised countries in the world, all with developed pension and social security arrangements. The experience of these countries is typical of many OECD countries, but may have limited relevance to countries in different circumstances, such as in some of the newer OECD Member countries.
>
> Caution is also needed in interpreting the results even within the nine countries. For example, a country might perform poorly on a particular aspect of the system when compared with the other nine, but might have performed very well if the comparison were with other countries or, indeed, with the OECD average. In other words, a relatively low ranking compared with the other eight does not necessarily imply that there is a problem that needs to be fixed. Policy action on other fronts, including outside the retirement income system, may have higher priority.
>
> **The use of relative standards**
>
> Analytic tools are used that reduce the possibility of making misleading comparisons. For example, following the usual practice, the income adequacy of older people is assessed in light of the incomes of other people in the country, not against any cross-national average or absolute standard.
>
> While this technique is essential in making meaningful comparisons, it is useful to recollect that the actual goods and services that an older person can consume depend not only on the share of national production going to older people, but also on the total amount of that national production. For example, the average disposable income of the retirement-age population in absolute terms is highest in the United States, Japan and Canada (at about $18 000 US a year in the mid-1990s, adjusted for purchasing power parities). This is well above levels in the Netherlands, Finland, Sweden or the United Kingdom (about $12 000 US). Yamada and Casey (2001) provide several examples of the results of using absolute measures, including their effect on low-income cut-offs.

comparisons based on the age group 65 to 74 and 75 and over. The aggregate "replacement" rates are somewhat lower for the oldest group,[3] but again not by a great amount.

Nor between replacement rates at different income levels

Even if quasi-replacement rates were adequate on average, there may be problems for people at different levels of income. Table 2.2 provides a rough sketch of this issue by comparing the disposable incomes of individuals aged 65 and over in each income decile, with the disposable incomes of their working-age counterparts. That is, the income of the lowest-income group of older people is compared

Table 2.2. **Disposable income of the population aged 65 and over by income decile**
(compared with population aged 18 to 64 in the same income decile)
Percentages, mid-90s[a]

	Canada	Finland	Germany	Italy	Japan	Netherlands	Sweden	United Kingdom	United States
Decile 1[b]	148	101	102	128	72	83	89	76	80
Decile 2	107	83	90	92	73	77	84	69	78
Decile 3	94	78	84	86	75	74	81	66	77
Decile 4	87	75	82	81	77	72	80	64	78
Decile 5	85	73	80	78	77	74	79	64	78
Decile 6	86	72	79	76	78	77	79	65	81
Decile 7	86	72	78	76	81	80	79	67	83
Decile 8	86	72	79	77	84	82	83	72	94
Decile 9	87	73	81	77	87	80	79	67	83
Decile 10	96	75	79	75	94	82	83	72	94

a) Disposable income of the retirement-age population in decile x divided by the disposable income of the working-age population in decile x.
b) Decile is based on each population income.
Source: Calculations from the OECD questionnaire on distribution of household incomes (1999).

with that of the lowest-income group of working-age people, and so on up the income scale. Note again that these are averages of groups of people and there might be quite different results if particular individuals were compared over time.[4]

Except in Japan and the United States,[5] the 1st and 2nd deciles of older people have the highest disposable income relative to their working-age counterparts. In the highest-income groups, older people have somewhat lower incomes than their working-age counterparts, but even here the figure is usually about 80% or even more. In Canada, Japan, and the United States, the richest of the retirement-age population have almost the same level of disposable income as in the working-age population.

The analysis of the rules of today's public pension benefits found in Chapter 3 also indicates that replacement rates are highest for low-income groups. Replacement rates from public pensions in all nine countries are higher for the lowest earners, except in the Netherlands where public replacement rates (of the quasi-mandatory occupational pensions including the public pension) are constant across all incomes, but high at 70%.

2.3. Success in meeting the goal of preventing low incomes in old age

The second main objective of retirement income systems is to eliminate the risk of very low incomes in old age. That is, if people were in economic difficulty before they retired, simply replacing 60 or 70% of their former income would not be enough. Indeed, the analysis of replacement rates above does suggest that replacement income may be above 100% for the lowest-income groups in many countries.

Chart 2.1 provides an historical look at the position of low-income older people. It shows trends since the mid-1970s in the mean disposable income of the lowest-income quintile of older people. The income of this group has been below 40% of average disposable income of the working-age population in Germany, Italy, Japan, the United Kingdom and the United States. In those countries, that level has been stable over the past decade at least. There has been an unusually large improvement in income levels for the lower-income group in Canada, moving from the worst position among the nine countries to the best, for reasons shown in Box 2.2.

Low-income cut-off lines are a standard tool for assessing the goal of eliminating very low incomes in old age. Since it is possible that many people are clustered around the low-income lines, these can sometimes produce misleading comparisons. They should be used in conjunction with other actions such as those found in Chart 2.1. There are many ways of calculating low-income thresholds, but an accepted approach is to examine the number of people who have less than 50% of the median

The Resources of Older People: Complex Systems and Successful Outcomes

Chart 2.1. **Mean disposable income of the lowest income quintile of people aged 65 and over**
Percentage of mean disposable income of people aged 18 to 64, mid-90s

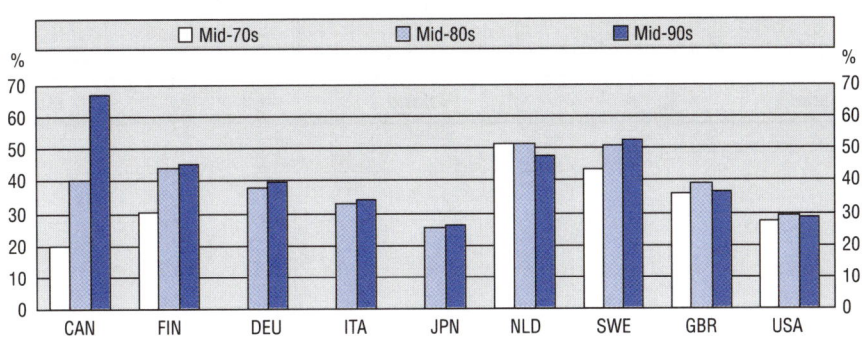

Source: Calculations from the OECD questionnaire on distribution of household incomes (1999).

disposable income of the entire population. This method is far from ideal,[6] but it is the only one that allows ready international comparisons. Chart 2.2 provides basic information by age groups:

- Take the Swedish case as an example. The dotted line, representing the mid-1970s, shows that most people who fell under the low-income cut-off were young people aged 18-25. Very few people in middle-age groups were below the low-income rate. The numbers started to increase at age 50 and were highest among those over age 75. By the mid-1990s (represented by the heavy line), overwhelmingly it is younger people who were below the low-income cut-off lines.

Box 2.2. **The case of Canada – the importance of the changing relative size of income sources**

Canada has shifted from having one of the lowest average replacement rates among the nine countries in the mid-70s to having the highest in the mid-90s. During the same period, there was a large decline in the number of older people living beneath the low-income cut-off line. These results can only be fully understood by examining changes that took place in the weight of the various sources of retirement income.

Several factors contributed to this positive outcome, including taxation, a growing weight of private pensions, a declining weight of working income and the design of public pensions. Basically, the income of all groups of older people improved (in part because of more private pension provision and the maturation of public earnings-related pensions), but the largest increase was among lower-income people.

An analysis (in Myles, forthcoming) of the components of the retirement income system, including a separate examination of the components of the public system, shows that the main factor in increasing replacement income among lower-income people has been the maturation of the earnings-related public pension.

As explained in Chapter 3 the low ceiling in the Canadian earnings-related pension means that it acts much as a flat-rate benefit for those with higher incomes and that the public system, taken as a whole, is highly redistributive. At the same time, working income (which increases inequality) was falling as a result of early retirement. The result was an increase in income equality among older people during a period when the income of older people was rising, on average, relative to that of working-age people.

There is no magic policy recipe in the Canadian experience – a large public system matures only once, and the decline in earnings as a result of earlier retirement may be undesirable on other grounds. The experience does, however, provide an example of how success can only be understood by examining all the components of the system and how they work together.

© OECD 2001

Ageing and Income

Chart 2.2. **Percentage of population that is below the low-income cut-off line**[a]
Mid-70s, mid-80s and mid-90s

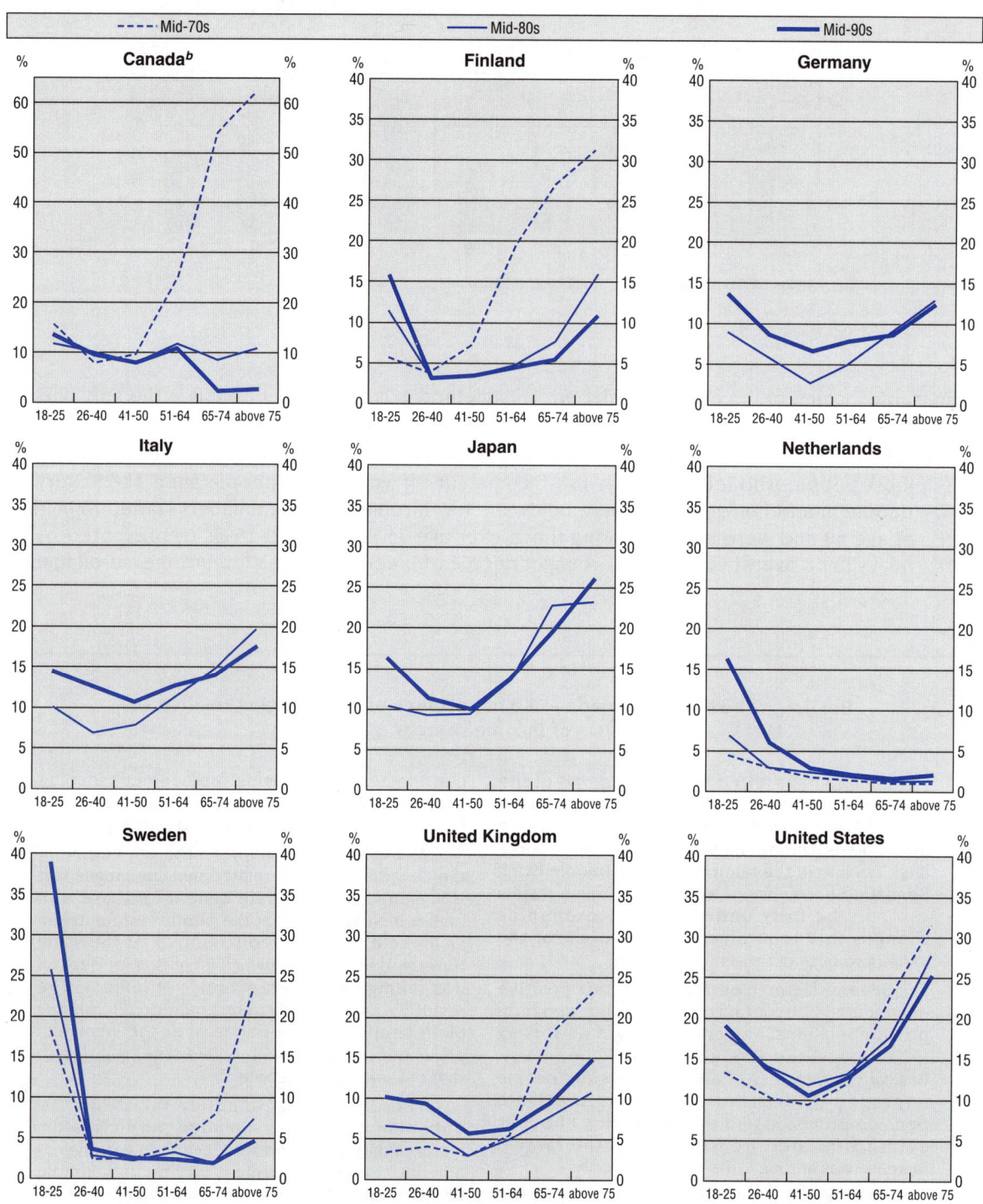

a) "Low-income cut-off line" means 50% of median disposable income of the entire population. So, the rate might be changed by population ageing, even if there were no change of substantial income levels in sub-population groups.
b) Measure of vertical axis is different for Canada.
Source: Calculations from the OECD questionnaire on distribution of household incomes (1999).

- The situation of older people has improved or remained stable in all countries. Finland and Canada show particularly large drops over recent decades in the number of older people living below the low-income cut-offs.
- In most countries, the curve today is like a shallow "U", with a higher incidence of low incomes among the young and the old. Canada, the Netherlands and Sweden are exceptions, with older people being the relative winners.

2.4. Why older people can have similar incomes in all countries, despite widely differing levels of public support

By the mid-1990s, the income needs of most older people were being met adequately and with dignity in all nine countries. This success is illustrated by Chart 2.3, which shows that, in the mid-1990s, the disposable income of people aged 65 to 74 (when, except in Japan, most people are retired) was between 80% and 100% of the disposable income of the adult population. Since the mid-1970s, the income of older people has grown relative to that of the whole population in most countries.

This outcome is the result of the balance of elements within the system, and cannot be seen by examining any one component, such as public pensions, in isolation. This section provides an overview of the share of these various components of the retirement income system, while later sections will examine how their role varies in different income groups in different countries. Chart 2.4 looks at social security income alone (mainly pensions), this time shown as a ratio of the working income of the population as a whole. Here there are large differences across the nine countries, both in the role of public pensions in the mid-1990s and in historical trends.

Chart 2.5 shows how sources of income for people aged 65 have evolved since the 1970s. It is important to note that all income is assumed to be shared within a household (including work-related incomes earned by non-elderly members of joint households). In the 1990s, working income played a significant role in several countries, especially in Japan and Italy. Capital income, mainly from private pensions, is important in about half the countries. Public pensions and social transfers play a large role in all, especially in Finland, Germany, Italy and Sweden. Working income played a much larger role in the household income of people aged 65 and over in earlier decades. Capital incomes have, on the other hand, risen over time with the growth of private pensions. In most countries, these two trends have been of about the same size (thereby leaving the share of social transfers about the same). In Finland, Italy and Japan, however, the drop in working income was offset by an increase in net social transfers.

To understand why older people in the nine countries have similar relative incomes, it is necessary to examine the mix of sources of that income among people for different income levels. Section 2.2 describes

Chart 2.3. **Ratio of disposable incomes of people aged 65 to 74 to people aged 18 and over**
Mid-70s, mid-80s and mid-90s

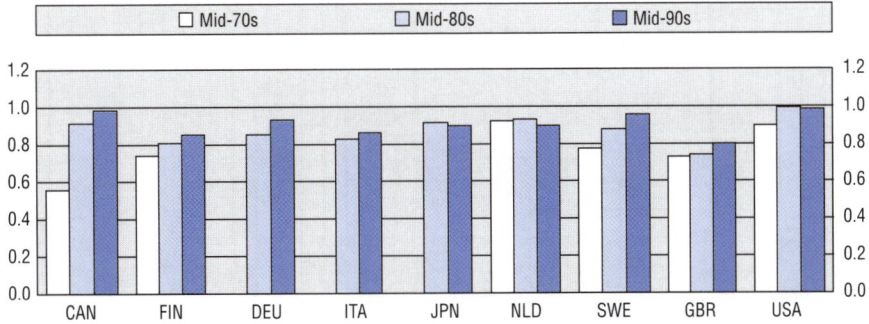

Source: Calculations from the OECD questionnaire on distribution of household incomes (1999).

Ageing and Income

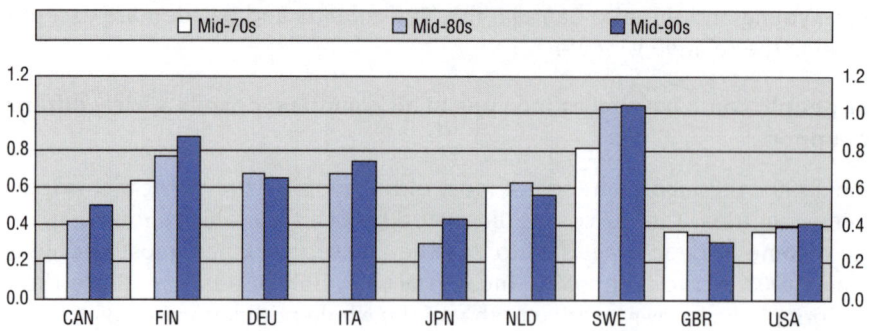

Chart 2.4. **Social security transfers, people aged 65 to 74**
As a ratio of the salary and self-employment incomes of people aged 18 and over
Mid-70s, mid-80s and mid-90s

Source: Calculations from the OECD questionnaire on distribution of household incomes (1999).

how total replacement incomes among older people are quite similar at different income levels. However, there are large differences in the sources of that income among lower- and higher-income groups. Chart 2.6 shows that low-income people in all countries usually have only one source of income – social transfers.[7] This has been consistently the case in recent decades – except in Japan, where reliance on these transfers grew over the past decade. Middle-income people also rely heavily on public pensions, although other sources begin to be more important. It is only among upper-income people that a more diversified system – particularly with a large role for working income – begins to emerge. In this respect, not much has changed in recent decades. As always, Japan is an exception with its higher reliance on earnings at all income levels.

A main explanation for the similarity across countries in the disposable incomes of older people, despite large differences in total public pensions and other social transfers, lies in the design of public pensions and the extent to which private pensions are mandatory. Chapter 3 shows that, in all countries, public and mandatory pensions are designed to provide reasonable levels of replacement income for those with lower incomes, but there are considerable differences in the level of income that is provided

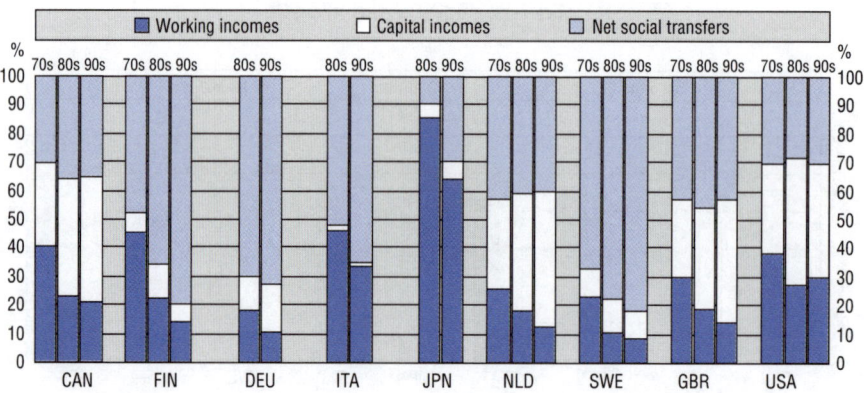

Chart 2.5. **Disposable income by source of income, age 65 and over**
Percentages, mid-70s, mid-80s and mid-90s

Source: Calculations from the OECD questionnaire on distribution of household incomes (1999).

© OECD 2001

The Resources of Older People: Complex Systems and Successful Outcomes

Chart 2.6. **Trends in income sources, by income group, age 65 and over**
Percentage of disposable income, mid-70s, mid-80s and mid-90s

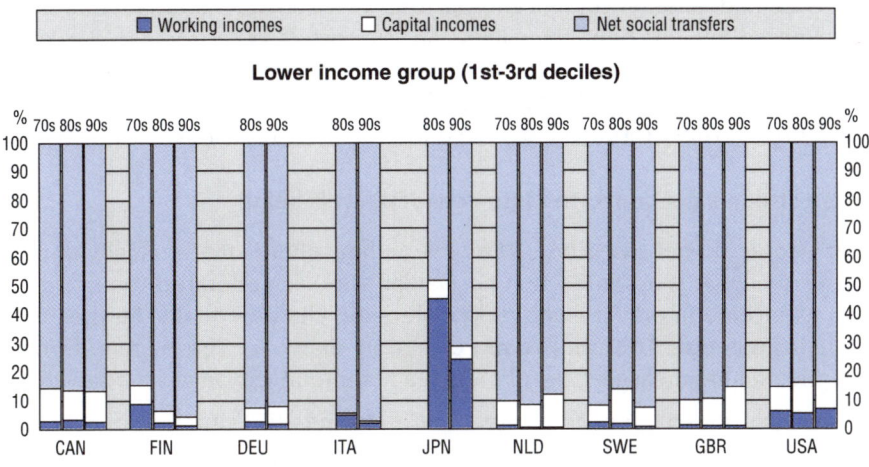

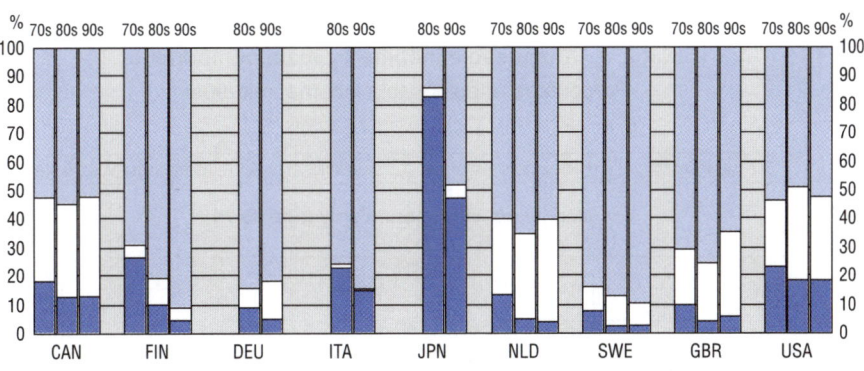

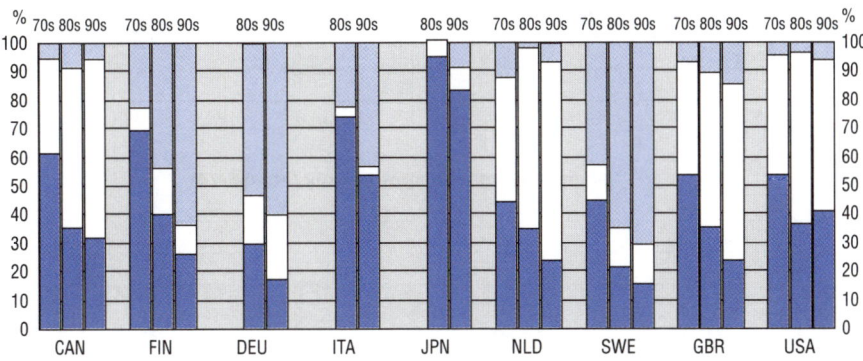

Source: Calculations from the OECD questionnaire on distribution of household incomes (1999).

to higher-income groups. In cases where the statutory system provides relatively low replacement income, the gap is filled by private arrangements and working income. The net effect is a similarity in the average income of older people across the countries.

© OECD 2001

Ageing and Income

The story behind this substitutability among sources of income is both complex and important to policy-making. The complexity lies, in part, in the fact that, in these data, income is assumed to be pooled at the level of the household, leading to the inclusion of earnings and other income of any non-elderly persons in the household. Another complicating factor is that there are alternative sources of income, such as disability or unemployment benefits, which can support early retirement. Work and the receipt of benefits can be combined in different ways. In addition, a change in the relative size of different sources of retirement income can, by itself, have complex effects on the measurement of replacement income and on income distributions. These topics are explored further in the remainder of this chapter.

2.5. How income streams get converted into economic well-being

Most older people do not live alone. They live in households that typically pool their incomes. In the data presented here it is assumed that no matter who has generated the income, or to whom the benefit is paid, all income in the household is pooled and shared equally. Further, there are economic advantages to living together. Two can live more cheaply than one. These are referred to as household economies of scale and are measured here through a technique known as an equivalence scale.

Chart 2.7 sorts out these household effects.[8] It examines the situation of couples. The top panel shows the situation of men aged 65 to 74 who are living in a two-person household with their spouses. Take the case of the United States. A little over 80% of the disposable after-tax income of an average

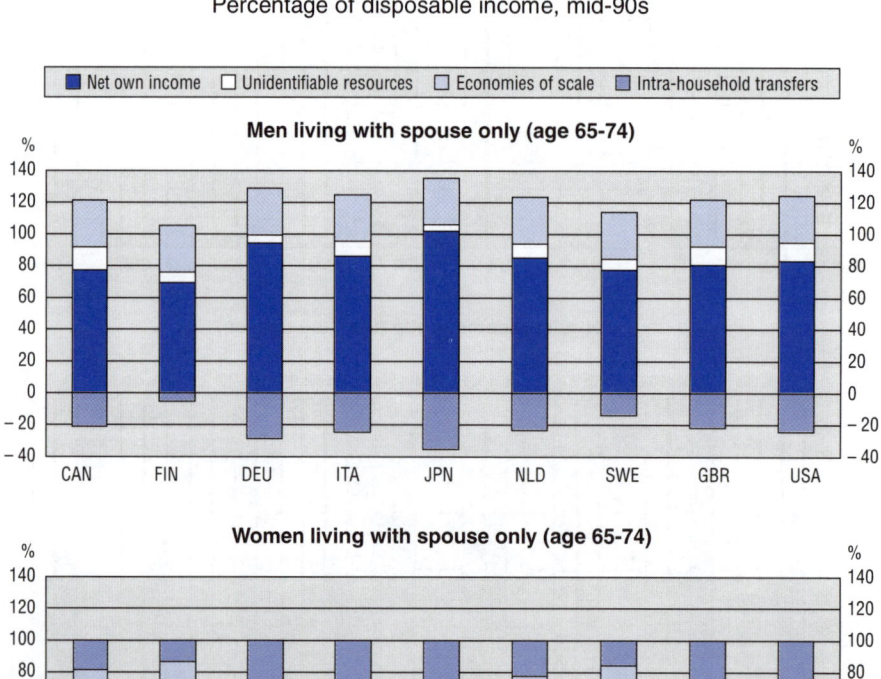

Chart 2.7. **Disposable income by main components**
Percentage of disposable income, mid-90s

Sources: OECD calculations based mainly on data from the Luxembourg Income Study. See Yamada and Casey (2001).

American man of this age would have come from his own sources (his own pension or work). He would make transfers, from his own income, to the spouse. These would be equivalent to over 20% of his disposable income. On the other hand, he would gain the equivalent of 29% of disposable income from the household economies of scale.[9]

The bottom panel shows the analogous situation for women aged 65 to 74 living with a spouse. Note that the transfers between men and women are not exactly the same in the two cases. These data are for individuals, not couples, and wives are often in a different age bracket from their husbands.

In all of the countries, married men make transfers to their wives (reflecting the higher wages of men overall), although in Sweden and Finland the extent of these transfers is somewhat smaller than in the other countries. Less than half of the disposable income of married women is own income; they benefit from both the economies of scale of the partnership and transfers made to them by their husbands.

Completing the circle – the components of "net own income"

When considering the economic well-being of older people, transfers *inside* households are most important, as are economies of scale associated with household size. However, when considering the sources of retirement income, it is often more useful to examine an individual's actual own income from various sources (with taxes shown separately). Chart 2.8 provides this extra information. It does this by examining the components of the "net own income" block in Chart 2.7. The chart shows that:

- Among men, own public pensions are by far the most important source of disposable income in Finland, Germany, Italy, Sweden and Japan.
- Among men, own private pensions are important in Canada, the Netherlands, Sweden, the United Kingdom and the United States. (Table A.8 in the Statistical Annex shows the percentage of income derived from private pensions for those who are in receipt of those pensions. It is considerable.)
- Own working income is an important source in Japan and the United States.
- Among the sources of women's own income, public pensions are important, and private pensions unimportant. However, neither is large in terms of its share in disposable income.

The interplay between external income sources and intra-household effects is important for understanding the situation of vulnerable groups, such as widows. It is also important in understanding how people can adjust their economic position by changing their living arrangements. This is described in the next section.

The central role of living arrangements: larger and smaller households

The role of household arrangements is important to policy. People can, and do, adjust their level of material well-being in retirement by making adjustments to various parts of the complex system that has just been described, including living arrangements. In international comparisons, understanding the household dimension is essential. Italy and Japan provide an illustration.

In most countries, about three-quarters of people near retirement age (between age 60 and 64) live in one- or two-person households, as shown in Chart 2.9. Their children have left home. Japan and Italy are exceptions. In these countries, only about 40% of people of this age live in one- or two-person households. People around retirement age in both these countries frequently have adult children living with them. OECD calculations show that some two-thirds of people in their late twenties in Italy are living with their parents, with the share of the same age group in Japan only slightly smaller. Elsewhere, the proportion rarely exceeds 10%. Details are found in Chart A.2 in the Statistical Annex.

In other words, there are more households consisting of three or more people among middle-age groups in Italy and Japan than elsewhere, reflecting a tendency for their children to remain at home, often until marriage. In the case of Italy, it is also argued that high youth unemployment rates – along with the relative absence of social security benefits other than pensions – mean that young people who are unsuccessful in entering the labour market must rely on intra-familial transfers and benefit from

Ageing and Income

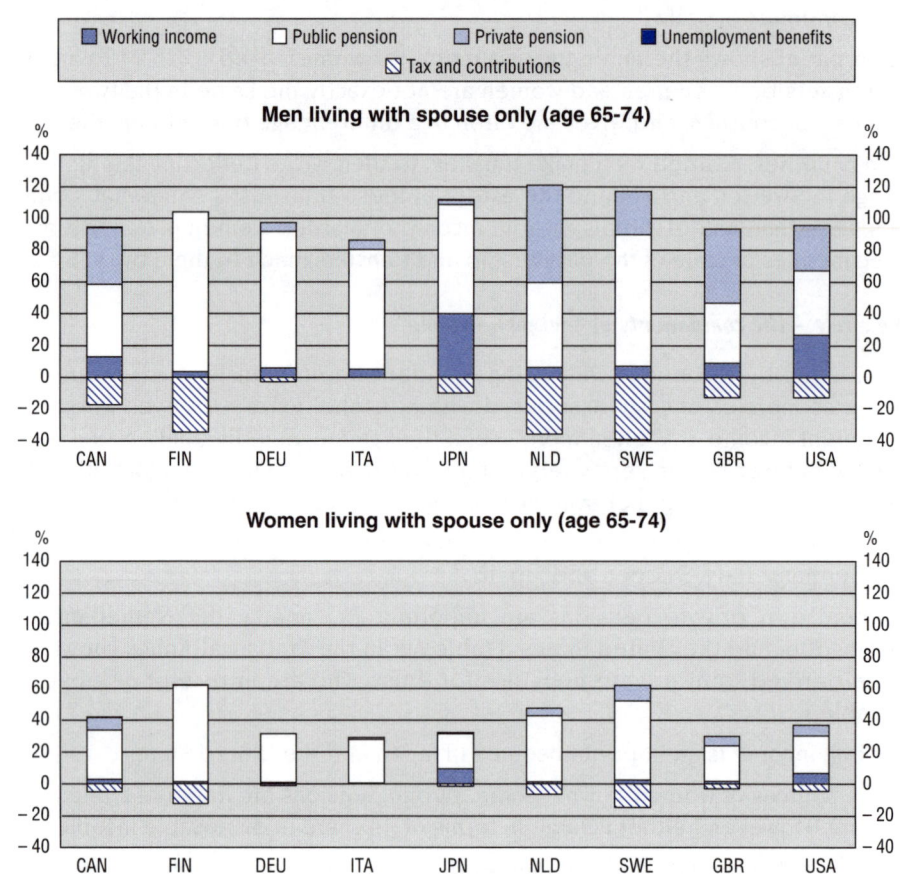

Chart 2.8. **Disposable income by "own" income components**
Percentage of disposable income, mid-90s

Note: Italian data are on a net income basis, because separate information on tax and contribution is not available.
Sources: OECD calculations based mainly on data from the Luxembourg Income Study. See Yamada and Casey (2001).

their parents' earnings and, later, pensions. In the case of Japan, housing costs are high and young people can enjoy a higher living standard if they live in their parents' house until marriage.

In Italy, households get smaller after the age of 50, following the pattern of most countries. In Japan, however, this does not happen. Beyond the age of 60 there is, in fact, an increase in the proportion of households made up of five or more persons. That is, in Japan, retirees often move in with their children, a process that occurs at a much later age, and to a much lesser extent, in other countries. The proportion of single older people living with other household members is also high in Japan. Table A.9 in the Statistical Annex provides details.

Living in larger households might be thought to point to low income levels and the consequent need to rely upon income from working children. Reality can be more complicated. Take Japan as an example. Household size reflects a complex inter-generational support system – supported by implicit inheritance rules – in a country where house prices are high, affordable accommodation is often small and/or distant from the place of work and care-giving takes place within the family (although professional care-giving is evolving as a result of new long-term care policies).

Chart 2.9. **Household size by age of individuals**
Mid-90s

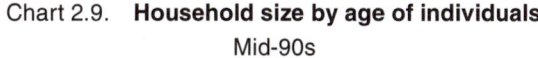

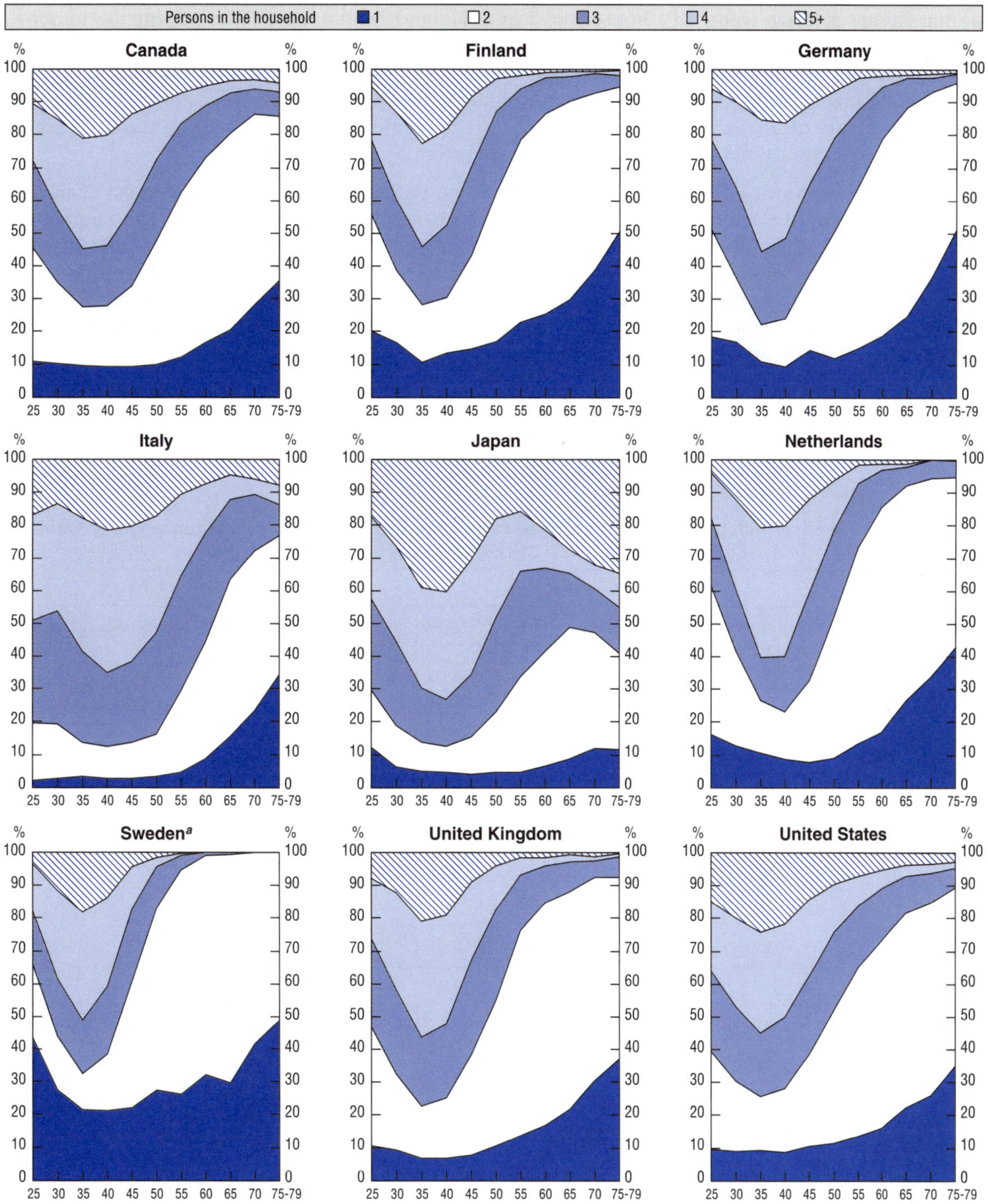

a) Since the numbers are obtained by income survey data, the numbers could be different from the National Census data. The Swedish definition of household in the survey is based on "tax units". Therefore, the data are less comparable with other countries.
Sources: OECD calculations based mainly on data from the Luxembourg Income Study. See Yamada and Casey (2001).

Ageing and Income

A *hypothetical example of the effects of shifting living arrangements*

In order to illustrate the possible effects of alternative household structures, a "pseudo-simulation" was calculated.[10] This shows what would happen if other countries were assumed to have the living arrangements of Japan (with large households) or of Finland (where most older people are in one- or two-person households). All other attributes of the population and the individuals were assumed to remain unchanged. This is an implausible assumption, since changing living arrangements would most certainly be highly correlated with other characteristics. However, the example is not intended to be a realistic estimate of what might actually happen. It is only intended to illustrate the possible scale of effects and the interactions with the tax and transfer system.

The results, shown in Table 2.3, are for people aged 65 to 79 – the years when most changes in living arrangements occur. The table shows that, if the United Kingdom had the same living arrangements as Japan, market income for older people would be over 50% higher. The income of the adult children (who would now be living with their retired adult parents) would be shared with those parents. After social transfers and taxes are taken into account, there would be a more modest increase in net income of 20%. Market income would be much less equally distributed, but the effects of social transfers and taxation would erase this added inequality.

Parallel results (but in the opposite direction and on a more modest scale) would occur if the United Kingdom had the same living arrangements as Finland – a country with somewhat fewer large older households.

Table 2.3. **Pseudo-simulation: countries assumed to have the living arrangements of Japan and of Finland**
Differences in mean incomes and Gini coefficients, people aged 65 to 79, mid-90s

	Differences of mean incomes (%)			Differences of Gini coefficients[c] (%)		
	The market income (mean value)	After receiving social security benefits (mean value)	After receiving social security benefits and paying tax and contributions (mean value)	The market income (labour incomes + private pensions + capital incomes + private transfers)	After receiving social security benefits	After receiving social security benefits and paying tax and contributions
	Japanese case					
Canada	38	15	13	–13	0	1
Finland	177	15	18	–22	–13	–7
Germany	159	19	9	–34	–13	–18
Italy[a]	20	–5		–1	10	
Japan	..	..	..	..	..	..
Netherlands	8	–3	–4	–10	5	9
Sweden[b]	16	4	3	–5	–4	–3
United Kingdom	52	24	20	–14	0	0
United States	25	9	7	–12	–3	–3
	Finnish case					
Canada	–11	–5	–5	4	0	–1
Finland	..	..	..	..	..	..
Germany	–3	–1	0	2	1	1
Italy[a]	–15	0		–1	–7	
Japan	–45	–20	–18	29	11	10
Netherlands	–2	–1	–1	0	–1	–1
Sweden[b]	–1	–1	–1	–1	–1	0
United Kingdom	–5	–3	–3	1	–1	–1
United States	–7	–4	–4	4	2	2

a) Italian data are on a net income basis, and therefore the two effects are not identifiable.
b) The reference unit in the Swedish income data is a "tax unit" rather than a "family" or "household". The data on Sweden are, therefore, less comparable.
c) A Gini coefficient is a standard measure of income inequality. A negative number means greater inequality.
Sources: OECD calculations based on data from the Luxembourg Income Study. See Yamada and Casey (2001).

The simulation illustrates a familiar policy paradox where, for example, an increase in public pensions could lead to lower measures of disposable incomes and greater inequality.[11] This might have happened, at least to some extent, in Japan. If other things were equal, a shift away from "re-merging" would reduce living standards among older people. In fact, the number of three-generation households in Japan has decreased almost 10% in the past decade, and it is possible that the maturing pension there has been a factor in providing the additional resources that have allowed more older people to live alone. The preferences of older people (and their adult children) for more independent living arrangements might, in some cases, have outweighed their preferences for higher income.

A similar pseudo-simulation (in Yamada and Casey, 2001) examined the consequences of assuming other countries had the same work patterns as a country where people worked later in life and a country where people retired earlier (again, Japan and Finland, which have the largest and smallest number of people working later in life). Unsurprisingly,[12] market income and measured inequality rose when people were assumed to work later and fell when they were assumed to retire earlier. However, again, these effects were greatly reduced by the workings of the tax/transfer system.

This discussion illustrates the care that needs to be taken in interpreting measures of outcome, particularly income distribution measures. Measures that show increased inequality, or even reduced levels of economic well-being, do not necessarily indicate a policy problem. They may, in some cases, simply be the consequences of achieving a more important objective, such as more independent living arrangements or a more balanced system with a larger role for private pensions and earnings.

2.6. Combinations of work, public pensions and private pensions

When the policy focus includes the transition to retirement and the various pathways from work-to-retirement, an even greater number of elements must be considered as part of the retirement income system. Various combinations of work, pensions and other benefits are possible,[13] and there is a degree of substitutability among these sources that must be taken into account in policy formulation. Chart 2.10, which provides a snapshot of men at successive ages, shows the main categories:

Older men who work

- *Workers without a pension*: The number of these "normal" workers usually begins to decline after the age of 50, with larger declines after the age of 50 to 54 (working non-pensioners).

- *Working pensioners aged 65 and over*: Japan has the largest group of men who both work and have a pension, but there are significant minorities in this group in the United States, Sweden and Canada as well.

- *Working pensioners under age 65*: The numbers are especially large in Japan and in Sweden (reflecting the large partial pension that then existed). In addition, there are significant numbers of men, especially in their early 60s, who worked and received a pension in the United States, the United Kingdom and Canada.

Older men who do not work

- *Non-working pensioners aged 65 and over*: These are "normal" retirees and constitute a clear majority of men over the age of 65 except in Japan.

- *Non-working pensioners aged 60-64*: There are also significant numbers of men between the ages of 60 to 65 who have ceased working and are drawing a pension. In some countries, but not others, this category contains men in a *disability benefit pathway to retirement*. In Germany, Finland, the United Kingdom and the Netherlands, disability programmes are important. In Canada, the United Kingdom and the United States, private or company pensions are important. It also includes men who are taking advantage of partial pension programmes.

- *Non-working pensioners under age 60*: The number of men in their 50s who are already pensioners and not working was particularly high in Italy, partly thanks to the former seniority pension scheme (now replaced) which gave benefits on the basis of number of years of contribution rather than

Ageing and Income

Chart 2.10. **Work and benefit status of men, older age groups**
Percentage of population, mid-90s

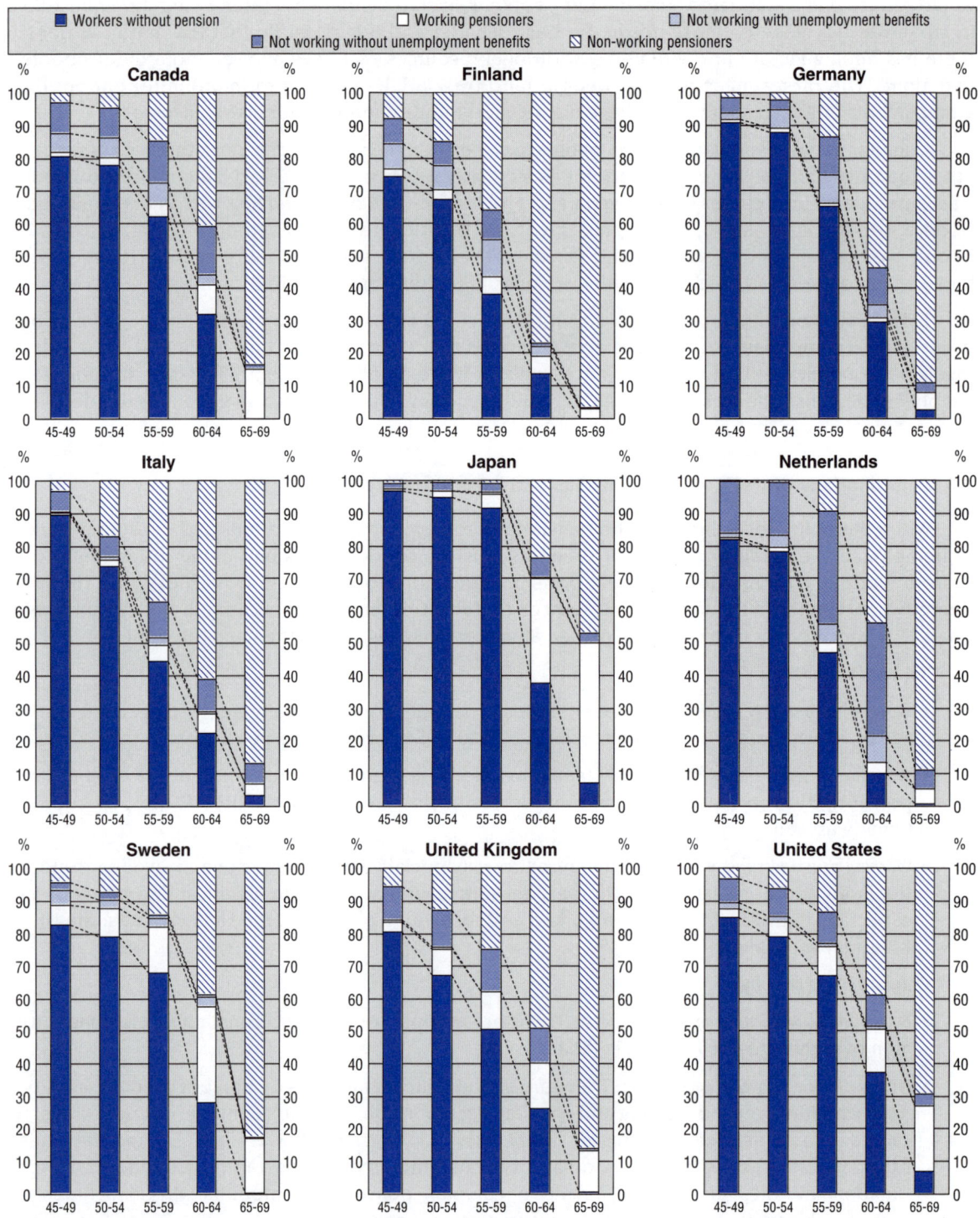

Note: "Pension" includes private pensions.
Sources: OECD calculations based mainly on data from the Luxembourg Income Study. See Yamada and Casey (2001).

age.[14] Numbers are also high in Finland, where there exists an early pension for the older unemployed, and in some countries with extensive private provision.

- *Not working with unemployment benefits*: About half of men that neither work nor have a pension are still attached to the labour force as indicated by receipt of unemployment benefits, although this varies by country. Numbers are relatively large in the Netherlands, where unemployment benefits can be drawn by people dismissed above age 57½ until they reach pension age at 65, and Germany, where an age pension can be drawn at 60 after one year of unemployment and older people are eligible for extended unemployment benefits. Finland provides an unemployment benefit for people in their late 50s that can be transformed into an "unemployment pension". Some people in this category do return to work, but for many unemployment benefits act in much the same way as early-retirement benefits. In Finland, in particular, the data must be understood in light of the high cyclical unemployment in the early and mid-1990s.

- *Other pathways*: There is a miscellaneous group of men without work and without pension or unemployment benefits. (In the chart these are referred to as "without unemployment benefits".) Other transfers often provide bridge income until normal pensionable age, such as disability benefits, mentioned above. Means-tested benefits are important in the United Kingdom and Canada. Other private transfers, including cash property income, are important resources in Canada and the United States for men aged 55-59, and in Canada, Japan, the Netherlands and the United States for older men. In Germany, private benefits provided as part of company outplacement packages are also important.

Table A.10 in the Statistical Annex provides various breakouts by age group of combinations of public and private pensions for very early retirees, early retirees, normal retirees and working and non-working pensioners. It shows the size of the pension for those who receive such benefit. These data are particularly useful in illustrating the role of partial pensions and private pensions during the transition process. Also in the Statistical Annex are a series of charts that examine income distributions in various categories:

- In Canada, Germany, Japan, the United Kingdom and the United States, early retirees tend to be less well-off than people who continue to work. On the other hand, in Finland, Italy and Sweden, early retirees often do better than those who continue to work. (Chart A.3 in the Statistical Annex).

- Continuing to work results in higher incomes for those aged 65 and over. It is not surprising that those who have income from both earnings and pensions are relatively better-off – over-represented in the high income quintiles and under-represented in the low quintiles (Chart A.5, second panel, in the Statistical Annex).

- Higher-income people rely, of course, on private pensions more than do lower-income people. Nevertheless, the recipients of private pensions are spread fairly evenly over the income distribution, apart from the bottom quintile. They are not concentrated in the top quintiles (Chart A.6).

- Private pensions also play an important role as a "bridge income resource" until non-working pensioners reach the normal pensionable age for public pension (Table A.10). This occurs in Canada, the Netherlands, Sweden, the United Kingdom and the United States.

This review illustrates the complexity of the retirement income system, especially during the transition to retirement. Retirement income policies should not be defined in terms of simple age cut-offs or simple "retired versus not retired" distinctions. Nor are pensions the only social programme that finances the transition to retirement. Chapter 5 provides information on various pathways, including disability benefits.

© OECD 2001

2.7. The relation between income sources, levels and distributions

The interplay among the various components of the system for different income groups is crucial to understanding the success of the retirement income system in meeting its low-income and income-replacement objectives. The practical importance of these interactions is illustrated in Box 2.2, which shows how the relative success of the Canadian experience reflects changes in the mix of components in the system in that country.

Perhaps the easiest way of understanding the importance of the changes in the mix of sources of income is to examine the factors that cause changes in income growth among older people.

Income growth: usually stronger among lower-income groups

Success in meeting replacement rate and low-income goals is ultimately a reflection of the growth in the mean disposable income in different older income groups. Looking at changes over the most recent decade, the income position of older people improved in all income groups between the mid-1980s and mid-1990s. Table 2.4 shows that higher growth took place mainly among lower-income groups in Canada, Finland and Japan. In Sweden and the United Kingdom, growth was strongest among higher-income groups. The situation was more mixed in Italy, and income gains were fairly equally distributed by income quintile in the Netherlands, Germany and the United States. (In these latter two countries and in Japan[15] income growth was stronger among the total population than among the older population.) The United States, the Netherlands and Japan are, of course, the three countries where aggregate replacement rates did not rise during this time period (see Table 2.1).

Table 2.4. **Real income growth, retirement age, by income quintile**
Percentages, total population and population aged 65 and over, mid-80s to mid-90s

	Total population	Q1	Q2	Q3	Q4	Q5
Canada	−1	19	11	12	7	2
Finland	11	14	15	14	10	10
Germany	19	24	26	25	26	19
Italy	7	10	10	6	9	17
Japan	21	29	20	12	14	18
Netherlands	19	11	13	13	14	15
Sweden	16	18	20	23	29	38
United Kingdom	21	14	24	32	33	30
United States	7	3	7	4	2	5

Note: Shaded cells indicate higher income growth than that of total population.
Source: Calculations from the OECD questionnaire on distribution of household incomes (1999).

The changing composition of the retirement income system

Chart 2.11 shows how each income component contributed to this income growth. The sum of each different box in each quintile is equal to the numbers in Table 2.4. In most of the countries, income growth among the older lower-income people comes from growth in social transfers and from reductions in direct taxes. However, offsetting changes in other components have also played a part. For instance, in Japan, the first three quintiles experienced almost the same growth in social transfers, but this was considerably offset in the third quintile by shrinkage of working income. The situation in the upper-

The Resources of Older People: Complex Systems and Successful Outcomes

Chart 2.11. **Real income growth, by income component and income quintile**
Population aged 65 and over, percentages, mid-80s to mid-90s

☐ Working income ☐ Capital income ■ Social transfers ☐ Tax

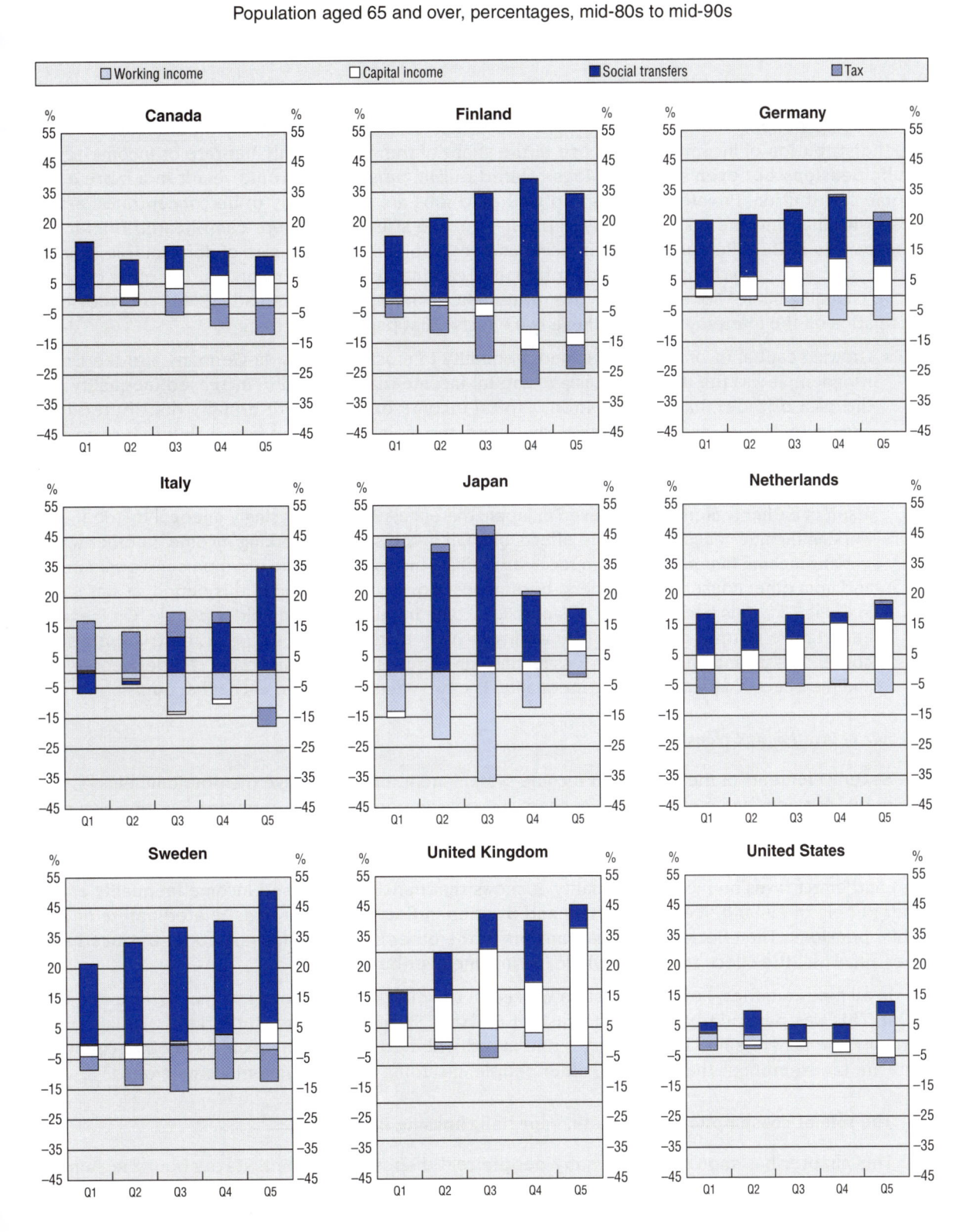

Source: Calculations from the OECD questionnaire on distribution of household incomes (1999).

income quintiles is quite mixed. Increased capital income played a major positive role in many countries, often partially offset by declines in working incomes. However, in most countries, increased social transfers also benefited higher-income groups, particularly in Sweden, Finland and Germany.

Not always self-evident distributional consequences

One might expect that an increase in the share of capital income or earnings would result in a less equal distribution of income, while a rise in the share of transfers (mainly flat-rate or income-tested public pensions but even some earnings-related public pensions[16]) would result in a more equal income distribution. Private pensions and well-paid jobs are more likely to be concentrated among those with high incomes. That usually happens, but the situation is more complicated than it first appears. Two quite different effects can occur as a result of a shift in the size of, for example, working income. One relates to changes in the distribution of earnings among older workers. The other depends on the changing share[17] of earnings in the retirement income package. Yamada (2001) provides more information on the interplay between these two effects. That paper shows that:

- Growing capital income has increased inequality in most countries. In Germany and the United Kingdom, it was the increased *share* of capital income that resulted in increased inequality over the past decade; taken in isolation, capital income became more equally distributed in its effects. In Sweden and Italy, on the other hand, the main effect came from a shift to less equality in the distribution of capital income.

- The contribution of employment income to inequality has been declining for two decades as a result of earlier retirement. However, in Japan, the effects of an increasingly unequal distribution of working income cancelled out the effects of a fall in the share of working income. In other words, working income (among those who received working income – both the older person's own earnings and from other household members) became less equally distributed in this period, as was shown in Chart 2.11. This had the effect of *increasing* income inequality among older people. On the other hand, more people retiring earlier and relatively fewer people living in multi-generational households meant that there was less reliance on earnings in the total income of older people. This had the effect of *decreasing* income inequality. The two effects cancelled each other out.

The role of taxation and transfers

Several elements of the retirement income system are intended to have distributional effects. Flat-rate public pensions and means-tested benefits and pensions are the main examples. Taxation also plays a significant role in the retirement income system, a role that is almost certain to grow in importance.[18]

Table 2.5 shows the effects of transfers (including all pensions – earnings-related as well as flat-rate) and direct taxes on income inequality. It shows that transfers increased income inequality among older people in Finland,[19] Germany, Italy and Sweden, reflecting the earnings-related nature of their public pensions. The effects of various transfers in the other five countries just about balanced each other out, with little effect, taken as a whole, on income distribution.

In all nine countries, however, taxation worked in the direction of making income distribution more equal. This was particularly true in the case of Finland, Sweden and the Netherlands. In Japan and Germany, the tax system played a smaller role in redistributed income. In Japan, as in other countries, there are tax exemptions that favour all older people, including those in higher-income groups.

2.8. The role of consumption and wealth, especially housing assets

This chapter has shown how for many people real disposable income stays about the same or increases when they retire. International data on consumption patterns shed some light on what happens to that income. Do they translate into actual higher levels of material well-being? There are many difficulties in interpreting existing data and linking it to income – including problems in the treatment of housing and health care. Nevertheless, recent OECD analysis (in Yamada and Casey, 2001)

Table 2.5. **Contribution of taxes and transfers to income distribution**
Gini coefficients for population aged 65 and over in each country = 100%, mid-70s, mid-80s and mid-90s

	Mid-70s		Mid-80s		Mid-90s	
	Contribution of social security benefits	Contribution of direct tax	Contribution of social security benefits	Contribution of direct tax	Contribution of social security benefits	Contribution of direct tax
Canada	−2	−26	−1	−31	0	−49
Finland	45	−67	63	−61	88	−60
Germany	..	..	53	−25	49	−13
Italy	..	..	10	−35	40	−40
Japan	..	..	7	−21	8	−21
Netherlands	9	−86	1	−84	0	−58
Sweden	79	−103	119	−101	99	−76
United Kingdom	−5	43	−4	−43	0	−34
United States	1	−35	5	−38	9	−37

.. Data not available.
Source: Calculations from the OECD questionnaire on distribution of household incomes (1999).

tends to support the conclusions based on income data that real living standards are about the same or increase somewhat once people stop working.

After making the same kind of adjustments that were made to the income data, available data suggest that the relative consumption of older couples (not counting expenditure for living accommodation) is at least 80% of that of younger couples with children and exceeds 100% in several countries (Germany, Japan, the Netherlands). Relative consumption of older singles is less than older couples, which is consistent with their lower incomes. Looking at housing, which is not included in the figures above, mortgage repayments are much higher for younger than older people. For countries where data are available, the estimated rental value of an owned house is higher among older people in most countries. For people who do rent, older people often spend more than younger people, although the pattern varies from country to country.

For many, wealth[20] is an important resource for retirement and a buffer against unexpected developments. There is, for example, considerable housing wealth even among low-income older people. The economic position of older people can be considerably better than is shown by income data alone, particularly when one considers housing assets. There are often barriers to being able to convert housing wealth into income but, as noted above, the imputed rental value of an owned house tends to improve the relative economic position of older people.

Table A.14 in the Statistical Annex shows proportions of "pre-retirement" and "post-retirement" households with financial wealth and housing wealth, by income quintile. It reveals, unsurprisingly, that most households at all income levels have at least some financial wealth (which includes money in bank accounts). In the mid-1990s, in nearly all income groups[21] over 90% of households in both the pre-retirement and post-retirement age groups reported financial wealth.

Fewer people have housing wealth, except in Finland, and it is somewhat more concentrated in higher-income groups. Nevertheless, some 70% or more of older couples in the lowest-income quintile still have housing wealth in most countries – somewhat lower in the Netherlands and Germany and somewhat higher in Canada, Japan and the United States.

Table 2.6 expresses financial wealth and housing wealth as a percentage of gross annual income in the mid-1990s. Financial wealth is relatively small, being less than a year-and-a-half's gross income in most cases. However, older people have greater financial wealth in Italy, the United States, the United Kingdom and Japan in post-retirement ages. Housing wealth is, of course, much larger, often three or four times annual gross income – lower in the Netherlands and Sweden and especially high in Japan. The Japanese figures reflect factors such as the high cost of housing in that country, the high value

Table 2.6. **Ratios of market wealth to gross income**
Households consisting of couples, mid-90s

	Financial[a] wealth-to-gross income ratio	
	Pre-retirement age head	Post-retirement age head
Finland	0.3	0.7
Germany	0.5	1.2
Italy	1.2	2.5
Japan	1.5	3.6
Netherlands	0.4	0.9
Sweden	–0.1	0.7
United Kingdom	1.5	3.3
United States	1.5	2.9

	Housing wealth-to-gross income ratio	
	Pre-retirement age head	Post-retirement age head
Finland	2.1	3.2
Germany	2.8	4.5
Italy	2.1	3.0
Japan	4.2	8.9
Netherlands	1.2	1.6
Sweden	2.1	1.7
United Kingdom	2.6	3.9
United States	1.5	3.0

Note: Canadian data not available.
a) Financial assets are in gross terms.
Source: OECD wealth data.

placed on home ownership and the lump-sum benefit paid at the mandatory retirement age that allows people to pay off their mortgages. Both financial and housing wealth are higher in the post-retirement age group than in the pre-retirement-age group (except for housing wealth in Sweden).

Chart 2.12 shows the total of both housing and financial wealth as a percentage of gross income. For each country, two bars are shown, one for the lowest-income quintile (left) and the other (right) for the highest-income quintile. Panels A and B compare pre-retirement age couples with couples of post-retirement age. Total market wealth is larger in the older age group, except for the lowest quintile in Italy and Sweden. Paying off mortgages is likely a main factor with respect to housing wealth. In most countries and most income groups, housing wealth exceeds financial wealth in all income groups. However, in the United States and the United Kingdom, financial wealth is greater in the highest-income group. A comparison of panels B and C shows that the wealth situation of older couples and older singles is quite similar.

Because the denominators used in Chart 2.12 are the gross income of each quintile, the expected large gap in wealth between the top and bottom quintiles is not seen. Chart 2.13 directly shows the diversity of the two types of wealth. Because of the small value of financial wealth in the bottom quintile, the ratio of mean financial wealth of the top to the bottom quintile may have little meaning, particularly the large differences found in Italy, the United Kingdom and the United States. More interesting is the much smaller gap in housing wealth. Even in Japan, where housing wealth has a relatively high value, the gap is relatively low.

The role of wealth is typically given limited treatment in discussions of resources to support retirement, often because of data difficulties.[22] This is unfortunate because wealth is important in several contexts. Financial wealth diversifies risks, as it can usually be converted to retirement income as required. Imputed rents of owner-occupied housing are important to the economic well-being of older people and, as noted, home ownership is common even among lower-income older

The Resources of Older People: Complex Systems and Successful Outcomes

Chart 2.12. **Market wealth-to-gross income ratio by household type**
In the top and bottom income quintiles,[a, b] mid-90s

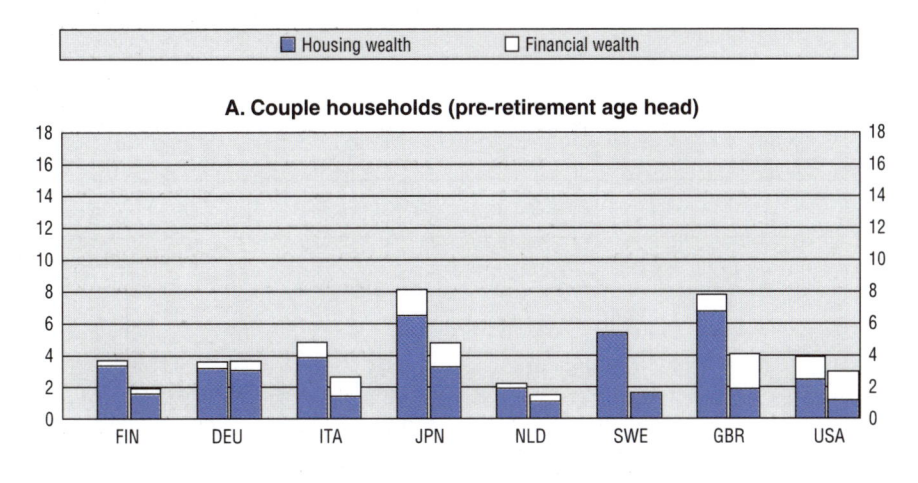

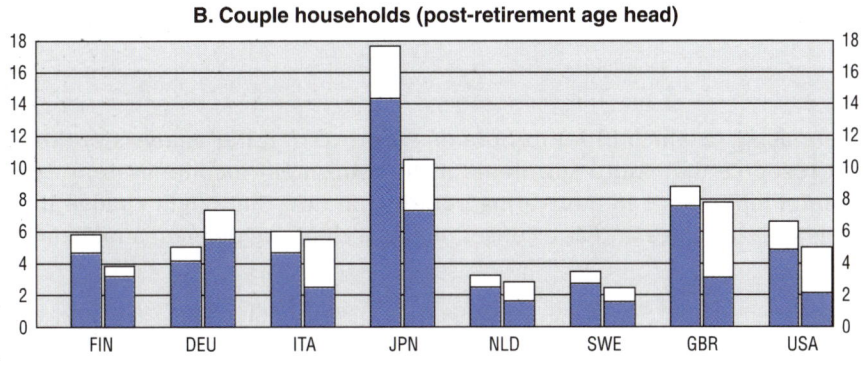

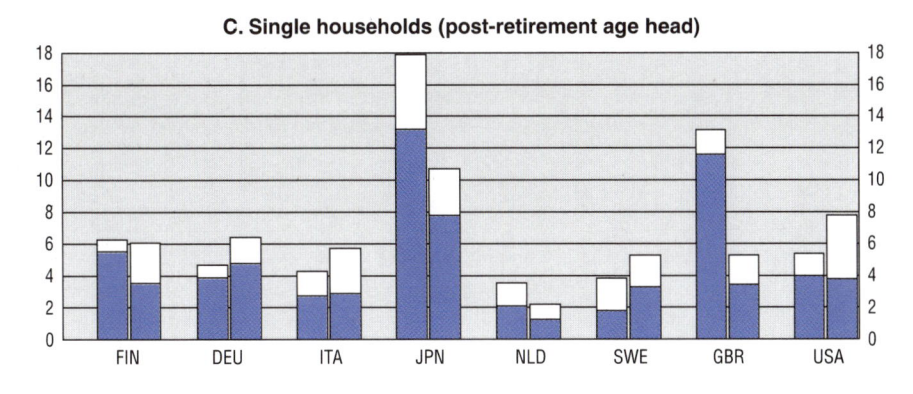

■ Housing wealth   □ Financial wealth

A. Couple households (pre-retirement age head)

B. Couple households (post-retirement age head)

C. Single households (post-retirement age head)

Notes: Data for Canada are not available.
Pre-retirement age group is about 51 to 59 (53 to 57 in Japan).
Post-retirement age group is about age 65 to 69 (70 to 79 in the United States).
a) The left bar represents the bottom quintile, the right bar the top quintile.
b) For the United Kingdom, the financial assets are in gross terms.
Source: OECD wealth data.

people in some countries. Moreover, housing assets might potentially play a larger role in the retirement income system, if there were ready means of converting housing assets to income. A review of policy alternatives, which was not undertaken here, would require an examination of such factors as the development of financial instruments (*e.g.*, reverse mortgages) and the availability of

Chart 2.13. **Difference in financial and housing wealth: top and bottom quintiles**

Ratio of the average wealth of the top quintile to the bottom quintile, couple where head is aged 65 and over, mid-90s

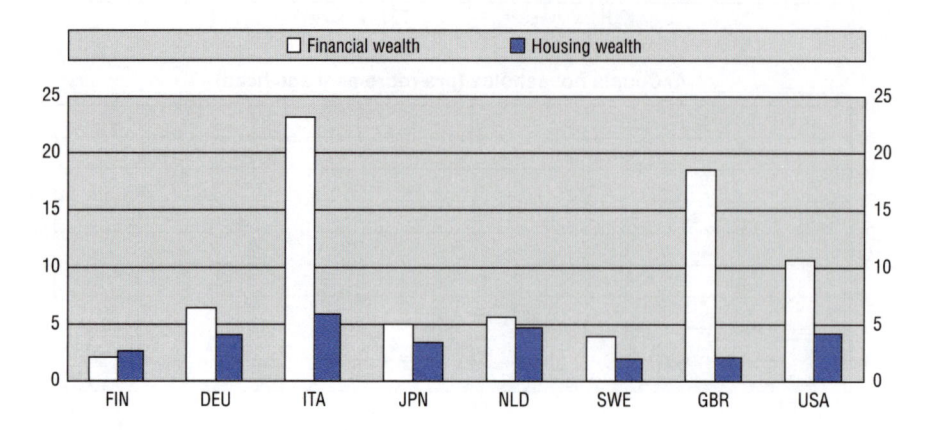

Note: Data for Canada are not available.
Source: OECD wealth data.

less expensive housing to which older people might move. A fuller analysis of the effects of wealth as a retirement resource that could supplement the retirement income system would also need to examine the role of inheritance in motivating people and how that might change in light of changing family and household structures and as a consequence of changing pension arrangements.

NOTES

1. A comparison of the average of a group of people of "post-retirement age" with a group of people of "pre-retirement age" in the same year will tend to result in quasi-replacement rates that are lower than real replacement rates (actual incomes of individuals before and after retirement) since, because of economic growth, the younger age group will usually have higher incomes than did the older group when they were at the same age.

2. Often lower replacement rates, of 70% or even 60%, are thought to provide a rule-of-thumb indication of adequate replacement levels. The actual situation would depend on an individual's income levels. The ILO standard of 40% refers only to the role of public pensions. See Section 2.8 for a discussion of the role of assets and consumption.

3. Note that these comparisons should be used with caution. Pension plans are not fully mature in all countries, and the oldest old are not necessarily covered by the same pension provisions as the younger old.

4. This comparison implicitly assumes that the income distribution hierarchy is reproduced in retirement, which is by no means always the case.

5. The data should be used with care. The comparison reflects the relative economic position of people in lower deciles in *both* the working-age and retirement-age population and thus does not provide a picture of any potential problems with low-incomes among retired people *per se*.

6. For example, even if there were no real change of income inequality in the society, the threshold would change over time as the population ages and living arrangements change. See Rainwater and Smeeding (1997).

7. A much more detailed breakdown of income sources by income quintile is shown in Chart A.4 in the Statistical Annex which shows the role of private pensions, means-tested benefits and taxes.

8. A weakness of the data shown in this chart is that it contains a miscellaneous grouping called "unidentifiable resources". It is small in total, but contains elements that are important for minorities of the older population. Means-tested benefits are the main example. Social assistance or income-tested pension benefits are an important source of support for many lower-income seniors. Table A.8 in the Statistical Annex shows the percentage of people in different older age groups who are in receipt of such benefits and their size for those recipients. The table shows that these benefits grow in importance in the oldest age groups, undoubtedly reflecting the age-related effect of widowhood and the cohort-related effect of the very oldest having accrued less substantial pensions. Relatively large numbers of people receive these benefits in Canada, Finland, Sweden and the United Kingdom and, in several countries (the United States, the United Kingdom), income-tested or means-tested benefits make up a significant share of the income of those who receive them. They are either part of, or complementary to, public pensions.

9. The determination of the equivalence scale is discussed in Yamada and Casey (2001). The one used here is based upon the square root of the number of people in the household, in this case two. The square root of 2 is approximately 1.41. (1.41-1)/1.41 is approximately 0.29. The results were tested using several conventional equivalence scales. No important differences resulted for the interpretation of the data.

10. In this simulation, individuals were simply re-weighted such that there is the same proportion of individuals in various categories of household living arrangements as in the reference countries.

11. Provided, of course, that the increase was not large enough to cover the added expenses of living independently.

12. As described in Yamada (2001), working income is the major source of inequality in countries where people work later in life.

13. Since original data sources are typically annual surveys, there could be a minor problem of response lag. For example, a person might be retired at the time of survey, but report earnings during the preceding year, prior to retirement. This is unlikely to alter the findings presented here in any major way.

14. This scheme has in practice been abolished since retirement with a seniority pension now requires a 40-year contribution period.

15. Except among those with lowest incomes.

16. The effect of earnings-related public pensions is usually to make the income distribution less equal, as can be seen by the data in Yamada (2001) for Sweden, Finland and Germany. However, this is greatly affected by the design of the earnings-related pension, especially in its use of ceilings – as explored in some length in Chapter 3.

17. Since earnings tend to be distributed more unequally than transfers, a fall in the share of earnings relative to transfers would result in a total package that was distributed more equally.

18. This discussion is about distributional issues. However, the role of taxation among older people is of obvious interest in terms of it being a growing source of government revenue. Of particular interest is the increasing role of income from private pensions which, while untaxed during the contributing years, are taxed when converted into retirement income. In several of the countries under review, these revenues will be sizeable. In the Netherlands, calculations by the CPB Netherlands Bureau for Economic Policy Analysis (2000) suggest that older people themselves will pay much of the added costs of ageing. They suggest that taxes paid on pension incomes will rise from 3.3% of GDP in 2001 to 8.4% of GDP in 2040. In Canada, as well, there have been calculations of the net tax gains as more older people pay income tax on their tax-deferred pensions. They conclude that, because of the robustness of the results to these and other assumptions, a wide range of tax expenditure projections is possible in this area.

19. The Finnish occupational pensions which are included here because they are statutory are, in reality, private.

20. The analysis of wealth data here updates earlier work reported in Disney, Mira d'Ercole and Scherer (1998). A fuller description can be found there. The pre-retirement group typically includes people from about age 51 to 59, and the post-retirement group 65 to 69 – although the American data relate to people in their 70s.

21. Exceptions are lower-income groups in Italy and the United States, lower- and middle-income groups in the United Kingdom and all income groups in Finland.

22. It is difficult to make consistent comparisons of wealth and income from available data sets. As well, an underlying problem is that many of the most important potential uses of wealth data are concerned with patterns of savings and consumption over the course of life. Most existing data refer to cross-sections only and provide only limited life-course insights. See Chapter 8 for potential solutions.

Chapter 3

THE DETERMINING ROLE OF PUBLIC POLICY

3.1. Introduction

Chapter 2 showed that there is much similarity among the nine countries in terms of the income situation of older people, despite large differences in the sources of that income, including public pensions. This chapter shows how current pension rules, together with related taxation policies, have a determining, if complex, influence on the overall mix of resources in retirement, on the adequacy of those resources for people at different income levels and on incentives to retire earlier or later. The chapter models the value of public and private pension benefits for typical workers at different earnings levels in the nine countries.[1] It shows replacement income levels from public and occupational pensions, net income after taxation and the work incentives associated with different arrangements. The exercise reveals many of the features and philosophies of the systems that are hidden in comparisons of the parameters alone.

Section 3.2 explains why modelling provides better comparisons across countries and what is included. This is followed by a comparison of pension replacement rates resulting from statutory or quasi-mandatory pension rules (Section 3.3) and from non-statutory occupational pensions (Section 3.4). Section 3.5 deals with the effects of taxes and net replacement rates.

Note that, for ready reference, a very short description of the systems in each of the nine countries can also be found in Annex I. For interested readers, a more complete description of the arrangements in each of the countries, and how these relate to the modelling results, is found in the last section of this chapter (Section 3.6).

The most immediately striking finding that emerges from this analysis is in the pattern of statutory pension values for people at different earnings levels. A key determinant is the ceiling on the earnings-related public pension scheme. These ceilings vary from just over average earnings in Canada to almost four times average pay in Italy. The quasi-mandatory scheme in the Netherlands and the mandatory scheme in Finland are basically uncapped.[2] This results in big differences in the (mandatory) pension entitlements of richer workers, while poorer workers' mandatory public benefits are much more similar between different countries.

A second finding relates to the importance of the interplay between public and occupational pensions, especially when the latter have wide coverage. The public schemes of Germany and Italy, for example, are large and based on social insurance principles. The result is a lower degree of redistribution than in countries such as Canada and the United Kingdom, where flat-rate basic pensions and income-tested top-ups target public pension benefits on the lower paid.[3] Since these schemes pay only a small benefit relative to pre-retirement earnings for higher-paid workers, they leave scope for private provision of benefits for these groups. In Sweden, Finland and the Netherlands occupational plans have nearly universal coverage either by statute or by agreement among the social partners. When these statutory or quasi-mandatory pensions are included with public pensions, pension values look similar to those in Italy. Finally are countries where occupational plans are large but cover only about half of the workforce or less (Canada, the United Kingdom and the United States). For those who are covered, including income from these private schemes means that the pattern of entitlements versus earnings would converge with countries with comprehensive public (or mandatory private) provision.

A third finding relates to the tax treatment of pensioners relative to workers. The principal difference in many countries is that pensioners pay fewer social security contributions or have no liability at all. Some countries, however, offer substantial income-tax concessions in addition. This means that net replacement rates (taking account of income tax and social security contributions) are higher than gross. It also means that the pattern of replacement rates against lifetime earnings is different when measured in net terms rather than gross.

Finally, the analysis begins to shed new light on the incentives to earlier and later retirement that flow out of the pensions and tax rules. Pensions can affect retirement decisions in many ways, including through ages of regular and early retirement, earnings rules, the generosity of replacement rates and level of pension wealth – the discounted value of pension benefits less the cost of obtaining them – that has been accumulated. It can be assumed that people will work longer if by doing so they increase their pension income or build up their pension wealth and will cease working when income no longer rises or wealth diminishes. However, there can be points when pension wealth is no longer accumulated (and even when pension wealth is decreased by further working) yet where retirement is unlikely because the pension income that would be received is too low or even zero. This may happen if the age of pension entitlement has not been reached. The way in which pension income and pension wealth develop and the way in which their levels interact with one another to influence the retirement decision are discussed in Annex II. This is work in progress. The results, when final, will represent a major advance over earlier work, particularly in allowing consistent cross-country comparisons of the retirement incentives (both income and substitution effects) embedded in the combined public and occupational schemes on a net basis. It appears that the incentives to early retirement arising from the pension wealth calculations vary considerably across countries and income groups. There are also important differences when calculated on a net and gross basis.

3.2. Modelling pension and tax rules – a better approach to cross-country comparisons

Pension systems: difficult to compare using traditional techniques

Pension systems differ substantially across the nine countries in the following major ways:

- *The role of the state*. Governments in every case provide support for the lowest-income workers in retirement who have little or no entitlement to earnings-related (public or private) pensions. Some countries do this through minimum pensions, whereas others provide support through minimum income guarantees, social assistance benefits targeted at older persons and general social assistance programmes.

- *The balance between pay-as-you-go financing and advance-funding*. This difference often follows the divide between public and private provision. However, there are also examples of partial funding of public pensions (Canada, Japan, Sweden, the United States) and of unfunded provision of private pensions (some occupational plans in Germany).

- *The balance between defined-contribution and defined-benefit schemes*. Defined-contribution pensions have begun to substitute for defined-benefit in Italy (only defined-contribution occupational and personal plans are now allowed), Sweden (in the new individual accounts replacing part of the public programme, and in occupational schemes), the United Kingdom (for the public and occupational schemes as well as among occupational plans) and the United States (in occupational schemes). Elsewhere, defined-benefit plans dominate in both public and private sectors.

There are many other differences in public policy approaches in areas such as taxation or the treatment of married couples. Consider the latter. Most earnings-related schemes use the individual as the unit of assessment. In countries with insurance-based systems, the same benefit formula applies to single people and couples alike. Japan and the United States are exceptions. In the United States social security pays a 50% dependant's supplement in respect of spouses who have no entitlement of their own (or only a small one). Canada's system combines many different elements. The basic pension is an individual entitlement, and the claw-back of the basic pension from higher earners through the tax system is based on individual income. The income-tested supplement, however, uses the couple as the unit of assessment. The benefit for a couple is 62% higher than that for a single person. The earnings-related pension is assessed individually with no extra payments for couples. Other income- or means-tested schemes – such as the United Kingdom's minimum income guarantee – use the couple as the unit of assessment. Finland's basic pension and Sweden's guarantee pension, however, claw back the benefit on an individual basis, not on the couple's income.

The effects of these different approaches are not easily captured by standard techniques that compare systems based on design parameters. As well, recent trends have undermined the usefulness of standard ways of classifying systems, such as pay-as-you-go versus advance-funded, defined-benefit versus defined-contribution or even the familiar three-tier[4] approach to describing pensions (public pension, occupational pension, individual pension). For example, the distinction between advance-funded and pay-as-you-go elements has been eroded by arrangements in which an advance-funded component has been incorporated within a fundamentally pay-as-you-go system (as with investment funds in the United States, Japan, Canada and the Netherlands). The concept of individual retirement accounts as a separate tier of the system has been similarly eroded by the incorporation of such accounts within the public pension system and occupational pensions (as in Sweden). The close linkage of defined-contribution and advance-funded elements on the one hand, and defined-benefit and pay-as-you-go elements on the other, has been blurred by the introduction of notional accounts (as in recent Italian and Swedish reforms). As already noted, the public-private distinction – at least as it relates to individual choice and replacement income levels – has been greatly blurred by arrangements where occupational pensions are, *de facto*, mandatory for employees in covered sectors (nearly all employees in Finland, the Netherlands and Sweden).

A *better approach*: *applying today's pension rules to hypothetical individuals*

This chapter provides a better understanding of the differences among the nine countries, not by analysing characteristics of the pension system's parameters – such as accrual rates, minimum pensions, indexation rules, eligibility requirements, etc. – but by using those parameters to actually calculate pension benefits of illustrative workers at different income levels. This allows an examination of, for example, the combined effects of public and occupational plans and of taxation. The results are typically expressed as "pension replacement rates"[5] (the ratio of the pension benefit to the individual's previous earnings), or the benefits are expressed in relation to economy-wide earnings.

It is important to bear in mind a number of limitations to the modelling, although there are fewer than in most approaches used to compare the systems. First, the modelling assumes that the structure of the pension system and its parameters remain unchanged in the future, although it does take account of any future changes that have already been legislated. Nevertheless, the frequency and the scale of past pension reforms suggest that future pension regimes will look very different from today's systems.[6] Second, it is not representative of the entire population, particularly those who do not have life-time careers. Third, it ignores the resources, other than pensions, on which older people can draw, such as earnings, investments and non-financial wealth, especially housing. A related issue is household economies of scale. Individual-level replacement rates ignore the sharing of resources with other household members. Nor does the modelling cover alternative paths to retirement, such as disability or unemployment benefits. The modelling therefore makes an appropriate complement to the household income data in Chapter 2, which do not have these limitations, but which are necessarily out-of-date – reflecting the characteristics of institutional arrangements of often many years in the past.

The modelling covers all the different components of the pension system, which can include:

- The flat-rate, universal, basic pension.

- Resource-tested public benefits, where the benefit is withdrawn from richer pensioners. These can be means-tested, where both assets and other income sources are taken into account, purely income-tested or tested only against pension income.

- Earnings-related public benefits (including the so-called notional-accounts based schemes in Italy and Sweden) which are (to a degree) the reverse of income-tested benefits, paying higher pensions to richer beneficiaries (those with higher earnings through their working lives).

- Employer-provided pensions, which are usually defined-benefit (they pay a specific sum or proportion of earnings for each year of membership).

- Mandatory personal pensions (which have a defined-contribution formula, so the pension benefit depends on contributions made and investment returns earned), known in the United States as "individual accounts".

As ever, there are many borderline cases. Earnings-related pensions in Finland and the Netherlands, for example, are ostensibly privately provided. But both the Finnish scheme, which is now statutory and mandatory, and the Dutch scheme, which results from collective bargaining, are best thought of as "quasi-mandatory". Similarly, almost all Swedish workers are covered by quasi-mandatory occupational plans. In contrast, employers provide occupational schemes voluntarily in Canada, Germany, Japan, the United Kingdom and the United States. The Dutch and Finnish programmes are therefore considered along with publicly provided earnings-related pensions in other countries, while private, voluntary occupational schemes are treated separately.

The defined-contribution schemes that are included in the calculations are the new mandatory scheme in Sweden and personal pensions in the United Kingdom. The latter are mandatory in the sense that people must make some provision for a second pension above the basic level, but this can be through the public-sector scheme, an occupational scheme or a personal pension plan.

The resulting pension values are presented in a standard format and on standard assumptions. Pension benefits are calculated for a full-career worker with earnings varying between 0.3 times and 5 times economy-wide average earnings.[7] Although most workers, of course, lie in the bottom part of this scale, a broad range of earnings was chosen to illustrate properly the impact of ceilings on contributions and/or pension benefits, which can reach nearly four times average earnings.

As noted previously, we have used today's system parameters along with any changes already legislated. For Italy, for example, the modelling shows the new system when fully introduced. Looking into the future, some countries adjust some parameters of their pension system in line with prices. This can have radical effects on the long-term structure of the scheme. The baseline results therefore assume that parameters will rise in the long term in line with earnings. Where pension programmes are income-tested, it is assumed that the worker has no non-pension sources of income.

3.3. Statutory entitlements vary considerably

Chart 3.1 summarises the difference in philosophy between mandatory pension provisions in the different countries. It looks at a full-career worker with earnings of various multiples of the economy-wide average: half, average, one-and-a-half times average and twice average. The vertical axis shows the corresponding individual pension value as a percentage of economy-wide average earnings. For technical reasons, the chart includes the (quasi-mandatory) occupational schemes in Finland and the Netherlands, but not in Sweden.

The largest differences in pension values are at higher levels of earnings. Italy's pension programme, for example, aims to provide a great degree of earnings replacement even for high-income workers. The mandatory occupational pension schemes of Finland and the quasi-mandatory occupational plans of the Netherlands have a similar effect. Canada and the United Kingdom, in contrast, show a much flatter profile for total mandatory pension benefits as earnings rise. Higher-paid workers in these countries are therefore left to make voluntary provision, either through individual savings or through occupational pension schemes. Japan, Sweden and the United States lie somewhere in between. In these countries the insurance component of the public pension system is more important, but the programmes are substantially more redistributive than in the three countries at the top of the chart. As in Canada and the United Kingdom, this has led to the development of private pension provision with broad coverage.

The Determining Role of Public Policy

Chart 3.1. **Pension values for illustrative workers earning between half and twice the economy-wide average**

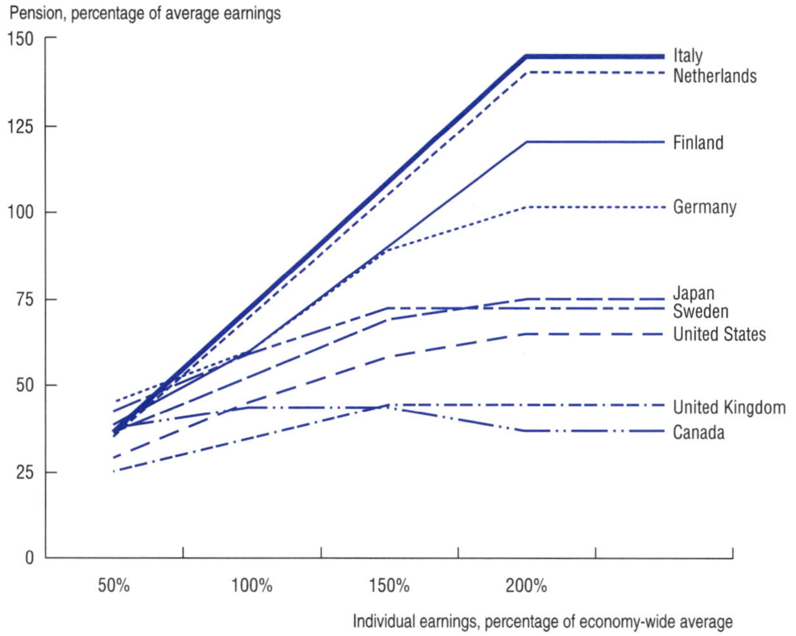

Source: OECD Secretariat calculations.

Charts 3.2 and 3.3 show the effects of various types of pensions in the nine countries. The first set of charts looks at the value of pension benefits as a proportion of economy-wide average earnings. The second shows the pension as a "pension replacement rate", that is, the value of the pension as a proportion of the individual's earnings. These charts further illustrate the essential philosophical differences between the countries' mandatory pension regimes. For low-income workers, pension benefits are fairly similar, typically around a quarter of economy-wide average earnings (although this varies between 20 and 35%). The differences are much larger at higher levels of earnings. However, it is important to recall the income-distribution analysis of Chapter 2. This showed that pensioners' overall income replacement rates were very similar across the nine countries, despite the major differences in their system. This is because higher-income workers tend to make voluntary provision, through occupational or personal pensions or other forms of saving.[8]

Ceilings playing a major role

A key variable determining these patterns is, as noted in the country descriptions, the country's *ceiling on benefits or pensionable earnings*. The importance of these parameters, set out in Table A.16 in the Statistical Annex is often understated. The six countries at the top of the table have pensions systems in which the mandatory portion has a relatively progressive structure of benefits, principally because they have relatively low ceilings either to pension benefits themselves or to pensionable earnings. These ceilings range from just over average earnings in Canada to 2½ times average pay in the United States.

At the other end of the spectrum, the Finnish scheme has no ceiling and the Dutch quasi-mandatory occupational schemes are usually uncapped.[9] At low levels of earnings, these two countries pay levels of benefits broadly similar to the six countries with relatively low pension maxima. But at high levels of earnings, benefits are constant in the first six countries, but continue to grow in these latter two cases. Italy lies somewhere between the two groups. It has a relatively high benefit floor,

© OECD 2001

Ageing and Income

Chart 3.2. **Mandatory pension benefits by earnings in nine countries as a proportion of economy-wide average earnings**

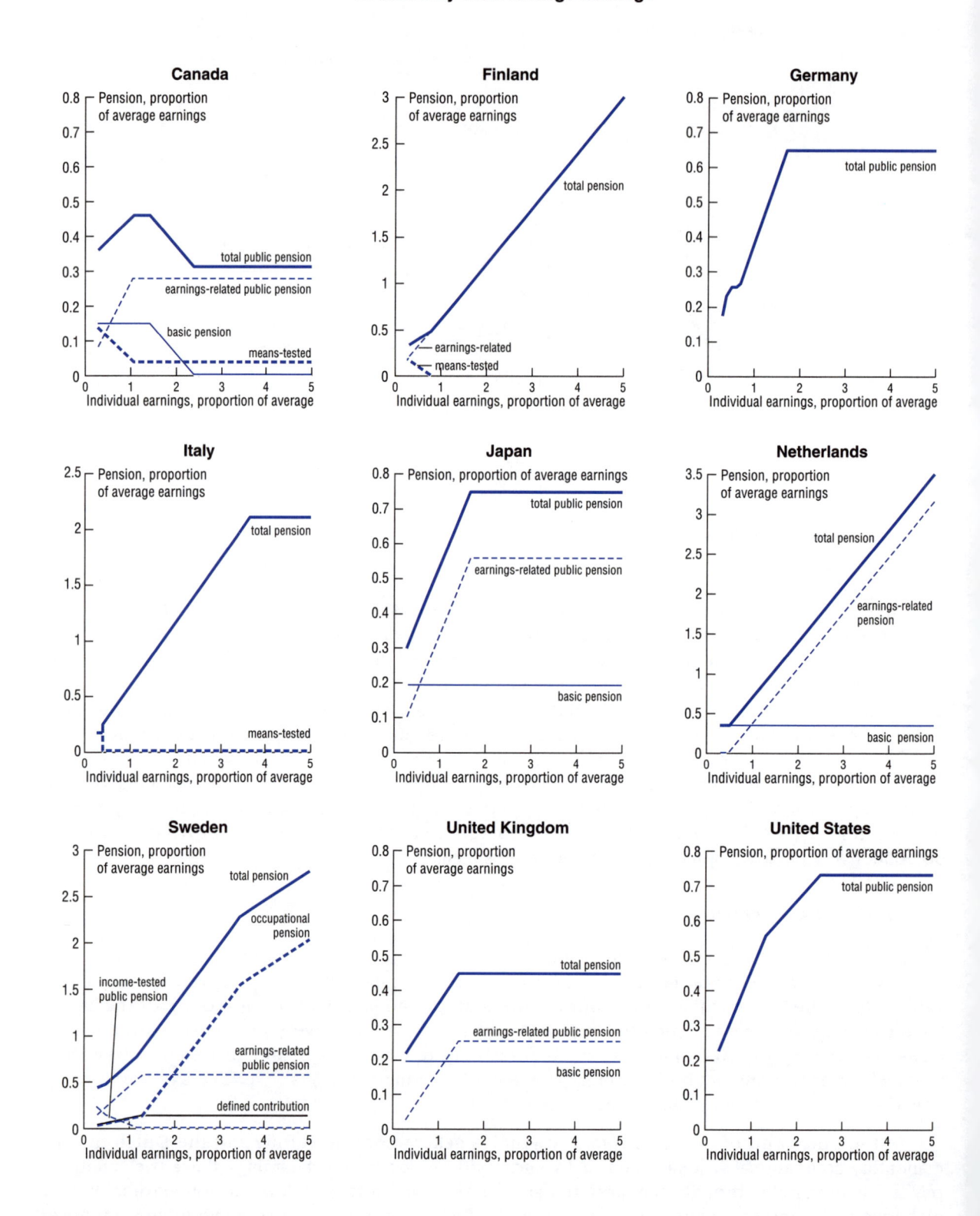

Source: OECD Secretariat calculations.

The Determining Role of Public Policy

Chart 3.3. **Mandatory pension benefits by earnings in nine countries as a proportion of individual earnings**

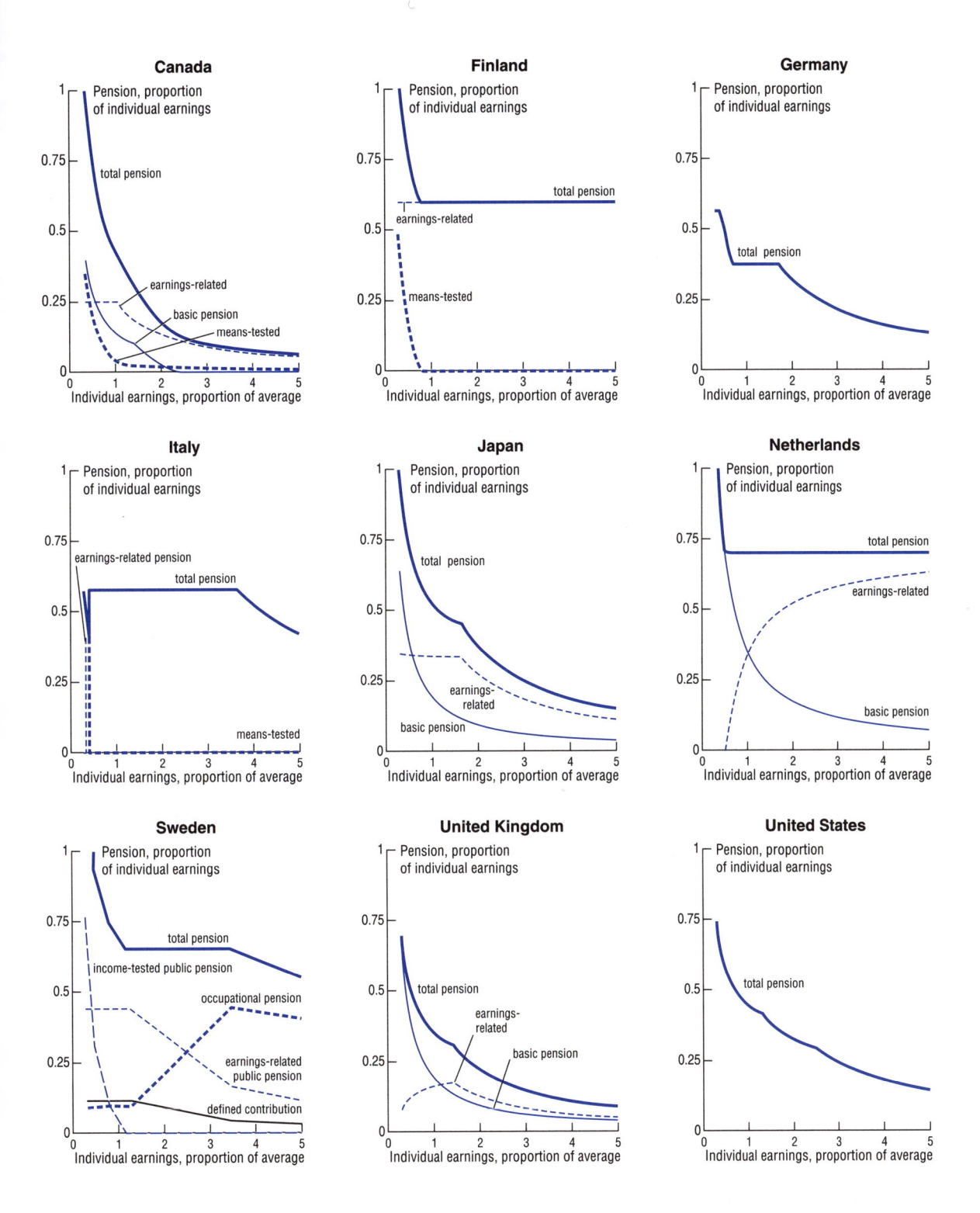

Source: OECD Secretariat calculations.

53

meaning that low-income workers receive only a small benefit from the public scheme. The ceiling, at 365% of average earnings, is also much higher than in the first six countries.

3.4. Non-statutory occupational pension benefits

Although they do not have complete coverage, occupational pensions are particularly significant in Canada, the United Kingdom and the United States, in terms both of their coverage of the workforce and their role in providing retirement incomes, as evidenced by Table 6.2 in Chapter 6. The majority of schemes[10] in each country provide benefits based on some measure of "final" salary. (This may, for example, be average earnings in the last five years.) The accrual rate is the main determinant of the generosity of the pension. A 2% accrual, for example, would imply 40 x 2 = 80% of final salary after a full 40-year career in the scheme. (The indexation of benefits is discussed in Section 7.8, while the integration of occupational pensions with the public scheme is discussed in Section 6.6.)

Chart 3.4 adds together the values of voluntary occupational pension benefits with mandatory pension entitlements to illustrate prospective total pensions for selected individuals in Canada and the United Kingdom. In the United Kingdom, the occupational pension scheme member foregoes his or her entitlement to the public earnings-related pension, SERPS, but is still entitled to the basic pension. The value of the occupational pension is proportional: the curve is a ray through the origin. This curve is also the value of the total pension in the model, integrated scheme, which deducts the value of the basic pension from the total benefit. Note that the modelling assumes that the individual spends eight years each in five different occupational pension schemes. Membership of fewer schemes across the career would result in a higher benefit, as explained in Section 6.6.

Integration of occupational pension benefits with public pension benefits is common in both Canada and the United States. Integration practice in the United States varies substantially, so it is difficult to devise a reasonable "model" procedure. In Canada, in contrast, the practice of applying a lower, 1.3% accrual rate to earnings below the ceiling for the public, earnings-related benefit is widespread. Chart 3.4 shows the results of modelling such a scheme. Even at the lowest earnings levels, the retirement income of occupational-scheme members is sufficient to float them off the income-tested supplement. The kink in the schedule for the occupational pension value at the ceiling of the earnings-related pension is readily apparent: here the pension accrual rate shifts from 1.3 to 2% of earnings. The pattern of total pension entitlement in both countries, once occupational schemes are

Chart 3.4. **Value of public and private pension benefits in Canada and the United Kingdom**
Proportion of economy-wide average earnings, full career in one occupational scheme

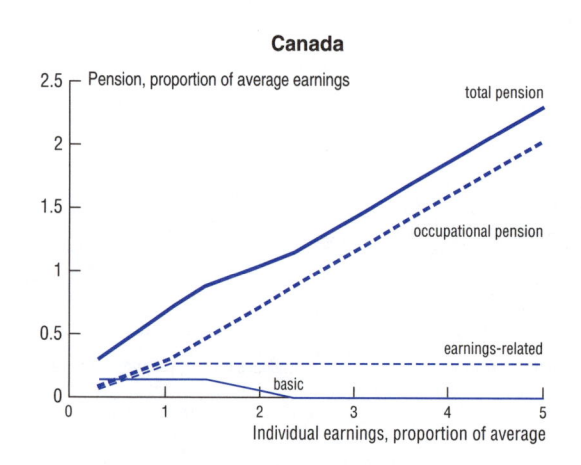

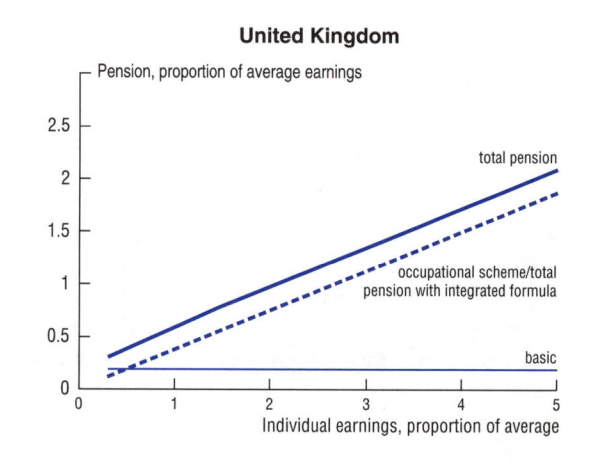

Source: OECD Secretariat calculations.

taken into account, is much closer to Finland and the Netherlands. This reinforces the point that differences in mandatory pension provision, particularly for middle- and high-income workers, tend to be closed by voluntary occupational pensions.

3.5. Tax treatment and net replacement rates

Personal income taxes and social security contributions have an important effect on the living standards of pensioners relative to the population as a whole and can affect retirement incentives. Again, there are huge differences between countries. Table A.17 in the Statistical Annex sets out the main concessions granted to older people in the various personal income tax systems. It is important to remember that income tax systems are progressive, and that the incomes of pensioners are typically lower than those of workers. Thus, pensioners tend to face a smaller tax burden than workers even in the absence of any specific concessions.

An additional fiscal advantage enjoyed by older people is that they are typically not liable for social security contributions. In most countries, social security contributions are levied only on earnings and not on pension benefits and other income sources. There are three main exceptions in the countries surveyed here. The Netherlands charges pensioners 11% of income for long-term health care insurance and survivors' pensions (compared with a total contribution of 27.5% paid by workers under the three general social security schemes). Finland levies the same sickness insurance contributions on pensioners' incomes as on workers', plus an additional 2.7% on pension income. Germany levies a similar charge for sickness insurance, plus a 0.85% levy to cover long-term care.

Chart 3.5 summarises the impact of the personal income tax and social security system on pensioners' and workers' incomes. The chart shows the average effective tax rates[11] on pensioners and workers, including the effect of the personal income tax, employee's social security contributions and, for workers, universal cash transfers (such as child benefits or family allowances).

In each figure, the thick line shows the pensioner's average effective tax rate (including personal income tax plus any social security contributions due). The thin line shows the average effective tax rate for the worker (again including both income tax and social security contributions). The dotted line shows social security contributions as a percentage of total income for the worker.

It is immediately apparent from Chart 3.5 that there are large differences between both the overall generosity of the concessions offered to pensioners, the pattern of the concessions with earnings and the sources of the fiscal advantages pensioners enjoy.

Canada, Finland and Sweden have the most highly targeted set of concessions. The patterns in the Netherlands and the United Kingdom are interesting because the gap between pensioners' and workers' average tax rates at first increases with incomes, due to the effect of social security contribution floors. As in Canada, however, targeting results from a mix of the withdrawal of additional allowances from richer pensioners and the effect of the social security contribution ceiling. The value of tax concessions to pensioners also increases initially with income in Germany and Japan. The United States offers the most valuable tax concessions across the income range.

Net pension replacement rates

The tax system has two main effects on pensioners' incomes relative to their incomes when they were in work. First, since income-tax systems are progressive and gross replacement rates are, over most of the income range, less than 100%, people will pay less tax on their pension than they did on their earnings when in work. Second, there is the range of concessions to older people, as discussed above. Again, this means that pensioners pay less tax than workers, even on the same income. Both these effects mean that net pension replacement rates are higher than gross.

This is illustrated in Chart 3.6. This combines the gross pension replacement rates from Chart 3.3 with the tax calculations underlying Chart 3.5. It gives both the gross pension relative to gross earnings, as in Chart 3.3, and the pension net of income tax (and any social security contributions) relative to net

Chart 3.5. Taxes paid by pensioners and workers
Average effective tax rate including personal income tax and social security contributions

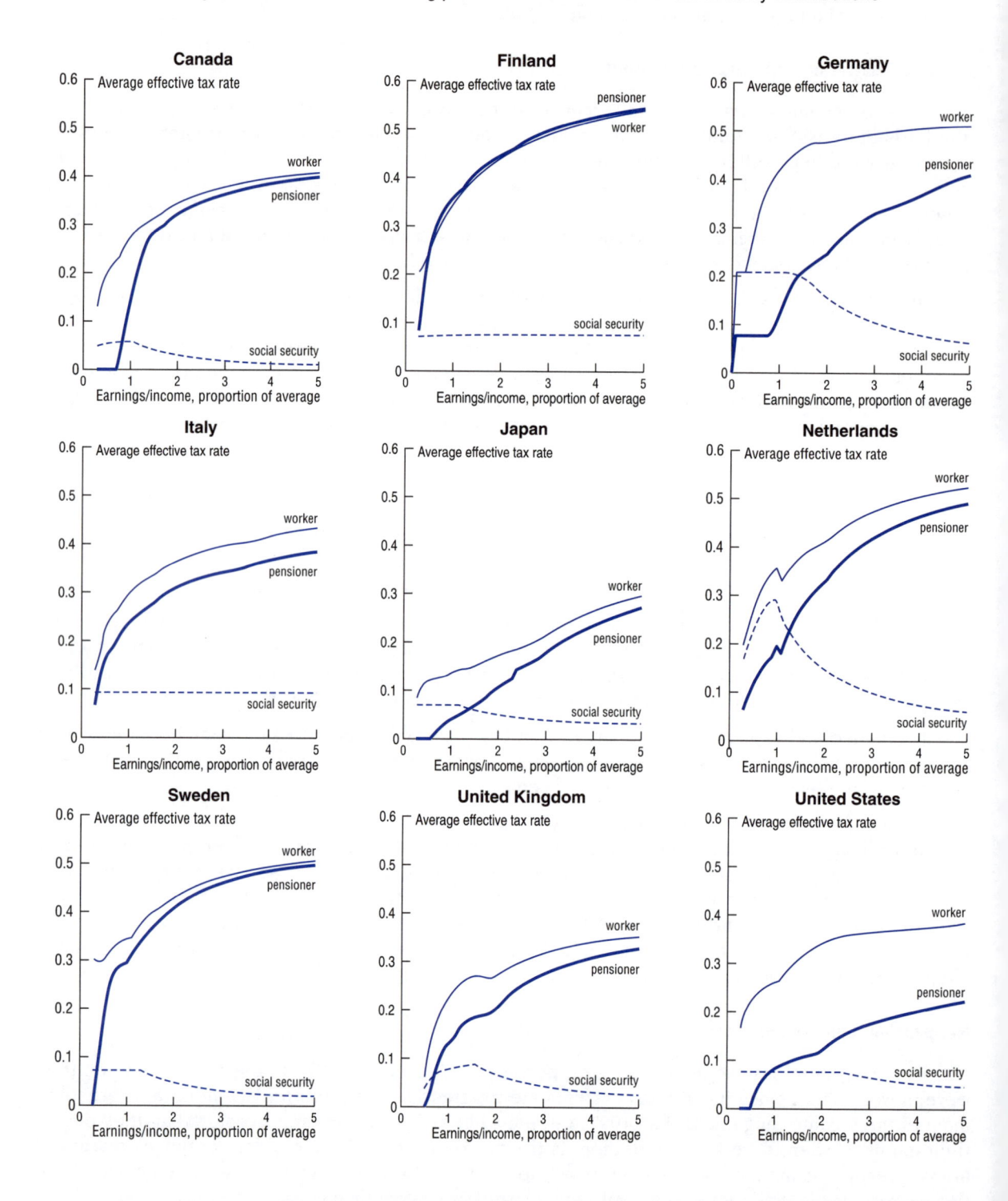

Note: The average effective tax rate lines for both workers and pensioners include both the effect of personal taxation and social security contributions. The dotted line shows social security contributions separately for workers. (In Finland, Netherlands and Germany pensioners also pay relatively small social security contributions, which are not shown here.)

Source: OECD Secretariat calculations.

Chart 3.6. **Gross and net replacement rates**
Pension entitlement as a proportion of individual earnings before and after income tax and social security contributions

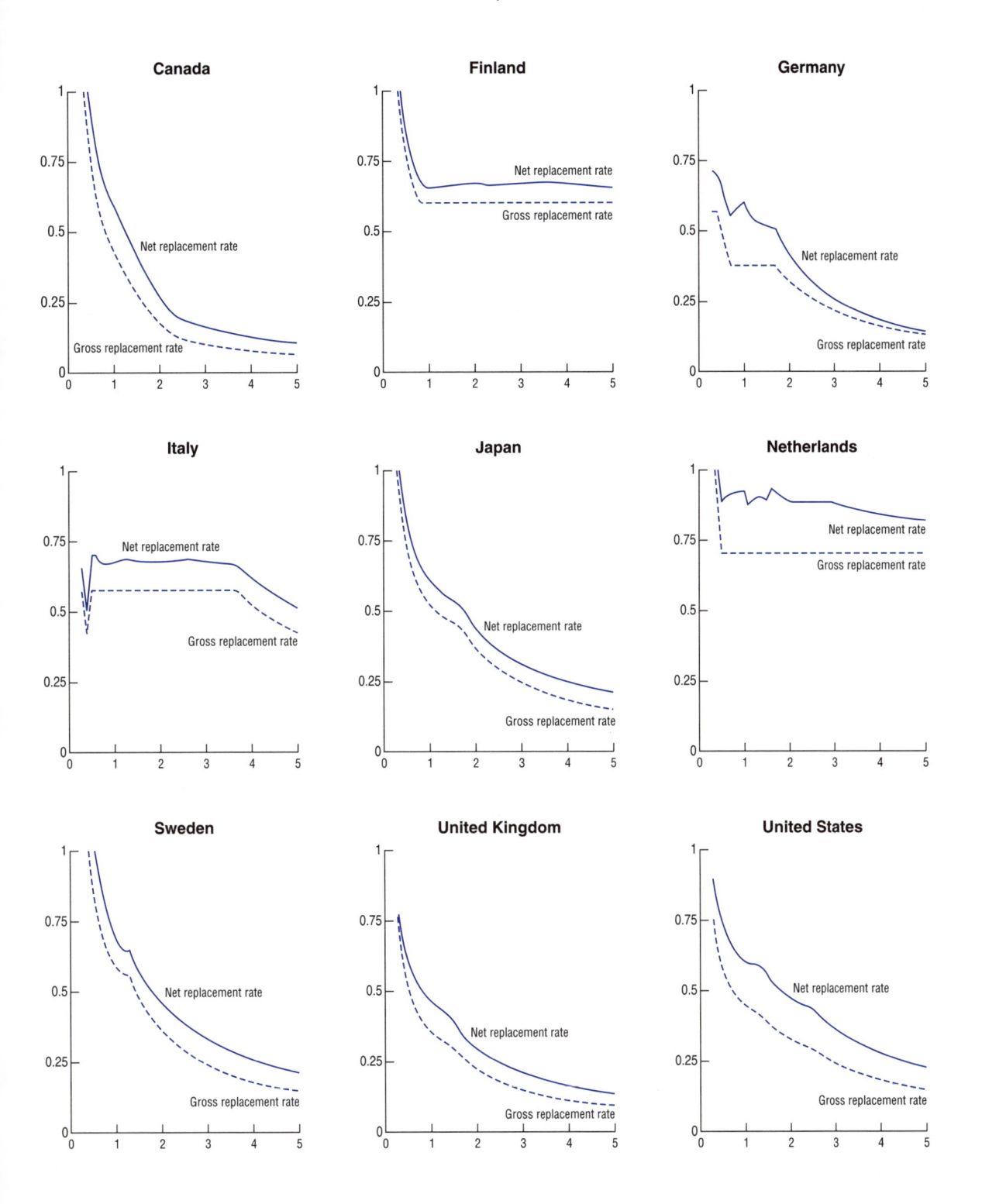

Source: OECD Secretariat calculations.

earnings (again after income tax and social security contributions). The charts confirm the important role that the tax system plays in supporting older people in all nine countries.

3.6. The experience of the individual countries

This concluding section is intended for reference purposes. It consists of a description of the basic arrangements in each of the nine countries and how they related to the modelling results. Readers interested in a shorter description of pension and early retirement arrangements in the nine countries will find a summary table in Annex I.

Canada

Public provision for retirement incomes in Canada is made up of three different components:

- First, a universal, basic pension, worth around 14% of economy-wide average earnings.[12] This is payable to everyone over 65, subject only to a residency test. This benefit is clawed back from richer pensioners – with incomes over around 1½ times average pay – with a 15% withdrawal rate.
- Secondly, an income-tested top-up, bringing single pensioners with no other income up to 31% of economy-wide average earnings.
- Thirdly, an earnings-related pension, based on average lifetime pay, with a target of 25% replacement rate relative to individual earnings. Earnings on which contributions and benefits are calculated are capped by a ceiling (about 107% of average earnings).

Less than half of the workforce is covered by employer-provided pensions. Individual provision for retirement can be made through tax-favoured pension savings instruments. The main parameters of the system (with the exception of the ceiling) are up-rated in line with prices, including the value of the earnings-related pension once it is in payment following retirement.

As is shown in Table A.16 in the Statistical Annex, Canada has the lowest ceiling of the nine countries in its earnings-related pension. The income-tested component is withdrawn from a lower-income level than in the basic scheme. However, in the absence of any private pension or investment income (a rather implausible assumption), it is still payable to those who had higher earnings during their working years. Adding the components together produces an interesting pattern. The value of the total pension at first increases with pay because of the earnings-related pension. Once the pay threshold for the earnings-related scheme is reached, the pension value reaches a plateau. Then the withdrawal of the basic pension kicks in. Once the basic pension is exhausted, the overall pension is flat, worth around 30% of economy-wide average earnings. In the presentation of Chart 3.3, the pension value is shown as an individual replacement rate: the ratio of the pension benefit to individual earnings. The income-tested and basic pensions together produce a rapidly declining replacement rate as earnings increase. The earnings-related pension offers a flat, 25% replacement rate at first, but the rate declines once the earnings ceiling is reached. Adding the components together, the Canadian public pension system is highly progressive, paying low-income earners much higher replacement rates than high-income workers.

Canada, along with Finland and Sweden, has the most highly targeted set of tax concessions. In Canada, the age credit is withdrawn once income exceeds 75% of economy-wide average earnings. The pensioner's tax burden moves rapidly towards that of workers over a relatively short income range, as can be seen in Chart 3.5. At the highest incomes, the difference in average tax rates is small because of the relatively low rate of social security contributions and the relatively low ceiling.

Finland

The picture for Finland is a stark contrast to the pattern of pension entitlements by earnings in Canada. Above three-quarters of average earnings, the income-tested pension is exhausted, and only earnings-related pension benefits are received. This makes for a very simple picture:

- There are nine different occupational schemes for different groups in the labour market. These schemes are part of the statutory system and provide an earnings-related benefit. The system targets a 60% replacement rate after a full career relative to average earnings in the last ten years. There is no ceiling to contributions or benefits. After age 65, the pension is up-rated by a mix of earnings inflation (20%) and price inflation (80%).

- The basic pension is a universal benefit, payable from age 65 subject to a residency test. The pension is tested against benefits from the earnings-related pension system but not against other income. The generosity of the system differs from one municipality to another to reflect regional differences in the cost of living. The basic benefit is between 19 and 22% of economy-wide average earnings. Once other pension income exceeds 2% of average earnings, the basic pension is reduced by 50% of the difference. This means that entitlement to the basic pension is exhausted once other pension income reaches 39 to 46% of average earnings (depending on municipality and marital status).

The absence of a ceiling to pension benefits and pensionable earnings means that the value of the pension continues to grow across the earnings range. Chart 3.3 shows that the Finnish income-tested pension boosts the pension replacement rate at lower levels of earnings, but above the threshold of three-quarters of average pay, benefits stay at 60% of individual earnings. The overall benefit structure is mildly progressive, but only because of the additional income-tested pension paid to people with the lowest incomes.

As with Canada and Sweden, tax concessions are highly targeted, as is seen in Chart 3.5. In Finland, the allowance is withdrawn at an even higher rate: 70%. Pensioners are also liable to social security contributions, and workers receive a deduction for work-related expenses. Thus, in Finland, higher-income pensioners face an average tax rate very slightly higher than that faced by workers.

Germany

The German public pension system has a single tier, combining insurance and some redistributive elements. It uses a points system: one point is awarded for a year's contributions at the average earnings of contributors under the ceiling. Contributions are levied on earnings between a floor of around 1% of average earnings and a ceiling of approximately 170% of average earnings.[13] Average covered earnings in 1999 were about 92% of the average production worker's pay, as measured by the OECD. The sum of points at pension age is multiplied by a "pension value".

There is no minimum pension, but low-income workers' points can be increased by up to 1½ times to a maximum of 75% of average earnings of contributors (*i.e.* 0.75 points) if they have contributed for 35 years. Vulnerable older people may also qualify for social assistance, which targets a minimum income of 13% of economy-wide average earnings for a single person. However, this is a very small group.

The pension is payable from age 65 with five years' contributions and from age 63 with 35 years' contributions. The pension-value variable is up-rated in line with net wages, which affects both the post-retirement benefit and the pre-retirement revaluation of earnings in the benefit formula.

Civil servants are covered by a separate scheme, while public-sector employees contribute to the general pension scheme and benefit from a supplementary occupational scheme.

The German public pension system is somewhat simpler to model than public schemes with two components, such as those in Canada and Finland. Nevertheless, the boost given to low-income workers' pension points gives the public pension a progressive formula (see Charts 3.2 and 3.3). Unlike the Finnish system, the German scheme has a ceiling to pensionable earnings, which means that the value of the pension is flat once earnings reach about 1¾ of the economy-wide average. Note that the pension entitlement at 30% of average earnings is sufficient to preclude entitlement to social assistance.

In terms of taxation, Germany follows a similar pattern to the Netherlands and the United Kingdom in that the gap between pensioners' and workers' average tax rates at first increases with incomes, due to the effect of social security contribution floors. Although there are no general concessions for pensioners, both public and private pension income receive favourable income-tax treatment. Public pensions in payment are treated as a notional annuity, and only the notional interest is taxable, not the notional return on capital invested. At age 65, for example, just 27% of the public pension is taxed.[14]

Italy

The Italian pension system has undergone two major reforms in the 1990s: the one described here is the system applying to labour-market entrants after 1996.

The pension age is 65 years, but pensions can be taken as early as age 57 with actuarial adjustments applied. The pension benefit is now strictly linked to the value of contributions paid. Contributions are up-rated in line with a five-year moving average of GDP growth until the year of retirement. The resulting sum, or "notional capital", is then multiplied by a "transformation coefficient", akin to the annuity rate in a true defined-contribution plan. Pensions in payment will be indexed only to the inflation rate.[15] Contributions are payable when earnings exceed around 40% of the economy-wide average. The ceiling on contributions is 365% of average earnings. The main social assistance benefit for older people guarantees a minimum income.

As in Germany, the new public pension system in Italy has just a single component. Italy applies a relatively high minimum both to contributions and benefits, meaning that very low-income workers are not covered by the public pension scheme. There is a jump in entitlements once pay reaches the threshold and contributions are levied and benefits paid in respect of the whole of earnings. At the other end of the salary scale, the high 365% ceiling on contributions makes the pattern of pension level with earnings much closer to systems without ceilings to mandatory pension benefits – Finland and the Netherlands – than it is to other countries with benefit limits. The relatively high floor to pension contributions means that the very lowest earners considered in Charts 3.2 and 3.3 will, in the new system, depend on social assistance for their income. The social-assistance level is, however, below the pension that would be earned for a full career of contributions at the contribution floor. This results in a jump in the value of total benefits at the floor. The strengthening of the relationship between contributions and benefits in the new notional accounts scheme results, by definition, in a less progressive structure of benefits at different earnings levels than in countries with basic, flat-rate or income-tested public programmes.

In Italy there are no specific personal income tax reliefs for older people, but the lower liability to social security contributions means that pensioners pay an average effective tax rate between 5 and 10 percentage points lower than workers. The advantage diminishes at higher earnings levels because of ceilings to social security contributions.

Japan

The public pension scheme in Japan has two basic components:

- The basic pension is payable from age 60. The pension age will increase to 65 for men in 2013 and for women in 2018. It is a contributory benefit, with 40 years of contributions needed for the full benefit. Workers earning below 26% of the economy-wide average wage are exempt and accrue basic pension rights at a third of the normal rate. The full basic pension is worth 19% of average earnings and is up-rated in line with prices.

- The earnings-related pension pays 0.75% of lifetime average earnings for each year of contributions, which falls to 0.7125% after the reform in 2000. Given a full 40-year career, the new replacement rate target is 28.5%. There is a ceiling on contributions and earnings eligible for benefits equivalent to 168% of average earnings. Earlier years' earnings are revalued in line with economy-wide average net earnings. Following the March 2000 reform, benefits in payment in the earnings-related tiers will also be up-rated in line with prices. The pension is payable from age 60, but this will increase to 65 by 2025, a slower time scale than the increase in pension age for the basic benefit.

At the lowest-income levels, most of the total pension benefit in Japan comes from the basic scheme. But beyond three-quarters of average earnings, the earnings-related pension dominates. There is, however, a ceiling to earnings-related pensions which caps pension benefits for people earning above 170% of the economy-wide average. The progressivity of this two-tier pension system is confirmed by the pension replacement rate relative to individual pre-retirement pay in Chart 3.3. The flat-rate nature of the basic pension means that the total replacement rate declines sharply at first. The earnings-related pension, which pays a flat replacement rate up to a ceiling, offsets this effect until the threshold is reached. After this point, the decline in the replacement rate with pay accelerates again.

In terms of tax concessions, the difference between workers' and pensioners' average tax rates peaks at 12 percentage points at gross income of two-thirds of average earnings. The relative value of the concessions then declines and is mainly a result of social security contributions at higher-income levels (see Chart 3.5).

Netherlands

The Netherlands also has a pension system with two basic components:

- The public pension is a flat-rate benefit, payable from age 65 subject to a residency test. The benefit for a single person is worth around 35% of economy-wide average earnings. It is up-rated in line with the net minimum wage.

- The private occupational pension system has broad coverage: 91% of all employees participate in an occupational pension scheme.[16] The system comprises some 64 industry-wide schemes (most of them set compulsorily on request of the social partners) and some 866 company schemes, which are all executed out of pension funds. Alongside this are some 30 000 smaller company schemes operated by insurance companies. Most pension schemes are defined-benefit; only 5% of employees participate in a fully or partially defined-contribution plan. Typical benefits are 1.75% of final salary for each year of service, giving a replacement rate after a complete 40-year career (including the public flat-rate plan) of 70%. Assuming that the fund is in a healthy financial position, pensions in payment are typically indexed to wages, although there is no legal up-rating requirement.

The total pension is simply the basic scheme plus an earnings-related top-up. The integration of the basic and the earnings-related schemes means that the earnings-related pension often pays nothing to the lowest-income workers. Unlike most of the nine countries examined in this report, there is no ceiling either to pension benefits or to pensionable pay. Chart 3.3 shows that this means that the system is only mildly progressive. Pension replacement rates are higher at low earnings because of the basic pension. At higher earnings, the basic and earnings-related pension replacement rates are the mirror image of one another, due to the integration procedure. So all workers with pay above 50% of the economy-wide average receive a flat, 70% replacement rate. Note that the model assumes that the individual remains in a single employer scheme throughout his or her working life. We return in Section 6.6 to the effect of transferring between schemes: the "portability" of pension benefits.

The patterns of tax concessions in the Netherlands, as in the United Kingdom, is interesting because the gap between pensioners' and workers' average tax rates at first increases with incomes, due to the effect of social security contribution floors.[17] As in Canada, however, targeting results from a mix of the withdrawal of additional allowances from richer pensioners and the effect of the social security contribution ceiling.

Sweden

The Swedish pension system has recently undergone a fundamental reform. The new regime, introduced in 1999, applies fully to people born in 1954 or later and partly to the cohorts born in 1938-1953. This new system has three main components:

- An earnings-related scheme based on "notional accounts" (similar to the new Italian system). Contributions of 16% of earnings are credited to the notional account, and indexed in line with a three-year moving average of economy-wide earnings. There is a floor and a ceiling to employee contributions and earnings eligible for benefits, of a little over 4% and nearly 130% of average earnings. At retirement, accumulated "notional capital" is converted to an annuity, with a coefficient related to contemporaneous life expectancy and a presumption of annual wage growth of 1.6%. After retirement, pensions are indexed in line with average earnings less a "growth norm" of 1.6%. So if real wage growth exceeds the norm, the real value of pensions will rise and *vice versa*. An automatic balance mechanism ensures the financial stability of the earnings-related system. The balance mechanisms states that if the ratio of total assets, *i.e.* the buffer fund and contribution assets over pension liability, drops below unity the balance mechanism is automatically activated. Indexation of pensions and notional accounts is then reduced according to the rules of legislation.

- A further contribution of 2.5% of earnings is credited into funded individual accounts. People have a broad choice of where these funds are invested. A public fund manager invests the assets of those who do not choose. At retirement, a new public agency will be responsible for converting the accumulated balance into an annuity. Alternatively, people will be able to choose a variable or "participating" annuity, where their funds continue to be invested by their chosen fund manager.

- Low-paid workers are protected by a minimum pension guarantee that is tested against the public earnings-related pension. For a single person, this guarantee is worth approximately 36% of average earnings. It is reduced at 100% against the first slice of public earnings-related pension income, and then at 48%. The guarantee level is, in contrast to the earnings-related pension, indexed to prices. There is additional social assistance for people who have not resided in Sweden.

Occupational pensions, provided under four main regimes for different labour-market groups, cover 90% of employees. These schemes are a mix of defined-contribution and defined-benefit. They are principally designed to provide a degree of earnings replacement for workers above the ceiling for the public plan.

The defined-contribution pensions are proportional up to the contribution ceiling. Hence the curves for Sweden in Chart 3.2 tend to begin as rays from the origin. The earnings-related pension is much larger than the funded pension. This is because it receives contributions of 16%, compared with 2.5% paid into individual funded pension accounts. Working in the opposite direction, we assume that the rate of return credited to the notional accounts (earnings growth) is below the rate of return on investments. Low-income workers receive a guarantee pension in retirement. This is reduced against public earnings-related pension income at two different rates, apparent in the kink in the total pension curve at around half average earnings. The individual pension replacement rate in Chart 3.3 confirms the strongly progressive role of the test against earnings-related pension incomes. The funded defined-contribution and the earnings-related pension pay the same replacement rate at earnings up to the ceiling, but the guarantee pension gives a substantial boost to low-income workers' retirement incomes.

Tax concessions in Sweden are highly targeted and follow a similar pattern to those in Canada, as can be seen in Chart 3.5 – although the withdrawal rate is higher than in Canada (65%) and the ceiling lower. Again, the difference in average effective tax rates at higher incomes is entirely due to social security.

United Kingdom

The United Kingdom's publicly provided pension has, again, two components:

- The basic pension is a contributory flat-rate benefit, worth around 20% of average earnings. This basic pension can be topped-up with a means-tested minimum income guarantee to give a minimum income of 22% of average earnings.

- The earnings-related second portion of the public programme targets a 20% replacement rate relative to average individual lifetime pay. The ceiling for benefits is around 1½ times economy-wide average earnings.

However, most workers are contracted out of this scheme into private pension plans. Most of these are employer-provided schemes, predominantly defined-benefit, although a quarter of the workforce hold personal pensions. People who are contracted out lose their public earnings-related benefit, but must make a minimum contribution to their personal pension or their occupational scheme must meet a minimum benefit standard.

The basic pension is flat-rate and the ceiling on the earnings-related component is quite low at 1½ times average earnings. Total benefits are therefore flat beyond this ceiling. Although means-tested benefits play a very important role in providing retirement incomes in the United Kingdom at present, a full-career worker earning 30% of economy-wide average earnings would just fail to be entitled to the main means-tested benefit. Expressing this as an individual replacement rate illustrates the highly progressive nature of the pension system in the United Kingdom (Chart 3.3). The basic pension delivers quite high replacement rates to low earners, and the relatively low ceiling to pension benefits means that the earnings-related scheme is progressive across much of the earnings scale.

The pattern of tax concessions in the United Kingdom is similar to that in the Netherlands, as can be seen Chart 3.5. The gap between pensioners' and workers' average tax rates at first increases with incomes.

United States

The public pension programme in the United States, known as social security, has a redistributive formula. The lowest-income bracket is replaced at a 90% rate, with bands of 32 and 15% replacement rates applying to higher earnings. The benefit ceiling is around 2½ times average earnings.

Social assistance benefits top up the incomes of old people with the lowest incomes to a minimum of 21% of economy-wide average earnings.

Around 40% of workers are covered by an employer pension scheme. Over half of these have a defined-benefit scheme alone, and almost a third defined-contribution, while 13% are covered by both types of plans. Tax-favoured individual pension arrangements also have relatively high coverage.

In the charts for social security, it is difficult to make out the 90% rate applied to the lowest band of earnings because it is close to the beginning of the curve. However, the shift from 32 to 15% produces a clear kink. Maximum pensionable earnings are around 2½ times economy-wide average pay. The result is a progressive benefit structure, with a monotonic decline in the individual pension replacement rate with earnings (Chart 3.3). This is driven in part by the progressive benefit schedule, which among the nine countries studied here is only found in Germany as well. The ceiling on pensionable pay, as elsewhere, also has an important effect. The social-assistance minimum, supplemental security income, is set at a lower level than the public pension entitlement of a worker with a full career on 30% of average earnings. However, some states' additions would be payable to lower-earners in these circumstances. California's supplement, for example, would boost the total income of pensioners who had earned less than 50% of average pay from around 20% of economy-wide average earnings to nearly 29%.

As noted above, the United States offers the most valuable tax concessions across the income range. The average effective tax rate on pensioners is nearly 20 percentage points lower than for workers. This is because of the range of deductions, credits and reliefs in the federal income tax and more generous concessions offered in the state income tax[18] (see Chart 3.5).

NOTES

1. The chapter summarises the more detailed findings of Whitehouse (2001).
2. In the Netherlands, there is no law concerning capping; it is a matter for the social partners. Most schemes are uncapped and, where this is not the case, the cap is a high level of income.
3. A complete analysis of the distributional impact of the pension system would also take into account contributions made as well as benefits received. Nevertheless, since flat-rate and income-tested pension benefits in Canada and the United Kingdom include financing from general revenues, their schemes would still be more progressive on this comprehensive measure.
4. The three-tier classification system has other weaknesses as well. It is not used in a consistent way within countries, and it ignores some of the most important elements of the retirement income system – earnings, disability, unemployment insurance and other means of funding early retirement.
5. The concept of "replacement rate", as used here, refers to an individual's income after retirement compared with pre-retirement income. It is not easy to measure directly, however. In Chapter 2, a "quasi-replacement rate" was used as a rough approximation. The average income for a group of people of "post-retirement age" was compared with the income of people of working age. In this chapter, the "pension replacement rate" does refer to specific individuals, but is limited to pension income only, not the full range of income from different sources.
6. McHale (1999) studies the impact of reforms on future pension entitlements in the G7 countries.
7. The average earnings data are the pay of the average production worker, as set out in OECD (2000c). For reference, Table A.15 in the Statistical Annex shows these earnings levels in the national currency and in United States dollars. Earnings have been translated into dollars using OECD purchasing power parities, which calculate the cost of a common basket of goods in each country. The table shows earnings net of taxes and social security contributions. Real earnings, both of the illustrative worker and the economy as a whole, are assumed to grow in the future at 2% a year.
8. This substitution is recognised in the pensions literature: see, for example, Disney, Mira d'Ercole and Scherer (1998) and Börsch-Supan (1998).
9. Although some are. There is no law regarding capping.
10. To value these pensions in the same way as the analysis above of public schemes (and the mandatory and quasi-mandatory occupational plans of Finland and the Netherlands), we again need to know the parameters, which unfortunately vary between plans. Table A.18 in the Statistical Annex sets out "typical" parameters based on surveys of plan rules in each country. Where possible, the proportion of members covered by plans with this rule is shown in parentheses.
11. These data have been derived from the tax equations developed by the OECD's Working Party on Tax Policy Analysis and Tax Statistics of the Committee on Fiscal Affairs. These algorithms were designed to produce the annual report (OECD, 2000c), which looks at the tax-benefit position of employees in different family situations and with different levels of earnings. We have extended these algorithms to a broader earnings range: between 0.3 and 5 times the pay of the average production worker, compared with the range of 0.67-1.67 times average earnings used in the report. The algorithms were further modified to look at the tax treatment of pensioners, including special concessions to older people, such as increased allowances, tax credits, etc. Certain types of income are granted additional concessions in some countries: for example, some kinds of private pension income. These features have been ignored and it is assumed that the pensioner's income is taxed at the normal rate.
12. Where possible, parameters are described at their 1999 level. References to proportions of "average earnings" relate to the earnings of the average production worker, as set out in OECD (2000c).
13. The ceiling varies with former East German and West German status; it also varies from year to year.
14. Chart 3.5 for Germany assumes that the pensioner is age 65 and that pension income, up to the ceiling of the public scheme, derives entirely from the public pension. (This is consistent with the treatment of other countries with such concessions.) Beyond the ceiling, it is assumed that all additional income is fully taxable.

15. The "transformation coefficient" takes into account an implicit average real growth rate of 1.5%, so the law establishes that the government can decide to adjust pension benefits according to the possible higher rate of GDP growth.
16. This high coverage is despite the fact that there is no legal obligation for an employer to provide a pension.
17. Note that the downward blip in average tax rates in the Netherlands at around average earnings is because people above this threshold are no longer liable for mandatory health contributions. However, people above this income level must pay for their own health-insurance arrangements.
18. It should, however, be noted that people of working age also have relatively generous deductions in the United States – for mortgage interest, for example – that are not captured in this analysis.

Chapter 4

THE NEED FOR REFORM

4.1. Introduction

The previous chapters described the wide range of resources available to older people and the complex ways in which public policy drives the operation of the retirement income system. Part II will turn to the ways in which the nine countries are attempting to manage this complexity. Population ageing and early retirement in particular will place considerable pressure on retirement income systems in coming years. The chapters of Part II will examine recent reforms that have been introduced in consequence.

Fiscal pressures have been a main factor in much recent reform. The present chapter begins with an examination of these pressures, the results of recent reforms and the likely fiscal payoffs from different types of future reform. It concludes that the fiscal situation has improved considerably as a result of recent changes, but that, in the absence of further change, large increases in public spending can still be anticipated in most countries. The changes that will bring the largest benefits by far are those leading to increases in the effective age of retirement.

The chapter returns to the three major challenges to the future of the retirement income system described in Section 1.3: re-balancing time spent in work and retirement, finding a new overall mix of resources available to older people (including greater reliance on private pensions) and, finally, continuing to provide adequate income to older people, including groups that may become vulnerable as a result of actions taken to meet the first two challenges. The extent of the challenges varies across countries, and the chapter ends with an assessment of their magnitude in each country. This provides a context for the discussion of actual reforms in the following chapters.

4.2. The projected results of recent reforms

There have been deep pension reforms in many of the nine countries in recent years. A dominant factor has been the need to prepare for the coming retirement of the "large generation" – the baby-boom generation that will be moving soon from work (and contributing to pensions) to retirement (and receiving pensions). The effects of population ageing have been re-enforced by long-term secular trends towards less work by men over the course of their lives (although trends appear to have changed recently, as will be described below) and by large increases in life expectancy. People are living longer after they retire. The resulting changes in the balance between time spent in retirement and in work will have consequences for all retirement income resources, public and private. However, most recent attention has focussed on the fiscal dimensions. The sustainability of public pensions has been a major theme in public debate. Recent reforms in all OECD countries, and the changing demographic and labour-market situation that underlies these reforms, have been described at length in *Reforms for an Ageing Society* (OECD, 2000a) and in many other documents at the national and international level.[1]

The OECD and participating countries have undertaken projections[2] of age-related spending (OECD, 2001a; Dang *et al.*, forthcoming) that take account of recent reforms. These suggest that, by 2050,[3] there could be significant increases in public spending of around 5 or more percentage points of GDP in Canada, Finland, Germany and the Netherlands. In Italy, where spending is now high, it will remain at about current levels, expressed as a percentage of GDP. At the other end of the spectrum, spending in

© OECD 2001

the United Kingdom is currently relatively low and is projected to stay low in the future, again at about today's level.

The final four columns of Table 4.1 show the factors that lie behind the total change between 2000 and 2050:

- The largest factor working in the direction of increased spending is, by far, the increase in the old-age dependency ratio[4] – the coming retirement of the large generation of baby boomers.
- A smaller effect (that usually works in an offsetting direction) results from increases in the ratio of employment in the population aged 20 to 64. This is caused by assumed increases in female participation and decreases in unemployment rates. This effect tends to be greatest where female participation is now relatively low and unemployment relatively high.
- Eligibility ratios – measured by the share of those receiving benefits in the 55-and-over age group – increase as a result of factors such as the greater employment of women and maturing systems. They are reduced by actions to increase the effective age of retirement. On balance, these factors are likely to increase spending except in the United States. (The eligibility and benefit ratios indicated are the results of the maturing of pension systems, changes in behaviour and the effects of reforms.)
- On the other hand, the projections suggest widespread declines in pension benefits relative to wages. (The benefit ratio is estimated as the average pension benefit relative to GDP per worker.) These result from reforms that shift indexation of benefits from wages towards prices, from longer required contribution periods for full pensions and from increasing the reference period for calculating benefits. On balance, these effects have outweighed effects in the other direction that are associated with changes in the age structure of the retired population, more female employment and longer contribution periods. Spending reductions associated with smaller average benefits are particularly large in Italy.

Caution is needed when interpreting such long-term projections. In the real world, programmes will not remain unchanged for 50 years. The simulations do not take changes in behaviour into account. The

Table 4.1. **Old-age pension spending**
Percentage of GDP, changes in percentage points[a]

	Level 2000	Change 2000-2050			
		Total change	Contribution of			
			old age dependency ratio[c]	employment ratio[d]	eligibility ratio[e]	benefit ratio[f]
Canada	5.1	5.8	5.1	0.0	1.3	–0.6
Finland[b]	8.1	4.8	5.2	–0.1	0.0	–0.2
Germany	11.8	5.0	6.4	–0.7	2.7	–1.9
Italy	14.2	–0.3	10.1	–3.2	0.0	–6.9
Japan	7.9	0.6	5.1	–1.2	0.9	–3.9
Netherlands[b]	5.2	4.8	3.8	–0.5	1.4	0.2
Sweden[b]	9.2	1.6	3.9	–0.5	0.4	–2.1
United Kingdom	4.3	–0.7	1.7	0.1	0.1	–2.5
United States[b]	4.4	1.8	2.4	–0.1	–0.3	–0.2

a) See OECD *Economic Outlook* (2001) and Dang *et al.* (forthcoming) for methodology and further explanation. Columns do not add up because of use of linear approximations.
b) Excludes "early retirement" programmes amounting to 3.1 per cent of GDP in Finland, 1.2 in the Netherlands, 1.9 in Sweden and 0.2 in the United States.
c) Ratio of those aged 55+ to the population aged 20 to 64.
d) Ratio of employment to population aged 20 to 64.
e) Share of those receiving benefits in the 55+ age group.
f) Average pension benefit relative to GDP per worker.
Source: OECD.

Table 4.2. **Average[a] effects of making different assumptions on old-age pension spending**
Percentage of GDP, 2000-2050

Alternative[b] assumptions	Old-age pension spending
Demographic assumptions	
Higher fertility rate. Fertility rates for all age groups are assumed to rise by 15 per cent until 2029 and remain constant at that level thereafter.	–0.6
Longer life expectancy. Mortality rates are assumed to rise by 30 per cent and 20 per cent respectively for males and females for all age groups by 2050. This corresponds broadly to an extra 3 years of life expectancy at birth for males and 2 years for females by 2050.	1.0
Higher migration flows. Net migration in numbers of persons gradually increase from the current (or estimated levels in the year 2000 to 50 per cent above the 2010 level), remaining constant over the rest of the period.	–0.5
Macroeconomic assumptions	
Lower participation rates for older workers. Participation rates of older workers (55 to 64) are 5 percentage points lower by 2050.	0.2
Lower female participation rate. Total female participation rates (20-54) are 5 percentage points lower by 2050.	0.2
Lower unemployment rate. Fall in the structural unemployment rate by the end of the period to level experienced in the 1960s (unemployment rates of 3 to 5 per cent).	–0.3
Lower productivity. Productivity growth is 0.5 per cent points lower starting in 2005 and ending in 2050. (In the baseline, labour productivity converges towards an annual growth rate of 1¾ per cent between 2020 and 2030.)	0.4

a) The average of selected countries. For details and further explanation see OECD *Economic Outlook* (2001) and Dang *et al.* (forthcoming).
b) The comparison is with the baseline shown in Table 4.1.

assumptions used by participating countries, while following standardised guidelines, may not always be identical. The effects of public pension changes could be offset by private pensions.

Despite these cautions, the projections result in important, practical conclusions. Table 4.2 uses alternative assumptions about the future to test the sensitivity of the projected public spending. Using any reasonable set of assumptions, the differences are not large enough to change the underlying story – that in many countries public pension spending will rise in the absence of further reform, that later effective retirement ages would be an attractive reform route and that action is needed quickly. The largest changes result from different[5] assumptions about future mortality and fertility – especially the consequences of increased life expectancy. Longer life, while a highly desired outcome, also means that the duration of time spent in retirement (and in receipt of a pension) could continue to grow significantly unless increases in the effective age of retirement are substantial.

4.3. Potential effects of further reform

The spending projections show the overall fiscal position to be more favourable than it appeared in the mid-1990s, which is a result of recent reforms and the improvement in overall budgetary positions. However, the projections also suggest that further reform may be needed in some countries if the negative effects of ageing on debt-to-GDP ratios are to be offset.[6] In a "stylised" country, the following scale of action would be needed to keep the debt-to-GDP ratio constant at around 55 percentage points of GDP in 2050:

- Average public pension benefits would have to fall by about 10% (assuming that this was the only change).

- The number of beneficiaries would have to fall (as a result of later retirement) by only about half of that amount, or 5% – since spending would be reduced and people would be working and contributing longer. A 5% cut in the number of beneficiaries is equivalent to a rise in the effective age of retirement of only about 10 months – a relatively small increase in light of historic patterns.

- The above simulations assume that reforms would be implemented in 2005. If the implementation of the reforms were delayed by ten years, the reforms would need to be one-quarter to one-third larger. A delay of 20 years would increase this amount to three-quarters.

If the reforms were to significantly reduce average benefits, they could undermine the basic income support objectives of public pensions and eventually create political pressures to reverse these policies. Hence, there would likely be pressure to fill the gap by encouraging private pensions and savings and by using other means to delay effective retirement ages and promote work among older people.

In summary, raising the effective age of retirement (and thus the age of receipt of pension benefits) would be a particularly effective steps from a fiscal point of view. Unlike benefit cuts, which could result in shifting responsibility from public to private finance, raising effective retirement ages could mitigate the effects of population ageing on total pension spending, public and private. The simulations suggest that relatively small increases in retirement ages could have large payoffs.

4.4. The scale of the challenges in the nine countries

The three challenges

This analysis suggests that a key first challenge for further reform lies in increasing the effective age of retirement: the work-retirement challenge. This makes sense for many social and economic reasons, as well as for fiscal reasons. Chapter 5 identifies realistic possibilities for change and describes recent reform directions.

A second challenge for future reform lies in helping older people achieve a better overall balance of resources. As the public role increases less quickly than was formerly projected, then other sources must be there to fill the gap. Greater use of earnings from working later in life is one means of diversification. Greater use of private pensions is another. The challenge for policy is to encourage access to a variety of resources that can best support people in different circumstances as they grow older. A broader range of resources diversifies risk. Recent policy directions are explored in Chapter 6.

A final challenge is to continue supporting the economic well-being of older people. Past success in meeting fundamental income goals may suggest there is no true "challenge" to be met today. However, pockets of low income do remain among older people. As well, reforms that reduce future public pension benefits may not be sustainable politically in the absence of remedial action. Reforms that increase the role of earnings and private pensions might, unless care is exercised, contribute to the rise of new vulnerable groups among the elderly. Necessary action is discussed in Chapter 7.

The scale of the challenges in the nine countries

If the scale of a particular challenge were relatively large in a country, then one might anticipate that the scale of the recent response might also be large. That has proven to be the general case. For example, the measures shown below suggest that, in the mid-1990s, Italy faced relatively more challenges than the other eight countries. And subsequent chapters will show that, indeed, Italy is also the country where recent reforms have been deepest.

Tables 4.3, 4.4 and 4.5 examine a set of indicators that corresponds to the challenges identified above. In the boxes, heavy shading indicates that there may be a larger challenge relative to the other countries.[7] Medium shading indicates a challenge that is close to the nine-country average, while light shading represents challenges that appear to be smaller than faced in the other countries. For the most part, the measures reflect the situation in the mid-1990s to provide context for the reforms that were introduced in recent years.

No country consistently ranks higher or lower on all measures, and there is considerable variability in the rankings even among the component measures that were selected for each challenge.

Two sets of measures were chosen for the work-retirement challenge in Table 4.3. One – the first four bars – relates to the fiscal and general economic pressures caused by changes in the total numbers

The Need for Reform

Table 4.3. **Work-retirement challenge**
Relative comparisons among the nine countries in the mid-90s

Larger challenge ■ Moderate challenge ▨ Smaller challenge ☐

	Canada	Finland	Germany	Italy	Japan	Netherlands	Sweden	United Kingdom	United States
% of pop. that is employed (current)	▨	■	■	■	☐	▨	☐	▨	☐
Ratio of retirees to employees (current)	☐	▨	■	■	☐	▨	▨	▨	▨
Public pension spending (current)	☐	▨	■	■	☐	▨	▨	☐	☐
Public pension spending (future change)	■	■	▨	▨	■	■	▨	☐	▨
Duration of complete retirement, men	■	■	■	■	☐	▨	▨	▨	▨
Recent change in age of withdrawal	▨	▨	☐	☐	■	☐	☐	☐	☐
Growth in older workforce	■	☐	■	■	▨	■	▨	▨	▨
Percentage of population 65+ part-time	▨	▨	▨	■	☐	☐	☐	☐	☐

Source: See Table A.19 in the Statistical Annex for sources of data and definitions.

Table 4.4. **The challenge of balanced resources in retirement**
Relative comparisons among the nine countries in the mid-90s

Larger challenge ■ Moderate challenge ▨ Smaller challenge ☐

	Canada	Finland	Germany	Italy	Japan	Netherlands	Sweden	United Kingdom	United States
Public expenditure on older people	☐	■	▨	▨	☐	▨	■	☐	☐
Size of the largest component	▨	■	▨	▨	▨	▨	■	☐	☐
Share from capital sources	▨	■	▨	■	▨	☐	▨	☐	☐

Source: See Table A.19 in the Statistical Annex for sources of data and definitions.

Table 4.5. **The challenge of economic well-being**
Relative comparisons among the nine countries in the mid-90s

Larger challenge ■ Moderate challenge ▨ Smaller challenge ☐

	Canada	Finland	Germany	Italy	Japan	Netherlands	Sweden	United Kingdom	United States
Quasi-replacement rates	▨	☐	☐	☐	▨	☐	☐	▨	☐
Percentage below low-income cut-off lines	☐	☐	☐	■	■	☐	☐	▨	■
Situation of lowest quintile	☐	☐	▨	▨	■	☐	☐	▨	■

Source: See Table A.19 in the Statistical Annex for sources of data and definitions.

of workers and retirees, *i.e.* the relative proportions of the two. The basic measure is the percentage of the adult population that is employed. A related measure that is more closely associated with retirement income policies is the ratio of retirees to workers – that is, an adjusted old-age dependency rate. Both of these apply to pressures on the entire retirement income system. The last two measures are narrower fiscal measures: public old age pension spending as a percentage of GDP. One is the current percentage, which reflects past programming. The other is the projected change from today's percentage of pension spending to peak spending.

Economic and fiscal pressures in the mid-1990s were highest in Finland, Germany and Italy. The absence of Japan from the list of countries facing strong dependency pressures warrants comment since Japan experiences great demographic pressure. However, the ratio of retirees to employees takes account of both population ageing and work-retirement patterns. The strong Japanese performance in the latter area compensates for the effects of population ageing. In Japan, the effects of population ageing on dependency ratios are already being felt; for the other countries these effects still lie ahead.

The second block of measures, which is drawn from Chapter 5, deals with the balance between work and retirement at the level of individuals. Here no country is without pressure, but the United States, the United Kingdom and Japan are in relatively better positions than the others. Again, the situation in Japan warrants comment. The measure, "the duration of complete retirement", mainly reflects the average age at which people completely withdraw from the labour force. The average age of withdrawal in Japan is much later than in the other countries. However, the following measure, "recent changes in the age of withdrawal from the labour force", does show a challenge for Japan, as it is the only country where the average age of withdrawal (for men) has been falling in recent years.

The measure of part-time work among people aged 65 and over warrants comment, since it results in a larger-than-average challenge for a country such as the Netherlands where part-time work is relatively common by most measures. "Age 65 and over" was chosen to ensure that it is a measure of the use of part-time work as a transition to working later in life after normal retirement age, and not of its use as a means of retiring earlier. In countries where very few people are actually working in any capacity after 65, the number of part-timers can appear large when expressed as a percentage of employees aged 65 and over, but low when expressed as a percentage of the total population aged 65 and over.

Table 4.4 outlines measures related to the challenge of achieving a greater balance of resources within the retirement income system. There are no surprises here. In the mid-1990s, the systems of Finland, Italy Germany and Sweden were dominated by a large public pension, with older people having relatively little income from working or capital sources. In Japan, working income tends to dominate, although that includes the own-income of older Japanese people who retire later and working income from other members of multiple-generational households.

Table 4.5 suggests that, in the mid-1990s, there were no large challenges in any of the nine countries in meeting basic replacement rate objectives, at least on average. There was more unevenness, however, in the situation of older people near the bottom of the income scale.

The three policy goals – encouraging later retirement, improving the balance of resources and maintaining adequate incomes among older people – can, in some circumstances, be in conflict. A dilemma of retirement income reform is that actions that are directed to one goal could, if taken in isolation, cause problems in achieving another goal. For example, unless care is exercised, a shift to greater reliance on capital sources, or reforms that encourage later retirement, could result in problems of income adequacy for vulnerable groups. The responses described in the following chapters therefore have often involved action on many fronts, reflecting this need to take account of multiple, and potentially conflicting, objectives.

NOTES

1. For ease of reference the basic data on demographic and labour force trends and future scenarios are shown in the Statistical Annex, where they have been updated to be consistent with the new scenarios presented in Chapter 5.
2. These projections are based on assumptions that are nearly identical to those in the middle scenarios in Chapter 5. They assume no change in existing policies but do take account of reforms that have been legislated but not yet implemented.
3. In Canada, Finland, Germany and the United States the projected levels are highest in 2050, while in other countries (Italy, Japan, the Netherlands, Sweden and the United Kingdom) the highest spending is likely to be reached earlier and will have fallen a little from its peak by 2050.
4. These calculations are similar to those in Chapter 5 in that they attempt to adjust for the fact that many people retire before the age of 65. Here this is accomplished by defining an old-age dependency ratio to be the ratio of those aged 55+ to the population aged 20 to 64. Chapter 5 compares retirees to employees directly.
5. The alternative assumptions for longevity and fertility were set to have a two-thirds probability of occurring on the basis of past projection errors.
6. While age-related spending can increase debt-to-GDP ratios, this does not necessarily imply that reform action need be limited to these age-related programmes. For example, there are comparable simulations in OECD (2001a) of the effect of an increase in the primary surplus that is sustained throughout the period.
7. As with any summary measures, comparisons need to be made with caution. A situation in one country might well appear to be a serious challenge when compared with the other eight, but it might look quite minor in comparison with less developed countries or, indeed, the OECD average. As well, countries have different priorities that are not reflected in such relative comparisons.

Part II
A COMPARISON OF POLICY RESPONSES TO KEY RETIREMENT INCOME CHALLENGES

Chapter 5

REFORMS TO RE-BALANCE WORK AND RETIREMENT

5.1. Introduction

Perhaps the key challenge posed by an ageing society is achieving a proper balance between the amount of time spent in work and in retirement. Effective retirement ages have stabilised or increased recently, but life expectancy upon retirement is also growing and may well continue to grow at rates beyond those that are typically projected. In most countries, working after age 65 is uncommon. There have been many reforms that are intended to support higher retirement ages. However, in the absence of further change, existing trends still point to the likelihood of even further growth in the proportion of life spent in retirement. The retirement income system still largely reflects the demographics and working life conditions of an earlier age. A common policy goal is to support a flexible, later transition to retirement, particularly for the types of people who now tend to retire well before age 65.

Pressures on the financing of retirement income will remain important as the large baby-boom generation reaches retirement age. Past reforms to increase effective retirement ages are still being offset in terms of their future fiscal effects by other trends that increase the numbers of people eligible for pensions, as described in Chapter 4. However, as the simulations in Section 4.2 showed, even relatively small shifts to higher retirement ages can have large fiscal effects in terms of reduced pension spending. Moreover, the potential gains are not only fiscal. Funds might be freed up for areas that may be of higher social and economic priority than ever-increasing public spending for longer periods of leisure in old age. Older workers can be an important, and possibly much-needed, source of future labour supply. Provided that work-retirement transitions are flexible, individual well-being can be enhanced as a result of greater choice in the way that work and leisure are mixed.

There remains a real question, however, about how much re-balancing of work and retirement is possible in today's economy. Despite the potential payoffs, in practice it is difficult to raise effective retirement ages. Given the labour-market and social security arrangements of today, many workers prefer early retirement to any alternatives, and many employers prefer to have the option of laying off older workers first during periods of down-sizing. Further, many of the most obvious reforms could, if taken in isolation, have negative effects on other goals, and in particular could create new vulnerable groups of retirees.

Section 5.2 assesses the size of change that may be achievable. The basic conclusion is that, over the longer-term, large changes are both possible and, indeed, have already begun to take place. The difficulty is to find a combination of policy actions that can effectively support later and more flexible retirement patterns. The range of possibilities is discussed in Section 5.3. Most countries have emphasised the "retirement" end of the work-retirement transition with reforms to retirement ages (Section 5.4) and especially to promote closer actuarial neutrality for pensions – closer linkages between benefits and contributions (Section 5.5). The highest priority has been on reducing the incentives that pull people into early retirement.

Another set of reforms has been directed to reducing the excessive use of alternative pathways into early retirement – early-retirement schemes and unemployment and disability benefits. Section 5.6 indicates that reforms to disability programmes have been a common theme. Section 5.7 deals with strengthening other routes to a more gradual retirement. Partial pensions, long considered a desired route, seem in practice to have been mainly used as a pathway to early retirement.

There has also been much reform activity at the workplace end of the work-retirement transition. Section 5.8 deals with initiatives that fit into a "workforce for all ages" category as well as measures that are more specifically related to older workers. In both cases, however, the initiatives tend to be somewhat diffuse and fit into the categories of research, co-ordination, promotion and smaller adjustments to pre-existing programming. No strong sense of common direction emerges as to the needed scale or focus of workplace-based policy initiatives.

5.2. The potential for major increases in effective retirement ages

As noted, while there are many reasons why increasing effective retirement ages is an attractive policy option, it has not always proved to be an easy objective to realise. While the work disincentives in pensions are large, there is a concern that remedial reforms could undermine the main income support goals of pensions. Reforms to alternative pathways to retirement such as disability benefits or unemployment insurance must be carefully co-ordinated in order to avoid hardship for the people for whom the programmes were intended – and to avoid simply shifting people from one early retirement pathway to another. Governments often have only indirect influence on factors affecting the supply and demand of older workers. Finally, early retirement is popular and, especially given recent labour-market conditions, it is often felt that public opinion would be hostile to reforms that would require people to work longer.

In these circumstances, there may be real constraints on the amount of change that can be achieved by reforms intended to re-balance work and retirement. Nonetheless, three factors provide grounds for optimism:

- Demographic pressures can be considerably eased by even quite small changes in effective retirement ages.

- In recent years, retirement ages have already been increasing in several countries at rates that, if sustained, could have large effects – more than offsetting the effects of ageing in some countries.

- Public opinion against working longer is not as firm as it first appears.

Maybe greater pressures than often recognised – but a wide range of future scenarios possible

Policy discussions of ageing pressures often rely on analysis that is based on demography alone. However, traditional demographically-driven dependency ratios (that compare the retirement-age population with the working-age population) understate the real pressure, since they do not take account of actual retirement ages. Chart 5.1 corrects for this by showing ratios of retirees to workers.[1] The middle scenario is distinctly higher than the traditional dependency ratios. On average in the nine countries, a traditional dependency ratio shows that the older population represents some 23% of the working-age population in 2000. The ratio of retirees to workers, 44%, is much higher. By 2030, the traditional dependency ratio reaches 42%. The middle scenarios for the adjusted ratios are significantly higher, ranging from 41% in the United States to about 100% in Italy – one worker for every retiree.

These ratios of retirees to employees give a more realistic (and pessimistic) view of the pressures on retirement income systems taken as a whole (and not only on public spending that was projected in Chapter 4). However, they also provide a better sense of how policy can respond to those pressures. There is nothing inevitable about the ultimate impact of demography and population ageing. The chart shows that a wide range of reasonable scenarios is possible, depending on assumptions[2] about the labour force participation of older workers. The scenarios reflect rates of change in the labour force patterns of older workers that are in line with those experienced in recent decades.

Trends towards early retirement in the decades prior to the 1990s made the demographic pressures worse. However, as discussed below, very recent trends in effective retirement ages are mainly having a positive, offsetting effect. Demographic pressures could be considerably reduced by continuing stronger demand for older workers combined with the reforms discussed in this chapter. In the scenarios that show the highest growth in employment rates among older workers, the ratio of

Chart 5.1. **Ratio of retirees to employees,[a] trends and scenarios**
1970 to 2000, and three scenarios to 2030

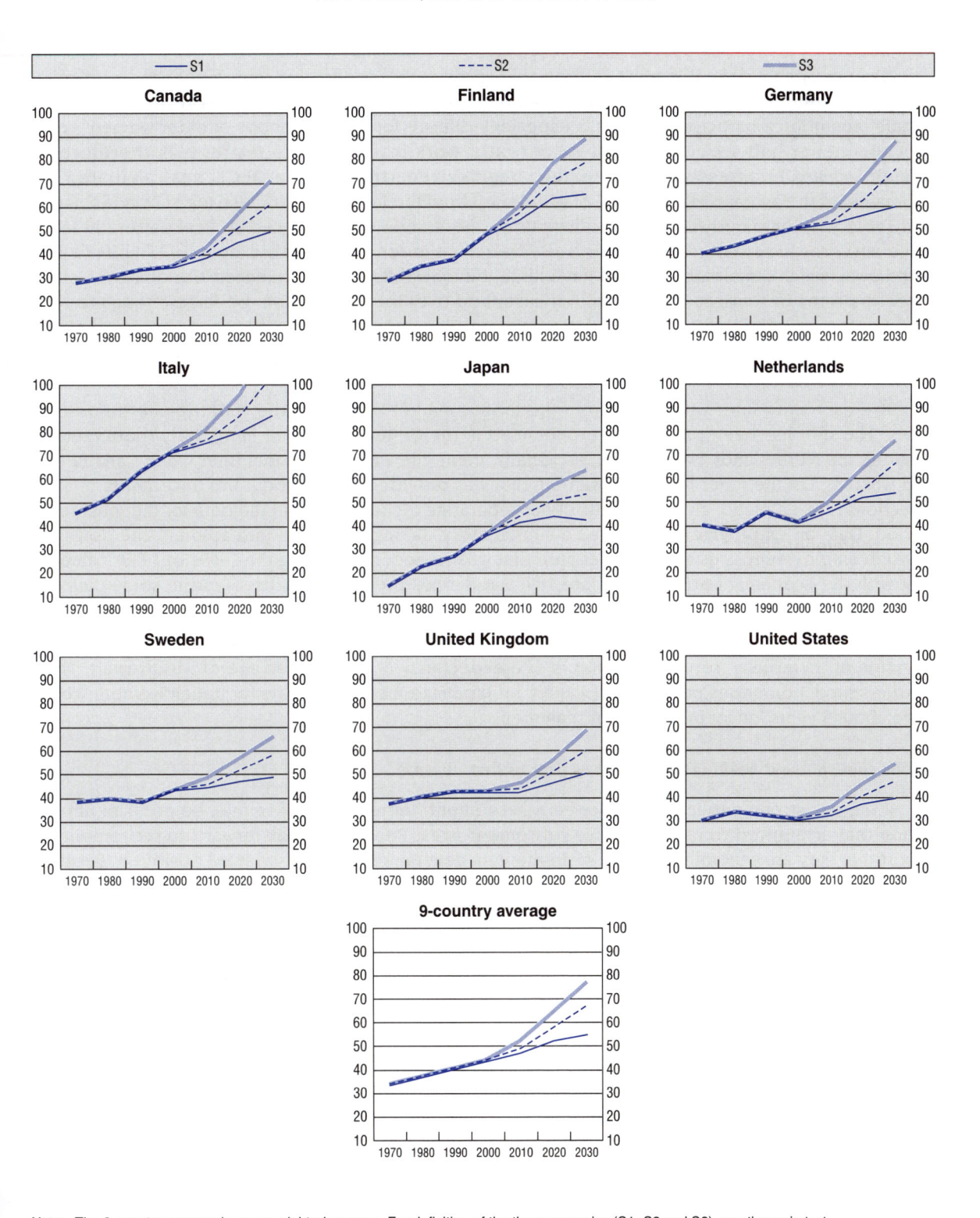

Note: The 9-country average is an unweighted average. For definition of the three scenarios (S1, S2 and S3), see the main text.
a) Retirees defined as number of people aged 55 and over who are not employed.
Source: OECD Secretariat estimates.

retirees to employees would still continue to grow in the nine countries but, in most, at rates that are not out of line with past growth rates.

Cyclically sensitive and increasing effective retirement ages

Given available data, it is quite difficult to directly measure effective retirement ages, particularly in distinguishing the effects of retirement among older women from overall patterns of increasing female labour force participation. This is especially difficult for today's cohorts of older women – many of whom never had a period of full-career paid work from which to retire. It is therefore not straightforward to assess when retirement begins. Nevertheless, the OECD has calculated new estimates[3] of the average effective age of withdrawal from the labour force. These are shown in Chart 5.2 and Table 5.1. Compared with earlier calculations, these show a pronounced cyclical pattern in labour force withdrawal rates. In many countries, there has been a noticeable post-1995 shift to later withdrawal, which if maintained could have large, beneficial fiscal consequences. Certainly, the size of recent patterns in some countries could, if sustained over the longer-term, be large enough to offset many of the negative effects of population ageing. The simulations in Chapter 4 showed that, in a hypothetical example, the fiscal effects of ageing could be offset by an increase of effective retirement ages of only one year.

The data show later withdrawal from the labour market in most of the countries in the past five years. The shift has been particularly pronounced in the United States (for men), Italy (both men and women), the Netherlands (women and, especially, men), the United Kingdom (men), and Canada (men and women). On the other hand, the warning that was provided earlier about the uncertainty of future directions is re-enforced, given the difficulty of separating cyclical effects in the data for the most recent period. Data on employment rates[4] tell a similar story. Taking all factors into account, the downward trend in employment rates among older men that was so dominant during the 1960s to 1980s came to a halt with the economic upturn of the late 1990s and since then has stabilised and in some countries even risen.

The final column of Table 5.1 translates these effective retirement age data into calculations of the duration of "complete" retirement (that is, life expectancy at the median age of withdrawal). These (under-stated[5]) durations range from 15 years for Japanese men to 26 years for Italian women. Women have about 5 years longer in retirement than men.

Public opinion about working longer: not as firm as first appears

If there is strong public support for early retirement, there would, of course, be political limits to action that attempted to raise effective retirement ages. People do look forward to retirement and report that they are generally happy in retirement. In general, retirement is viewed positively. People in the European countries that are examined here reported that they look forward to retirement, regardless of actual differences in national retirement ages.[6] In Canada almost half of retirees said they enjoyed life more than in the year before they retired. Those who enjoyed retirement less often reported health reasons as the cause. In the United States, analysis of many polls suggests there is little support for raising the age of eligibility for social security.[7] Indeed, it is one of the least favoured reform options, even if it were to be introduced gradually. US survey data show that workers there want to retire early – at, or before 55, in many cases, and just under 60 years on average.

The preference to spend more time in paid work declines with age and, in most countries, falls to under 10% of people aged 65 and over (see Table A.13 in the Statistical Annex). By labour force status, the desire for more paid work is, unsurprisingly, highest among the unemployed and, in most countries, lowest among retired people. Retirees were most interested in paid work in Italy (22%), the United States (11%) and Germany (10%). Preferences have not changed greatly in recent years.[8]

On the other hand, Table 5.2 shows that a very different set of responses were given when people were asked what they would choose if they could decide on their own work situation at present. When asked in this manner, most retirees (and most people over the age of 65) said they would prefer to have

Chart 5.2. **Average ages of withdrawal from the labour force: trends**
Dynamic estimates, men and women

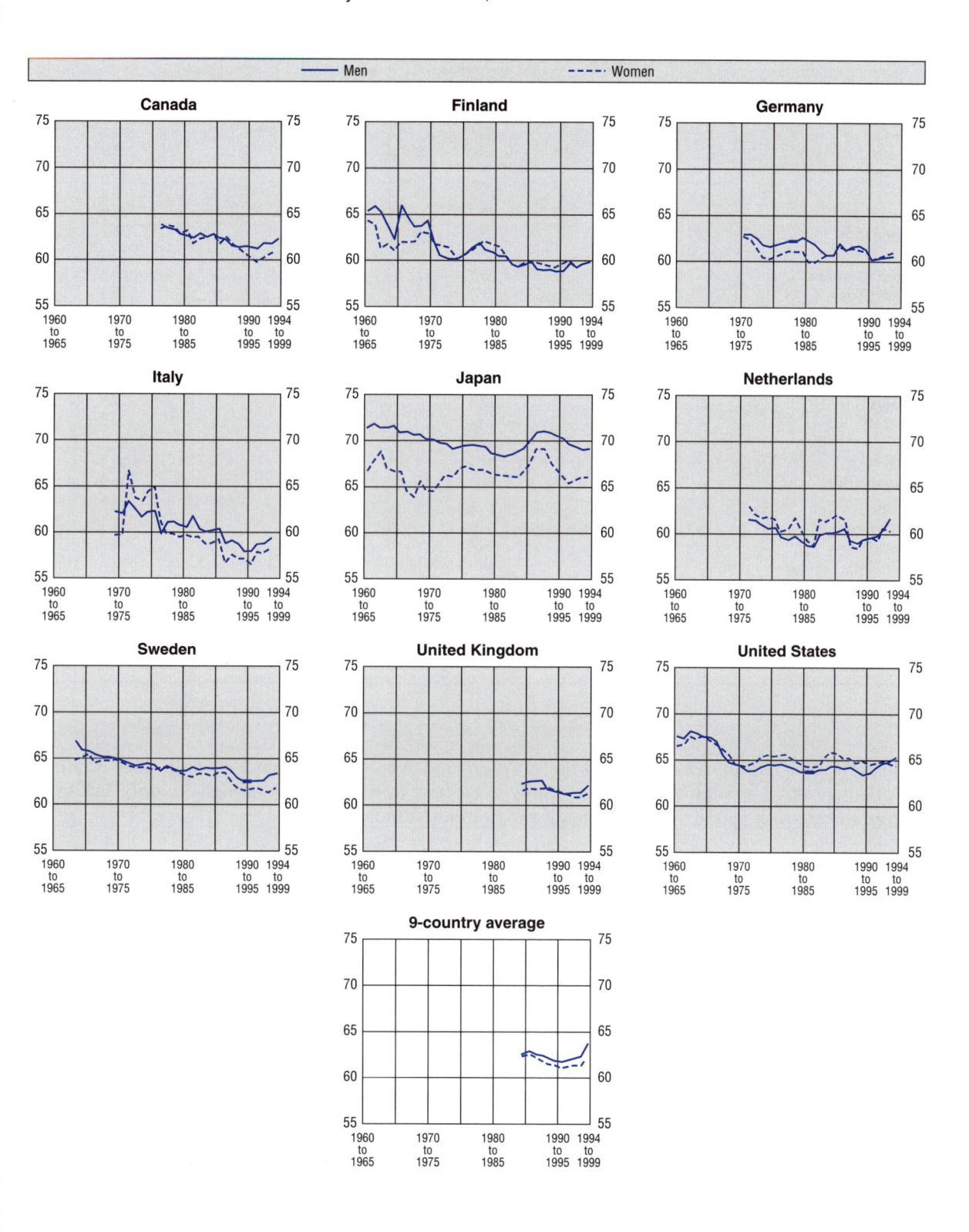

Table 5.1. **Age of withdrawal from labour force[a] and retirement duration**
Years spent in "complete" retirement, men and women, 1999[b]

	First and third quartiles: a quarter of the population		Median age of withdrawal	Duration of "complete" retirement
	withdraws earlier than age	never withdraws or later than age		
Men				
Canada	57.8	66.5	62.4	18.2
Finland	56.0	63.0	59.6	18.9
Germany	57.4	63.9	60.3	18.8
Italy	54.5	63.4	58.8	20.7
Japan	62.7	77.7	68.5	14.9
Netherlands	57.8	64.1	60.4	18.2
Sweden	59.9	66.7	63.7	17.5
United Kingdom	57.8	66.5	62.6	16.8
United States	59.4	71.4	64.6	16.3
Nine-country average	58.1	67.0	62.3	17.8
Women				
Canada	56.8	65.2	60.8	23.5
Finland	56.8	62.5	59.8	23.7
Germany	57.8	62.4	60.1	23.2
Italy	53.4	61.9	57.9	26.2
Japan	59.1	73.2	64.7	22.3
Netherlands	56.9	62.4	59.8	23.2
Sweden	59.1	65.3	62.7	22.0
United Kingdom	57.2	64.5	60.4	22.3
United States	59.0	68.8	63.4	20.4
Nine-country average	57.4	65.1	61.1	23.0

a) This table shows the median age at which people completely withdraw from the labour force. Take men in Canada as an example. Half of Canadian men leave the labour force at age 62.4 and live another 18.2 years without working. A quarter of Canadian men leave the labour force before the age of 57.8 and another quarter after the age of 66.5.
b) 1998 for Germany and the Netherlands.
Source: Scherer (2001).

paid work. The numbers of retirees who reported they would like to have no paid work at all was surprisingly small – ranging from lows in Italy (13%) and Germany (17%) to highs of only 38% in the United Kingdom and 36% in each of Canada and the United States.

Similar results are found when employees are asked if they themselves intend to work after retirement. Many do, often for economic reasons. US polls (Rix, 1999) taken 20 years ago indicated that just over half of pre-retirees would like to work after retirement, preferably in part-time or less demanding jobs. Today, over 70% of workers indicated they expected to work after retirement. A 1998 US survey (American Association of Retired People, 1999) found the figure is even higher among the baby-boomer generation, currently aged 36 to 54. Over 80% of them said that they plan to work after retirement. However, in reality, the numbers of people who follow this route has been small, at least until now.

What accounts for these seemingly contradictory findings? Part of the explanation is that people were likely thinking of hypothetical, highly desirable jobs that were particularly suitable for them – ones that are in limited supply for most people. Another survey response would seem to bear this out. As shown in Table 5.3, only a relatively small number of retired people felt that it would be easy to find an acceptable job – likely a realistic answer given the labour force situation of many of the countries in 1997 when these questions were asked. The most optimistic were older Americans, a third of whom thought it would at least be fairly easy to find a job. Indeed, the job market was stronger in the United States than in the other countries.

Reforms to Re-balance Work and Retirement

Table 5.2. **Public views on own preferred labour force status, 1997**

Percentage of people picking the labour force status they would wish, in answer to the question
"Suppose you could decide on your work situation at present, which would you choose?"

	Canada	Germany	Italy	Japan	Netherlands	Sweden	United Kingdom	United States
Percentage of those aged 50-64 choosing:							
A full-time job	54.0	53.5	47.0	55.8	43.8	54.6	44.0	51.4
A part-time job	28.5	35.7	39.3	24.9	27.1	40.1	37.4	33.2
A job less than 10 hours a week	8.0	2.9	6.0	12.5	8.1	3.0	5.4	5.5
No paid job	9.6	7.9	5.7	6.9	11.7	2.2	13.2	10.0
Percentage of those aged 65+ choosing:							
A full-time job	20.5	57.0	36.5	39.2	32.3	45.0	31.5	24.9
A part-time job	30.0	19.1	46.6	16.9	13.9	33.7	21.9	27.5
A job less than 10 hours a week	12.7	5.3	2.7	14.8	3.5	9.0	8.3	14.8
No paid job	36.8	18.5	10.4	29.1	31.3	12.4	38.3	32.8
Percentage of current retirees choosing:							
A full-time job	19.4	55.9	40.3	41.3	42.4	43.6	33.1	24.1
A part-time job	29.8	24.1	38.1	16.3	12.8	32.2	21.4	24.1
A job less than 10 hours a week	15.0	2.9	4.1	15.0	3.2	10.2	7.8	15.9
No paid job	35.9	17.2	13.3	27.5	26.8	14.0	37.7	35.9

Source: International Social Survey Programme, 1997.

Table 5.3. **Public perceptions on ease of finding a job, 1997**

"If you were looking actively, how easy or difficult do you think it would be for you to find an acceptable job?"
Percentage saying very and fairly easily

	Canada	Germany	Italy	Japan	Netherlands	Sweden	United Kingdom	United States
50-64	25.8	6.0	10.0	5.8	12.6	17.5	15.7	44.7
65+	12.9	7.0	9.3	1.6	14.3	12.4	9.5	29.3
Retired	23.9	7.8	9.0	2.5	16.1	10.8	9.7	32.7

Source: International Social Survey Programme, 1997.

In summary, the main public concern is not directed so much to working later *per se* as it is to the lack of suitable jobs for older people. These concerns are likely to be reduced to the extent that reform agendas stress older worker issues. In fact, a recent OECD review (OECD, 2000a) showed quite mixed public reactions to reforms that raised pension ages, with an unexpectedly low negative reaction in several countries.[9]

5.3. What can countries do?

This chapter covers responses across the whole work-retirement spectrum – in the workplace itself, in the various transitional pathways to retirement and in the work incentives in pensions themselves.[10] However, as most of the countries have recognised, while trends towards ever-earlier retirement have stabilised, there remains a culture of early retirement that requires action on many policy fronts.

Public pension reform can take various forms

At a fundamental level, pensions must have a large effect on labour-market participation. It is precisely their purpose to provide income so that people can stop working in their older years.

© OECD 2001

Similarly, the purpose of disability and unemployment benefits is to support people – young or old – who cannot work. What is less clear is the extent to which the rules and incentives of pensions and other income security arrangements work, in combination with other incentives, to cause people to retire at a particular age, and which features have the largest effects.[11] The goal of reform is not to remove all work disincentives, but rather to prevent the average duration of retirement from continually growing (or possibly to reduce existing durations somewhat) and to remove unintended incentives that induce people to retire more abruptly or earlier than they would otherwise choose.

Intuitively, the first important step to reverse the trend towards earlier retirement would seem to be an increase in the standard age of pension entitlement. The evidence shows, however, that the large majority of workers have left the labour force well before the official retirement age in most OECD countries. Workers who remain on the job forego pensions and continue to pay contributions, but in most systems pension rights increase little or not at all during these additional years. Thus, the earliest age at which benefits become available is an important parameter of pension policy.

Annex II discusses work incentives – pension replacement rates and pension wealth effects – in the actual arrangements in the nine countries. Lower pension replacement rates may encourage workers to stay in employment longer. Accumulated pension wealth usually falls with continued work once a certain age has been reached, giving an incentive to retire. Although much more empirical work is needed for a full understanding of the actual effects of pension design on retirement decisions, past work suggests that these could be large. This is important given that, as discussed in Chapter 4, only relatively small changes in retirement ages are needed to achieve large future effects.[12] Note, however, that some desirable reforms will not have the full fiscal effects outlined in Chapter 4, where it is assumed that working longer involves a longer contributory period and a correspondingly shorter period in receipt of benefit. It is possible, for example, to have arrangements where older people both work part-time and receive a partial pension.

Actuarially correct reductions for early retirement may stop workers from retiring much earlier than the standard retirement age, especially if they do not have other sources of retirement income to make up for a lower pension. However, alternative sources of income frequently do exist, and action on other fronts is also needed. Further, even more needs to be done if workers are to be encouraged to stay in the workforce beyond the age of 65. Most countries do raise pension benefits for workers who decide to stay on beyond the official retirement age, but these increments are in most cases not high enough to make a difference in the worker's retirement decision.

Reforms to alternative pathways to retirement: more specific to national circumstances

Moving to a public pension system that applies actuarially correct adjustments for early and late retirement will help, but by itself will not succeed in removing all incentives to retire early. Often there are multiple pillars in the pension scheme, with the retirement incentives in other pillars countering those in earnings-related public pensions. Additional important incentives to retire early are often found outside of the pension system. Alternative pathways such as disability programmes, special pensions for unemployed older workers or other benefit programmes serve as quasi-retirement programmes in many countries by bridging the gap until workers reach the minimum retirement age. Their importance varies widely across countries, as is shown in Chapter 2. Changes to incentives in the pension system may put more pressure on these alternative bridges to early retirement.

Early-retirement incentives are not only offered by public pension systems but also by occupational and personal pension arrangements. In most countries, company defined-benefit schemes are used as a tool to reduce the number of older workers. Retirement is often allowed before the standard retirement age with little or even no reduction of benefit levels. Some schemes are designed in a way that workers reach the maximum benefit before the standard age, in which case working longer brings no extra benefits. While such arrangements are made between the company and the worker and thus constitute private contracts, they are still subsidised by the public, which loses contribution revenue through early retirement.

The incentives to retire in occupational pensions depend significantly on their characteristics and how they are integrated with public pensions. In some cases, a private pension can be used to finance a period between early retirement and receipt of public pension.[13]

Partial retirement policies are another option to keep older workers in the labour market, although they have had limited success, as described later. Under such schemes, workers are entitled to either a full or partial benefit while continuing to work part-time. One approach is to offer partial pensions calculated according to the reduction of hours worked and the worker's earnings prior to retirement, allowing workers to continue to earn credits for their later full retirement benefit. Another route are pension schemes that make the receipt of a normal or early-retirement pension dependent on an earnings test; workers are allowed to earn income only up to a certain threshold, beyond which they are not eligible for benefits. The exemption amount thus gives workers the possibility of working beyond retirement. A still further approach is to pay subsidies to employers to encourage the hiring of new part-time employees to make up for the reduction in working hours.

Workplace reform must take place through less direct action

Most countries have recognised that reform must also encompass the issue of older workers' employment. Age discrimination legislation is one route. Beyond that, much of the responsibility for action rests with workers and employers, with relatively limited room for government policy to take a direct role (apart, again, from government's role as a large employer in its own right). Possible avenues include steps to reduce the cost of older workers, such as hiring subsidies, active labour-market programmes and employment services for older workers, and information and promotional campaigns to address a culture of early retirement. Much of the most important action – lifelong learning and flexible working arrangements – is not limited to older workers only, but must apply to workers of all ages (Section 5.8).

5.4. Pension ages

Most of the nine countries have a standard retirement age of 65 years at which full benefits become available for men and women, often with some special rules allowing earlier retirement for civil servants or special occupational groups. Japan still has an official retirement age of 60 years. Other exceptions are women in the United Kingdom, Germany and the old Italian system who can still retire at age 60 with a full pension. But all four countries have taken steps to gradually raise the standard retirement age for men and women to 65 years. In Japan, this will be done by 2025 for men and 2030 for women; in the United Kingdom, women will retire at 65 in the year 2020; and in Italy, the uniform retirement age will be phased in with the new system. Germany still has several other exceptions that enable workers to retire with a full pension before the age of 65 if they have a minimum contribution period or if they were unemployed or disabled before. These exceptions will be phased out by 2011. Only one of the nine countries, the United States has decided to increase the age of entitlement to full benefits beyond the age of 65. By the year 2022, it will have increased to 67 years. In Sweden, a proposed labour protection law would give employees the right to remain in employment until the age of 67.

The ages for early retirement in the nine countries range from 57 years under the new Italian system to 62 years in the United States and in Germany (by 2012). Most other countries allow early retirement at 60 years with permanent actuarial benefit reductions.

Entitlement ages in occupational pension schemes vary substantially both between countries and within countries. In the United Kingdom, for example, about half of private-sector schemes have a standard retirement age of 65, while most public-sector schemes still apply the age of 60. The majority of schemes – 60% in the private sector, 90% in the public sector – allow early retirement. In the private sector, about two-thirds of those plans with a standard age of 65 years allow early retirement at age 60, but one-fifth allow retirement as early as age 50. In the United States, about half of the company schemes have 65 as the retirement age, about 20% 62 and 10% 60. Almost all occupational plans offer early-retirement benefits, which are usually conditioned on a combination of a worker's age and years of

© OECD 2001

service. In Canada, the standard retirement age in occupational schemes is 65 years, but typically early retirement is possible starting at age 55.

Most countries also set a retirement age for personal retirement arrangements by applying tax penalties to savings that are withdrawn at younger ages. In the United Kingdom, due to the opting-out provision personal pension arrangements are part of the "official" pension system. Personal pensions can be drawn at age 50 provided that this does not threaten adequacy of retirement income at age 65.

As noted, direct reform of official retirement ages can only be a partial answer, since in most countries many people retire before the official retirement age. A full solution must also address the incentives to early retirement in pensions, alternate benefit streams and the workplace itself.

5.5. Repairing work incentives in pensions – linking benefits and contributions

The design of pensions, particularly with regard to how directly benefits are linked to contributions, can result in markedly different labour-market incentives. For people under the age of 65, the incentives for people to retire are dramatically lower in a simplified, but typical, defined-contribution model (where benefits are directly tied to contributions) than in typical defined-benefit arrangements. It is not until people reach their later 60s that incentives to retire in typical defined-contribution arrangements become greater than in their defined-benefit counterparts.[14] Actual pension arrangements are, of course, much more complex than shown in any simplified model. As well, many of the features of defined-contribution arrangements can be mimicked by traditional pensions, and defined-contribution models have other weaknesses. Often, too, incentives arise from a combination of different pensions. Nevertheless, there are strong reasons underlying why reforms directed to increasing work incentives tend to tighten the linkages between benefits and contributions.

In terms of recent reforms, the most fundamental changes in the contribution-benefit link occurred in Italy in 1995 and in Sweden in 1999, as both countries switched their public pension systems from defined-benefit schemes to notional defined-contribution schemes. The effects will not, however, be fully felt for many years. Each insured employee's contributions are recorded in an individual account that will "earn" interest. Since both countries continue to finance pensions according to pay-as-you-go principles,[15] however, their defined-contribution schemes are "notional" in the sense that contribution credits (rather than financial assets) are accumulated in the workers' individual accounts.

When a worker retires, the balance of the individual account will be converted into a stream of monthly pension payments using a "transformation coefficient" that depends on the worker's age at retirement and the cohort-specific life expectancy at that age. In Italy, the transformation coefficient will be adjusted to increases in life expectancy (together with changes in GDP, salary and employment) at 10-year intervals. The adjustments will be negotiated between the social partners. In Sweden, the applicable life expectancy will be based on the previous five years' unisex mortality table.

These reforms will make the systems approximately actuarially neutral. The benefits in the new systems are not only linked very closely to the age at which a worker chooses to retire but also reflect increases in life expectancy over time. Benefits will be lowered gradually to compensate for the fact that retirees receive pensions over a longer period. Since adjustment in Italy is not automatic, however, much of the system's effectiveness will depend on the social partners' ability to reach agreement on such benefit reductions. In Germany, too, an attempt was made in 1999 to introduce a "demographic factor" into the benefit formula to take account of increasing life expectancy; the measure met with strong political resistance and was abolished after the change of government.

In Italy, systemic change came after a series of reforms in the 1990s which, taken together, have been the most fundamental of all the countries analysed. Historically, both the conditions of entitlement and levels of benefits in Italy have offered strong incentives to retire at the earliest possible age. The series of reforms, ending with the very close link of contributions and benefits, has hugely improved the long-term incentives of the pension system, more so than in Sweden where there had already been a link, albeit much looser, between pensions and contributions.[16] The Italian reforms were acceptable politically only with a very long transition period from the old to the new system. Only in 2035 will all workers be under the new pension rules, and only around 2050 will all pensioners be receiving their pension under the new rules.

Other countries introduced smaller reforms that made a closer link in their public systems. Finland, for example, lengthened the income period on which the earnings-related pension is calculated from the last four years to the last 10 years.

There have been relatively few policy responses in the nine countries with respect to improving the work-retirement incentives in private pension schemes. An exception is the Netherlands, a country with high levels of early retirement, where early-retirement schemes[17] are now being phased out. These schemes were introduced as a result of collective negotiations to curb unemployment in the late 1970s. They are now in effect in many branch and employer-sponsored plans and are *de facto* early-retirement schemes. The government is encouraging the social partners to convert the schemes to flexible pension schemes in which actuarial adjustments are made for early retirement.

In most countries, however, employers continue to facilitate early retirement by offering company pensions with no or low actuarial reductions before the standard retirement age. In some countries, for example the United States, occupational defined-benefit schemes may well be used to circumvent age-discrimination rules by offering generous early-retirement benefits; in Japan, lump-sum benefits are frequently used as a means to promote early retirement and restructuring. In Germany and Japan, for example, occupational pension plans of the defined-contribution type, which by definition link contributions and benefits, are not even allowed yet. There are proposals in both countries to implement such schemes, but no decisions have been taken.

Another source of early-retirement income is private voluntary schemes, such as personal retirement savings plans or life insurance contracts. Here, too, governments are trying to move the incentives towards later retirement. In Finland, for example, tax relief for voluntary retirement arrangements was reduced, as it was believed to provide incentives for early retirement.

Actuarial adjustments for early and late retirement

Only four of the nine countries have public systems that are approximately actuarially neutral with respect to early retirement. In the United States, public old-age pensions are permanently reduced by 0.56% per month of anticipated retirement; this means that a worker who retires at age 62 instead of age 65 will receive 80% of a full benefit. (The age of full benefit is gradually increasing to age 67.) This reduction is considered about appropriate, taking into account current life expectancy at retirement in the United States. In Canada, the earnings-related pensions are reduced by 6% per year of early retirement.

The reforms in Italy and Sweden that were described above have also removed the previous system bias towards early retirement. In the new Italian system, workers are allowed to retire starting at age 57 with a minimum contribution period of five years. Since the new system is based on defined-contributions, the pension benefit will be reduced accordingly. The reduction results from the transformation coefficient and is therefore not set in advance. If the resulting benefit is below a minimum threshold, however, retirement will not be allowed until the age of 65 years. In Sweden the situation is similar. The new pension system will allow flexible early retirement with actuarial adjustments. Early retirement is possible starting at the age of 61 with a permanent benefit reduction of almost 30%; the guaranteed minimum pension, however, is not payable before the standard retirement age of 65.

In the Netherlands and the United Kingdom, public pensions cannot be taken before the standard retirement age. All early retirement has to be financed privately or through occupational schemes. In the Dutch quasi-mandatory occupational schemes, retirement can often be earlier, with actuarially neutral adjustments. In Germany, pension benefits are reduced only by 3.6% per year; retirement at 62 instead of 65 years would thus lead to a reduction of about 11%, which is substantially lower than that required for actuarial neutrality. In Finland, the reduction depends on the type of pension and on the age of the worker; the basic pension is reduced between 4 and 6% per year, and the earnings-related pension between 5.6 and 6%. In Japan, retirement before the age of 65 will be penalised with a 6% reduction of the basic pension for every year of anticipated retirement, and after 2025 the earnings-related benefit will not be payable before age 65.

Occupational schemes in the nine countries offer early-retirement benefits under a wide variety of conditions. Comprehensive data on the actuarial adjustments applied in such plans are not readily available in most countries. In the Netherlands, where occupational plans cover almost all workers, early retirement is possible in most schemes, although other programmes such as the collective pre-retirement (VUT) programme and disability benefits are more widely used to exit the labour market. Most occupational pension schemes apply actuarial reductions to early-retirement benefits, but the collective pre-retirement programmes are seldom actuarially neutral.[18] Early occupational pensions are usually not adjusted actuarially. No assessments can be made in Germany, Japan and Italy, as information on the plans' characteristics is not collected on a regular basis.

Better data are available for the United Kingdom, the United States and Canada. In the United Kingdom, actuarial adjustments to benefits often depend on whether the retirement comes at the employee's or the employer's request. Only 4% of schemes with a normal retirement age of 65 pay full benefits to workers retiring voluntarily at age 55. But 40% will pay full benefits if early retirement comes at the employer's request. In the United States, the most common adjustment factor is 6% per year of early retirement, which is slightly lower than the one applied in the public pension system. In Canada, the picture is more varied. In some private occupational plans, pensions are actuarially reduced, and in some benefits are paid without reduction. Some plans even provide additional bridge subsidies until 65; often this is done by waiving integration with the public pension benefit until age 65. About half of the Canadian occupational schemes are estimated to provide unreduced benefits once minimum service requirements are met.

Turning to arrangements for later retirement, the public earnings-related pension in Canada and the German pension system reward each year of deferred retirement with a 6% benefit increase. The basic pension in the United Kingdom is increased by 7.5% per year. Finland has a 12% increase per year, but its effect is limited since there is an overall benefit ceiling set at 60% of pensionable wages, thus discouraging work at later ages. In the United States, the accrual rate for older workers is gradually being increased from 5% of the earnings base per year to 8% per year for workers attaining age 66 in 2009 or later. Japan recently lowered its rate of increase; now every year of later retirement is rewarded with a benefit increase of 8.4%. Until 1999, a five-year deferral resulted in a pension increase of 88%. The new Swedish system offers substantial incentives to remain in the labour force beyond the age of 65 – a worker continuing until age 70 sees his/her pension increased by almost 60%. The new Italian system will offer no incentives to work beyond the age of 65 since there are no actuarial adjustments in the transformation coefficient after the standard retirement age span.

5.6. Closing or restricting pathways to early retirement

This section examines reforms aimed at restricting pathways such as disability benefits and unemployment benefits and at promoting rehabilitation to enable workers to avoid dropping out of the labour market unnecessarily. Section 2.6 presented household data on the way that income is provided to people during the work-retirement transition, including the various combinations of income, pensions, unemployment and other benefits. A weakness of the household data presented there was the absence of separate measures of people in disability benefit pathways, a common pathway to retirement in many countries. (Disability programmes were typically included with retirement pensions.) Chart 5.3 corrects this by comparing trends in various benefit streams, including disability benefits, based on recent information from administrative sources from those countries that could supply the data.[19]

The data on beneficiaries in Chart 5.3 suggest a substitutability among benefits in the age group 55-64 years.[20] Countries with a small number of disability beneficiaries tend to show a high proportion of people with old-age pensions and unemployment benefits. For example, Sweden, Finland and the Netherlands show high levels of disability beneficiaries and relatively low levels of old-age pension

Chart 5.3. **Trends in beneficiaries, for persons aged 55-64, 1975-1999**
Percentage of employed

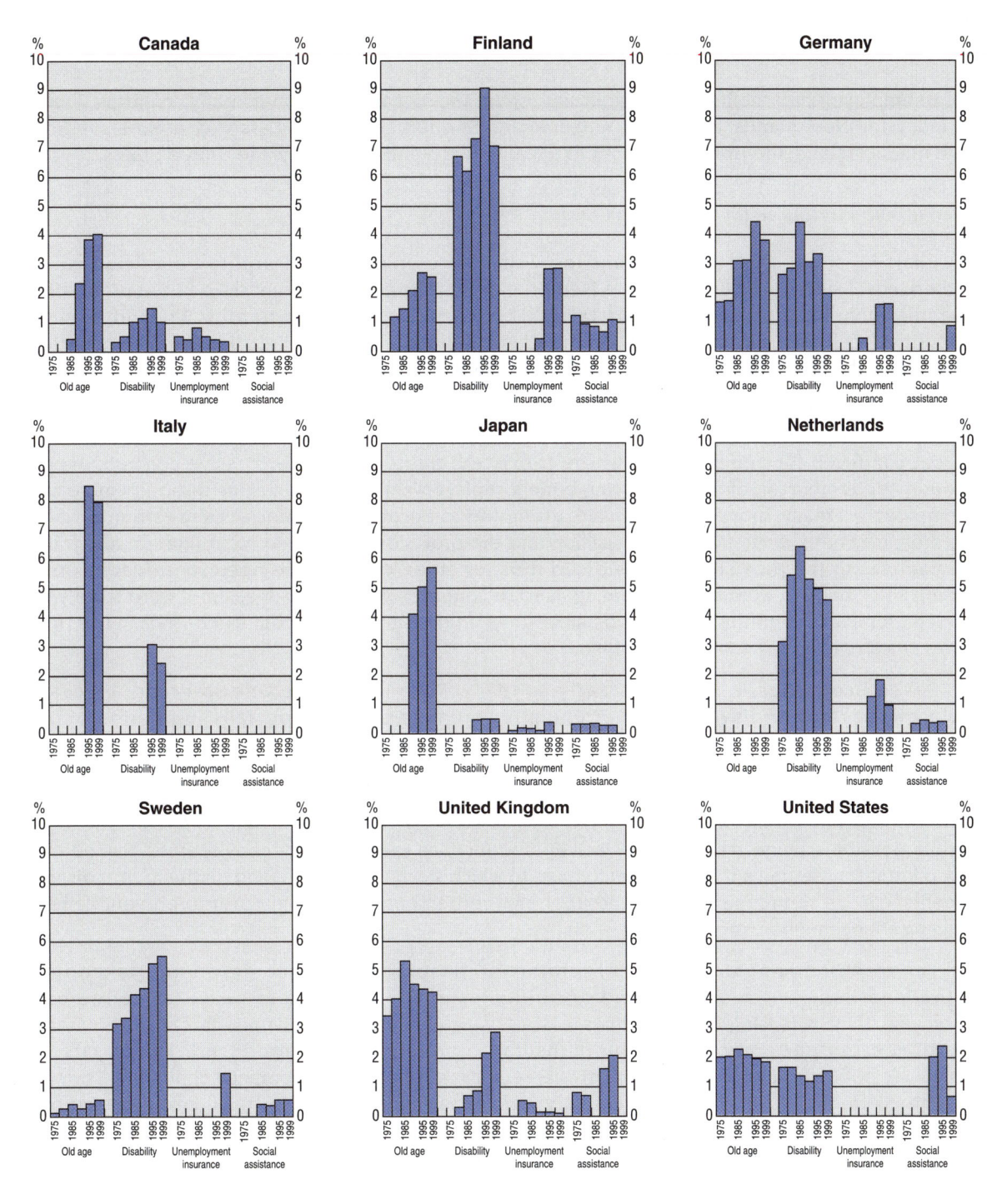

Notes: Canada: Social assistance not available. Finland: Old age and disability beneficiaries not available for 1975; unemployment insurance beneficiaries only available from 1990. Germany: Unemployment insurance beneficiaries not available for 1975, 1980 and 1990. Italy: 40-64 instead of 55-64; old age and disability beneficiaries only available from 1995; unemployment insurance and social assistance beneficiaries not available. Japan: Old age and disability beneficiaries only available for 1990, 1995 and 1999. Netherlands: Unemployment insurance beneficiaries only available from 1990. Sweden: Unemployment insurance beneficiaries only available in 1999; social assistance only available from 1985. United Kingdom: Disability and unemployment insurance beneficiaries not available in 1975; social assistance not available in 1985. United States: Unemployment insurance beneficiaries not available; social assistance not available in 1975.
Source: OECD Secretariat calculations from national data submissions.

beneficiaries in this age group. The United Kingdom shows the opposite pattern, with relatively few beneficiaries on disability and unemployment benefits and high levels of old-age pensions in the 55-64 age group. (The United Kingdom trend has changed, however, with an increasing number of disability beneficiaries and a falling number of old-age pensioners.) Japan and Italy[21] also show large proportions of old-age pension beneficiaries in this age group.

Unemployment benefits play a significant role in the 55-64 population in many countries (Finland, Germany, the Netherlands, the United Kingdom and Sweden), while social assistance plays a relatively large role in Finland, the United Kingdom, the Netherlands and, especially, the United States.

Reforms concentrating on the disability pathway

Chart 5.3 shows that, among countries with a large number of disability beneficiaries – the Netherlands, Sweden and Finland – the Netherlands has shown a significant drop in the proportion of disability beneficiaries since the mid-1970s. There has been no clear trend in Finland, while the proportion has been rising in Sweden. The trend is also up in the United Kingdom, but at a lower level. In Germany, there is no clear trend in disability benefits.

Starting in the mid-1980s but particularly in the 1990s, most countries took steps to reduce the stream of beneficiaries flowing into disability programmes. Actions included abolishing the labour-market condition for benefit award where it existed, tightening administrative controls over the disability determination process, reducing benefit replacement rates and making disability more costly to employers. Finally, most countries have attempted to encourage beneficiaries to return to work. In this area, measures range from moral suasion and the provision of targeted rehabilitation and training programmes to the provision of subsidised jobs for older workers. The need for initiatives to get beneficiaries back to work has been recognised in countries where such measures were largely non-existent, for example in the Netherlands since 1998, in the United Kingdom since 1997, in the United States since 1992 and in Canada since 1996.

Several countries, *e.g.* Italy (as early as 1984), Finland and the United Kingdom, cut the replacement rates of disability and/or unemployment pensions, especially in relation to other potentially accessible benefits. The Netherlands and Finland also raised the minimum ages at which income-bridging arrangements through unemployment or special early-retirement benefits can be used to exit the labour force. Dutch employers and unions are encouraged[22] to move – within the ten-year period in which fiscal facilitation of the pay-as-you-go early-retirement scheme will be ended – to a flexible pension scheme, which applies actuarial reductions to benefits for early retirees. Sweden went a step further by setting a maximum percentage to which sickness benefits (and, in the future, disability benefits) can be supplemented from occupational retirement schemes in order to prevent generous bridging arrangements.

The most fundamental structural reforms of disability insurance were undertaken in the Netherlands. The Dutch sickness and disability insurance programmes were transferred to the employers, thus increasing the companies' cost of using disability as an avenue to early retirement. In addition, experience rating of disability insurance premiums was introduced. The transfer of a previously public insurance scheme to private-sector insurance and reinsurance companies, however, still means that costs are borne collectively rather than individually. Initially, costs to employers seemed very low, but preliminary evidence suggests that this was primarily due to insurance companies under-pricing their products in a new market. It remains to be seen whether higher premiums will lead to lower disability rates.

In Finland, the government has also made disability insurance more costly for employers by requiring a higher level of pre-funding and thus higher contribution rates; this action aims at lowering the incentive for employers to use disability insurance to shed workers. Other countries, for example Italy in 1999, have increased the costs to employers by giving them more responsibility for rehabilitation and job retention policies.

Most countries have also implemented reforms to restrict access to disability benefits. Benefits are now largely awarded only under medical conditions. While this helped reduce inflows into the disability programme initially, several countries are now reporting increased numbers of less easily identifiable diseases, such as mental conditions. Several countries, for example the United States, have also introduced more frequent medical reviews of disability cases, or largely abolished the award of permanent benefits (Italy, the Netherlands, planned in Sweden).

Increasing rehabilitation measures

An increased emphasis on rehabilitation and general training to improve the skills and employability of disabled persons, and particularly older people, is observed in all countries. Some countries, such as Germany and Sweden, have long had a strong emphasis on rehabilitation measures. However, the evidence on the effectiveness of reintegration and training programmes has not been very encouraging so far. The US disability programme, for example, has several incentives for return to work. Beneficiaries are allowed a 9-month trial work period without benefit reduction, are offered extended health insurance coverage through Medicare after they return to work, and are allowed to deduct disability-related work expenses in determining the substantial gainful activity. But these steps have not been very effective with respect to beneficiaries' reintegration into the labour market. Currently, only about 0.5% of disability beneficiaries leave the disability rolls to take up work, but the impact of these reforms will have to be measured over a longer period of time. The Finnish programme, which includes subsidised jobs, has shown some positive results with younger disabled workers, but the success rates for older workers have been low (Gould and Saurama, 1999). Japan too is stepping up efforts to promote the employment of older workers through a range of different programmes.

Preventive rehabilitation measures are another important approach for retaining older workers. The effectiveness of such action is seen not in return-to-work statistics but in lower disability incidence rates. Immediate success stories are unlikely, however, since the creation of a rehabilitation culture and the development of a market for rehabilitation services take time.

Unemployment benefits

Another pathway to early retirement is provided through unemployment benefits. Many countries make such benefits available to older workers over a longer period and at less stringent job-search conditions than those applied to younger workers. Some countries have special unemployment pensions, which are provided outside of the public pension system and aim at bridging the time until a worker becomes eligible for an early old-age pension. Before recent reforms in Finland, for example, a worker could become unemployed at the age of 53 (today about 55) and bridge the time to retirement with extended unemployment benefits and subsequently an unemployment pension. Special early-retirement schemes also exist in some countries, partly as a response to increasing numbers of older workers in the disability and unemployment programmes. In the Netherlands, for example, a separate scheme for early retirement was set up as a result of collective negotiations; it aimed explicitly at reducing unemployment and displaced disability insurance as the most important avenue to early retirement. Conditions depend on the industry, but usually workers are eligible to retire at age 60. In Japan, the duration of benefits for those who experienced mandatory retirement was lowered in 2001.

5.7. Gradual pathways to retirement

In the absence of institutional constraints, such as fixed retirement ages or incentives in pensions and other programmes, it might be expected that the interplay between the supply and demand of older workers[23] would result in a gradual decline of work in older age groups and a gradual decrease in the share of work that was full-time, full-year in character. There appears to be nothing in the pay, productivity, sickness, skills, work-leisure or other fundamental factors[24] that could account for the abrupt transitions from work to retirement mainly at age 65 and earlier that still are common today. This section examines reforms directed to easing these institutional constraints and to encouraging more people to work longer, but on a more gradual basis.

Ageing and Income

It is useful to recall that, in some countries, the concept of flexible retirement, and the legitimacy of any work while in receipt of a pension, is quite recent in policy discussions. There was often a view that pensioners would be taking jobs away from younger people or that receiving a pension while still working was a form of double-dipping. More recent public opinion surveys[25] have shown that this is no longer the case in most of the nine countries.

Part-time work and self-employment are often cited as potential means of gradual retirement – possibly bridging a full-time career and full retirement. The evidence described below suggests that, given today's incentives and preferences, this is not yet a common pattern. Indeed, Table 5.2 above shows that most retired people expressed a preference for having full-time over part-time work,[26] with work at a job of less than 10 hours being the least favoured. Canada is the main exception to this pattern, with part-time work being preferred to full-time, while in the United States they are equally desired.

Part-time work: mainly a device to retire earlier, not later

Table 5.4 shows that the percentage of employees who work part-time rises in older age groups. Among people aged 55 to 59, about 18% of men worked part-time in the Netherlands, but the share is under 10% in most countries. By age 65, over half of workers were part-time in about half the countries. However, that is mainly because full-time workers had withdrawn from the labour force, as indicated by

Table 5.4. **Employees working part-time**
Percentages, 1999[a]

	Men			Women		
	55 to 59	60 to 64	65+	55 to 59	60 to 64	65+
Canada						
% of employees	7.7	14.8	34.3	27.9	39.8	53.0
% of population	5.1	6.4	3.0	13.2	9.6	1.6
Finland						
% of employees	9.1	28.6	54.5	16.5	32.1	60.0
% of population	5.0	6.6	2.1	9.0	6.8	0.6
Germany						
% of employees	4.0	11.6	48.0	44.6	63.2	72.1
% of population	2.9	3.3	2.1	21.8	7.6	1.1
Italy						
% of employees	3.8	6.3	13.9	14.1	12.5	18.4
% of population	2.0	1.8	0.8	3.2	0.9	0.3
Japan						
% of employees	11.3	23.9	40.7	39.5	46.0	55.4
% of population	10.3	15.5	13.2	23.2	17.6	8.0
Netherlands						
% of employees	17.7	33.8	..	75.2	82.8	..
% of population	11.2	7.3	..	22.9	6.6	..
Sweden						
% of employees	8.8	23.7	..	36.2	50.1	..
% of population	6.7	11.8	..	26.3	21.3	..
United Kingdom						
% of employees	10.0	20.0	67.3	51.8	67.9	88.0
% of population	6.7	9.1	4.9	26.8	16.3	2.8
United States						
% of employees	7.3	15.1	48.1	22.0	33.2	61.5
% of population	5.4	7.8	7.6	13.2	12.4	4.9

.. Data not available.
a) 1998 for the Netherlands.
Source: OECD full-time/part-time database and UN demographic database.

the second set of figures for each country. These show part-time workers as a percentage of the total population of the respective gender and age group. The figure is much lower, of course, and is quite similar across the age groups. Typically there is a growth in the numbers working part-time between the ages of 55-59 and 60-64, and then a somewhat greater decline after the age of 65. Part-time work may be a route to retiring before 65, but not for continuing work after 65. OECD analysis[27] has also shown that people do not generally shift to part-time work as "bridge jobs" between full-time work and full retirement.

Sweden, Finland, Japan and the Netherlands stand out in terms of the amount of part-time work. The first two have a partial pension system. Japan has an "earnings rule" that governs pension entitlements between the age of 60 and 65 and which encourages part-time work. In the Netherlands, part-time work among men at all ages is high. Earlier OECD analysis (OECD, 2000a) shows a dramatic decline over recent years in part-time work among older men in Sweden, which is likely associated with the curtailment of partial pensions discussed below.

No shift to more self-employment in later life

Self-employment is a potential way of working later on a more flexible basis. It might be thought that some employees with accumulated pension rights in their main career job would be interested in shifting to self-employment after leaving that job – receiving both the pension and the income from self-employment. However, in reality, this is not a common pattern. The situation for self-employment is similar to part-time employment, as can be seen in Table A.6 in the Statistical Annex. Self-employment does rise as a percentage of employment in older age groups. As a percentage of the whole population, however, self-employment falls. This suggests that self-employed people retire later than salaried employees, but that, on average, there is not a shift from employee status to self-employment. The exception is a rise in the percentage of men who are self-employed between the ages 55 to 59 and 60 to 64. However, the percentage falls after age 65 in all countries.

Indeed, the earlier OECD analysis referred to above (OECD, 2000a) concludes that there is net outflow from self-employment, as self-employed people retire or move to employee status. Japan is an exception; more men there do move from employee status in a "career" job to self-employment in their older years as a "bridge" to retirement.[28]

Reforms – partial pensions and other action

The above-mentioned reforms that link benefits and contributions in an actuarially neutral fashion should support the emergence of more gradual arrangements, to the extent that people indeed prefer these routes. In some cases, gradual pathways are supported by specific policies. Partial pensions are an example, but they tend to support a gradual early retirement. They have not been used to encourage people to continue working later in life on a more gradual basis. Other approaches have included the removal of earnings rules that discouraged work after retirement and, in the case of Japan, increased efforts to provide alternative work for older people.

Sweden has a part-time pension scheme that allows workers to reduce their hours of work and receive a benefit to replace part of the lost earnings. However, the part-time scheme was closed for new entrants in 2001, and the last participants will be phased out in 2004. The share of part-time work among older workers is still high in Sweden, but it has been declining significantly since 1995 when the replacement rate provided by the scheme was reduced from 65 to 55% (Latulippe and Turner, 2000). Due to the actuarial adjustments, the new Swedish old-age pension system will offer significant incentives to workers to continue working beyond the earliest retirement age.

Finland's part-time pension scheme was reformed to provide an incentive to take up this scheme rather than full-time unemployment or disability programmes. The minimum age for the scheme was gradually lowered from 60 years in 1994 to 56 years in 1998. As a result, the number of part-time pensions awarded in 1999 exceeded the number of people with disability benefits.

Germany introduced several options for part-retirement in the 1990s. Under a scheme started in 1992, it is possible to take one-third, one-half or two-thirds of a regular old-age pension before 65 and to continue to work part-time. In 1997, another part-time early-retirement scheme was introduced for which any employee over the age of 55 is eligible.[29] In addition, a recently-enacted law gives all employees the right to ask for conversion of their full-time job to a part-time job.

The labour-market situation of older workers in Japan is quite different from that in the other countries, as seen in Box 5.1. In Japan, a partial pension[30] is available in conjunction with full-time as well as part-time work, thereby compensating older workers for the wage reductions that occur after they leave their regular career jobs.

Box 5.1. **The situation of older workers in Japan is quite different**

The high employment rates of older workers in Japan stand in contrast with the other eight countries, as are the government policies in support of older workers. The country never experienced high unemployment of younger workers and thus early retirement was never introduced as a general policy to combat youth unemployment.

The mandatory retirement age from a "career job" is low (it is currently 60, having risen from 55), but working longer is nevertheless common. Until the retirement age, lifetime employment arrangements with a single employer are common. After that, people often move to employment with a related, subsidiary or sub-contracting firm under one of several arrangements. Companies assist their older workers in finding such bridge jobs, which has lowered resistance against wage reductions in post-career employment.

Self-employment has also been high traditionally in Japan. As shown in Table 5.4 and A.6, self-employment and part-time work are important among older people, including those over 65.

Recent reforms have gradually increased the pension age. It is expected that firms will adjust and raise retirement ages as well, and the overall retirement age may be adjusted in another decade or so, as the situation warrants. Indeed, various sectoral arrangements have already extended the retirement age beyond 60. As well, partial pensions are available to encourage working after 60 and those working will be less penalised by an earnings rule.

Active labour market policies, training and employment services for older workers have been strengthened. There are wage subsidies to private-sector firms for hiring older people and a subsidy to older people taking a new job after age 60 that helps compensate for a drop in wages. The partial pension can also act as a *de facto* wage subsidy for people aged 60 to 64.

Seniority pay is also common in Japan and that, in principle, should work against the employment of older workers. However, the Japanese authorities indicate that the wage gap between the ages has been decreasing in recent decades and is expected to continue to do so. Some companies, for example, have, on an individual basis, dropped the weight of age and experience in the salary-determination formula.

The "end of lifetime employment" has been much discussed in Japan in light of recent restructuring. However, current data and field research show that, in down-sizing, large firms have continued to rely on hiring cuts and transferring employees to related firms or subsidiaries. Job retention rates remain high. In the medium-term, pressures may mount as a consequence of factors such as declines in the relative size of the retail and agricultural sectors, where many older workers are employed. However, there is little evidence of a decline at present.

The United States abolished the earnings test[31] in 2000 for all pensioners aged 65 and older. For pensioners up to the age of 64 a withdrawal rate of 50% is applied, while those aged 64 and 65 see their benefit withdrawn at a rate of one for three. Only wages and income from self-employment are counted for the purposes of the test, however, and there is an exemption threshold.

5.8. Promoting a workforce for all ages

The work-based challenge: more related to learning than age

As noted, there is much concern about the likely availability of jobs for a growing number of older workers. Chart 5.4 illustrates the potential scale of the problem, if indeed there is a problem, by showing the share of employment that is accounted for by people aged 55 and over. Japan is the only country to have seen a large rise in the share of older workers over the past 30 years. In the early-retirement scenarios for 2030, the share of older workers will likewise not differ greatly from that today or in 1970 in most countries, apart from Japan. In later retirement scenarios, however, the rising share of older workers does move beyond historical patterns in several countries.

While the number of older workers is likely to grow, recent OECD studies[32] do not point to fundamental problems in absorbing more older workers. There will be relatively fewer alternative sources of labour supply – younger people and women. The available evidence does not point to any basic problems related to productivity,[33] pay or skills acquisition, apart from those associated with the lower educational levels of older people.[34] More generally, there is need for a better empirical understanding of the interaction among the factors that affect the demand for older workers – for example, the extent to which learning, job retention or sickness are related to each other, to physical age and to the age of expected retirement. The OECD will commence shortly a thematic review of the obstacles facing older workers in Member countries that will analyse the determinants of demand for older workers in more depth.

Many of the employment problems of the existing generation of older workers seem to be rooted in their relatively low level of foundation skills such as literacy and numeracy. Older workers today had less opportunity than younger workers to undertake formal education when they were young, and low educational attainment has acted as a barrier to access training to maintain or increase their skills. Table 5.5 shows that workers aged 55 to 64 have significantly lower educational attainment than workers aged 25 to 49, although the differences are less pronounced in Germany and the United States. The gap in educational attainment between older and younger workers tends to be greater for women than men. Employed people in the older age group usually have much higher educational attainment than retirees of the same age.[35]

Training, and formal adult learning in general, does fall off quite sharply at about the ages when people are retiring. The resources for lifelong learning are unevenly distributed within countries and, in general, the older part of the population tends to lag behind in resources for training. Chart 5.5 shows that Finland has the highest proportion of persons enrolled in adult education[36] and training up until the age of 49, and thereafter Sweden shows the highest proportion. Finland also has an early age of retirement. All countries show major drops when people are in their later 50s. A likely explanation is that the incidence of training reflects the expected age of retirement in a country, not the actual ages of the individuals.

Note, however, that it is only lifelong learning that holds the potential to address problems of skill gaps among people of different ages. Greater investment in learning among young people may well be justified in its own right. However, if increased learning were limited only to the young, it would widen, not narrow, the learning gap between younger and older workers. On the other hand, training directed exclusively at older workers would likely have relatively small payoff in the absence of learning activities among workers before they become older.

Promoting a workforce for all ages – at all ages

The key labour force actions that would strengthen the position of older workers are ones that take place before workers become old, such as lifelong learning, or that apply to workers of all ages, such as flexible work arrangements that allow part-time work or other flexible working patterns. OECD Ministers have endorsed the concept of lifelong learning as an essential approach to ensuring that all young people and adults acquire and maintain the skills, abilities and dispositions needed to adapt to

Ageing and Income

Chart 5.4. **Percentage of the workforce aged 55 and over**
1970, 2000 and three scenarios to 2030

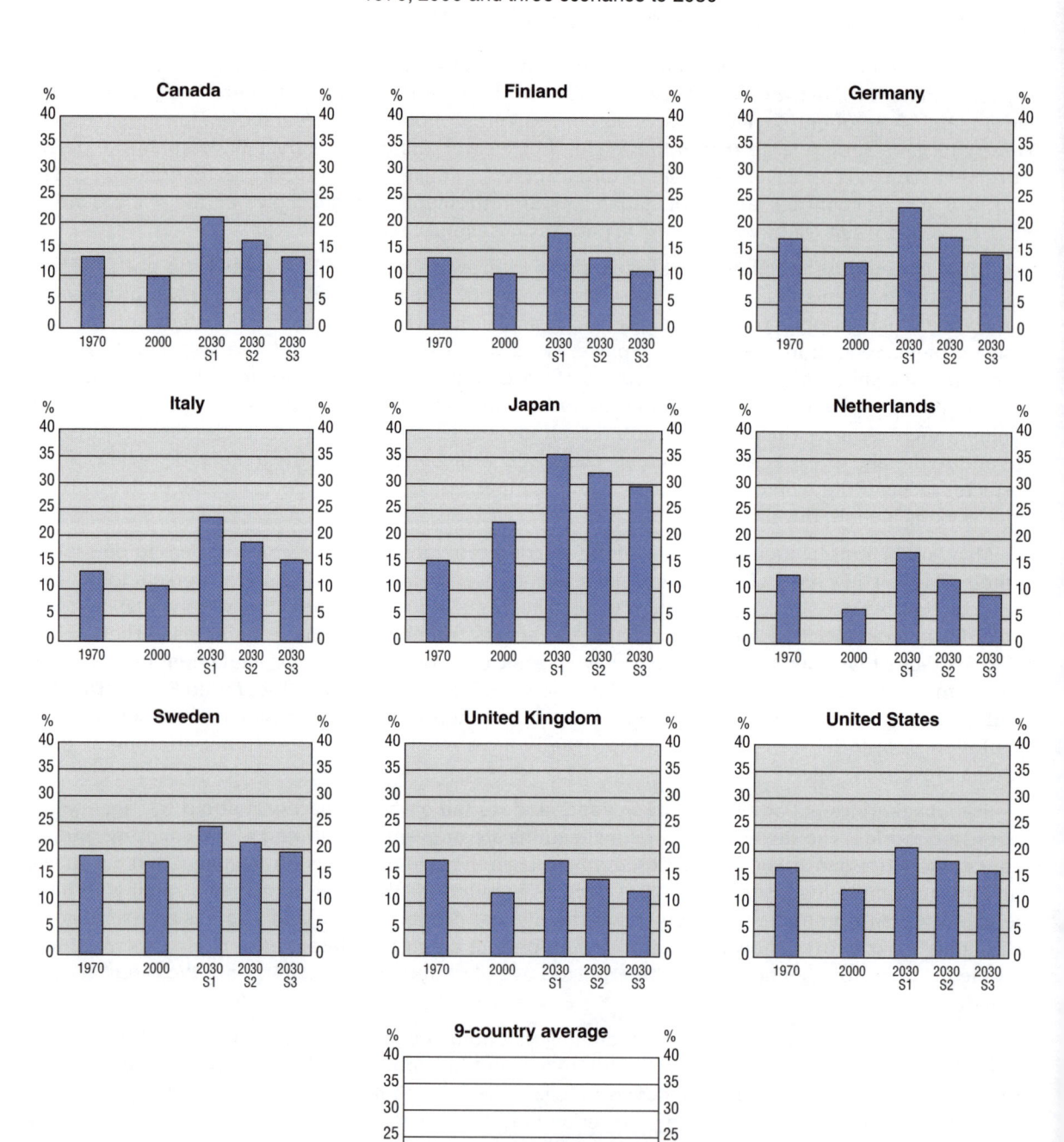

Note: The 9-country average is an unweighted average.
Source: OECD Secretariat estimates.

Table 5.5. **Younger and older workers, and older people not at work, by educational level**
By gender, percentages,[a] 1999

	Employed people aged 25-49[b]			Employed people aged 55-64			People aged 55-64 and not employed		
	High	Medium	Low	High	Medium	Low	High	Medium	Low
Both sexes									
Canada	58.6	28.8	12.6	46.8	23.5	29.7	33.2	21.9	44.9
Finland	38.0	45.0	16.9	30.3	25.4	44.1	13.9	24.9	57.9
Germany	26.3	58.0	13.0	28.1	47.0	18.9	12.4	48.9	31.2
Italy	12.9	43.1	43.5	12.1	22.0	62.1	3.0	12.3	74.4
Japan	37.9	49.9	12.2	16.5	44.9	38.6	10.4	45.9	43.7
Netherlands	27.4	46.9	25.5	27.2	36.2	36.3	11.3	31.8	56.8
Sweden	33.0	52.1	14.7	24.8	43.0	32.0	13.1	38.9	46.7
United Kingdom	29.8	52.5	9.3	20.6	37.7	26.4	9.3	20.0	26.5
United States	40.1	50.7	9.2	33.7	53.0	13.2	20.0	53.6	26.4
Men									
Canada	57.4	28.1	14.5	48.2	20.4	31.4	38.8	19.6	41.6
Finland	32.4	48.2	19.2	32.8	23.8	43.4	14.2	23.4	58.7
Germany	28.8	56.7	11.9	34.7	45.6	13.8	19.3	53.4	19.9
Italy	10.9	39.4	49.1	12.3	21.4	62.7	3.2	14.5	75.3
Japan	40.0	47.3	12.7	20.6	43.9	35.5	13.8	40.9	45.3
Netherlands	27.2	45.7	26.8	29.7	39.0	30.9	15.6	40.4	43.7
Sweden	30.2	52.6	16.9	23.3	41.7	34.9	14.4	37.3	47.0
United Kingdom	29.7	52.9	8.0	22.1	41.8	21.3	16.7	33.7	36.5
United States	38.8	50.5	10.6	37.3	48.3	14.4	21.6	50.8	27.6
Women									
Canada	60.1	29.5	10.4	44.8	28.1	27.1	29.5	23.4	47.1
Finland	44.3	41.3	14.3	27.8	27.1	44.9	13.6	26.2	57.1
Germany	23.2	59.6	14.6	17.3	49.3	27.4	7.3	45.5	39.5
Italy	16.1	49.3	34.2	11.5	23.5	60.6	2.8	10.8	73.8
Japan	34.7	53.8	11.4	9.9	46.5	43.6	9.2	47.6	43.1
Netherlands	27.5	48.5	23.8	21.8	30.0	48.2	8.4	26.1	65.4
Sweden	35.9	51.7	12.3	26.4	44.3	28.9	12.0	40.4	46.4
United Kingdom	30.0	51.9	10.9	18.5	31.6	33.9	4.5	11.1	20.0
United States	41.6	50.8	7.6	29.4	58.8	11.8	19.0	55.4	25.6

a) Percentages do not necessarily add up to 100 due to non responses.
b) 25-54 instead of 25-49 for Japan.
Sources: OECD database on labour force statistics.

continuous changes in jobs and career paths. Within countries, the concept of lifelong learning has received wide support, and there is an emerging attempt to define and operationalise lifelong learning in national policies.[37]

Most reforms have not targeted particular programmes on older workers, who are as heterogeneous as any other group of workers, but have instead attempted to ensure that older workers are not excluded from such programming. In many countries, there are general age-related co-ordination mechanisms or strategies to provide communication and harmonisation of action on many fronts affecting older workers. In a number of cases, special bodies (often reporting to the Prime Minister's office or other senior levels) have been established to provide co-ordination.[38]

"Workplace for all ages" policies can, however, be supplemented by special measures designed specifically for older workers. In nearly all cases, countries have established specific research agendas addressed to a better understanding of the situation of older workers and of the work-retirement situation. In many there are promotional activities addressed to overcoming ageist workplace practices

Chart 5.5. **Participation in adult education and training**
Percentage, by age groups

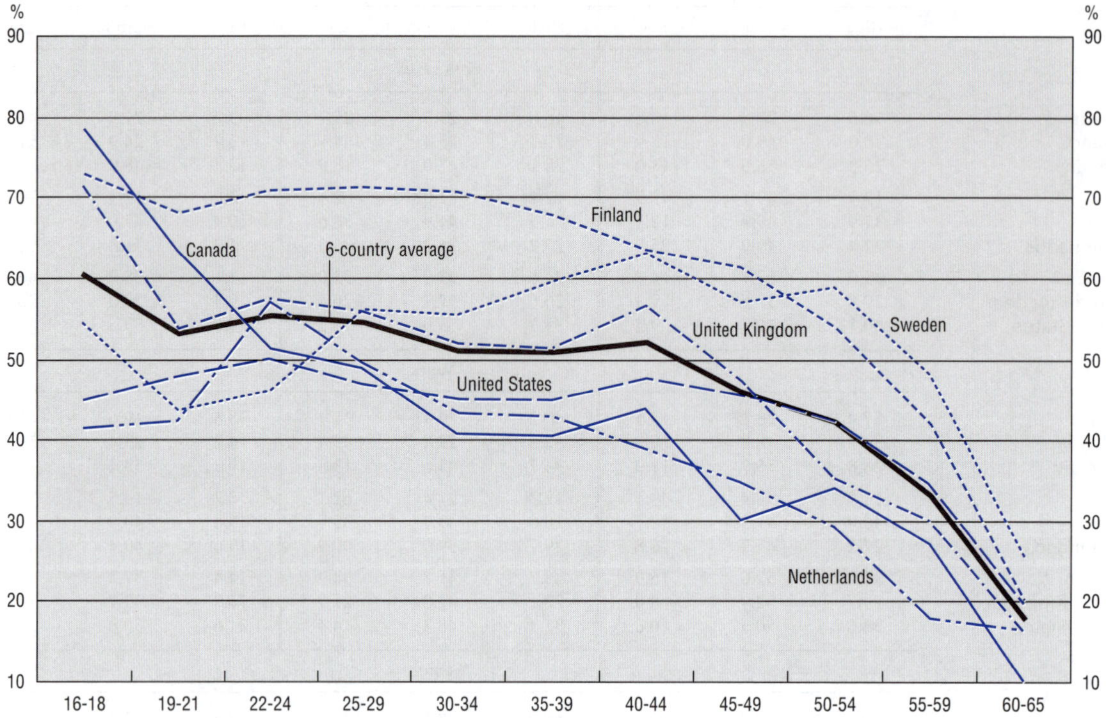

Source: OECD education database and international adult literacy survey database.

and to encouraging best practice in the employment of older workers. However, beyond research and promotion, no clear sense emerges from the review of the nine countries on the importance that should be attached to such supplementary policies.

Quite different policies exist, for example, with respect to preventing age discrimination. Some countries have not yet moved in this direction. Canada and the United States have legislation that prohibits age discrimination. The evidence suggests that it likely does not have a major direct effect, but it may be a useful part of a larger programme to change an ageist culture in the workplace.[39] The United Kingdom is evaluating its Code of Practice on discrimination, and the possibility of new measures is being considered. In Sweden, there is a proposal to enforce a right for people to work until 67.

Targeted labour protection legislation is used in some countries. In Sweden "first in last out" labour protection legislation has contributed to relatively high employment rates among older workers. However, this does not mean that the legislation is uncontroversial. It might result in insider/outsider problems that hamper mobility. Such actions must be assessed in terms of their overall effects on the labour market and not only on any one group in the labour market.

Active labour-market policies specifically targeted on the older unemployed are used in different forms in many of the countries.[40] Many of these are, however, quite modest. While there are few evaluations, it is likely that their effects are small. Taken to an extreme, steps to protect or support only older workers could entrench ageist attitudes. This could happen, for example, if there were additional training opportunities for older workers beyond those available to other workers with similar needs for skills upgrading.

What is needed is a cultural shift in workplace arrangements for older workers, but a full consensus has yet to emerge on the role of government policy in helping introduce this shift.[41] Indeed, there often appears to be an asymmetry between the views expressed in the official statements of employer organisations and governments about age discrimination and the importance of retaining older workers and the actions of individual employers and governments in their capacity as large employers facing the need to downsize.

Active ageing

A number of the studied countries place policies that support more active labour-market participation of people as they grow older into a policy framework referred to as "active ageing". This is a broader framework that also supports a more active life of older people in unpaid work, in providing care for others and in voluntary activities in the community. Many proclamations by national and international bodies support the goal of promoting an active life of older people in society as well as in the labour market. There is also an attempt to address the concern that there may not always be enough jobs for older workers – by recognising that a more active life does not necessarily require paid work.

Earlier OECD work (OECD, 2000a) examined internationally comparable data on how people of different ages actually allocate the 24 hours a day that are available to them to a variety of work, personal and leisure activities. It concluded that the time that was once spent in paid work is not used in unpaid work or voluntary activities. The retirement income system is, for the most part, supporting people who are mainly engaged in passive pursuits. Nor do there appear to be any strong trends away from passivity, despite the growing duration of retirement and the improved health of retirees.[42] The data are consistent with the hypothesis that people do not take on new activities when they retire. If they volunteered before they retire, they are likely to continue to do so afterward. This suggests that, if active ageing agendas are to succeed, they should focus on people as they grow older, not when they have reached old age.

Chapter 8 returns to the potential use of the active ageing concept as a way of defining the scope of reform agendas. To date, however, the concept has proved more useful in the areas of health and social cohesion, and has not been used to any significant extent in framing labour-market and retirement initiatives.

NOTES

1. A retiree, for the purpose of this chart, is defined as anyone aged 55 and over who is not employed. See Tables A.1-A.5 in the Statistical Annex for supporting data on the age structure of the population, life expectancy and employment ratios. The resulting demographic and labour-market pressures can be expressed in a variety of ways. Chart A.8 in the Statistical Annex calculates scenarios for the number of employees supporting each retiree, while Chart A.9 shows scenarios for the percentage of the total population that is employed.

2. The middle scenario is based on the same assumptions as the baseline projection in Chapter 4. The higher scenario assumes that the labour force participation rates of men in older age groups grows such that by 2030 it returns to the same level as in 1970. The lower bound is the symmetrical opposite. The upper and lower bounds for women assume participation rates for older women that are 5% higher and lower by 2030.

3. See Scherer (2001). Scherer provides a dynamic estimate, derived by comparing age groups five years apart, and adding the resultant estimates of net withdrawal rates over all age groups. These ages at which people withdraw from the labour force are sometimes referred to as effective ages of retirement. However, retirement in this sense is defined narrowly, to include people (over the age of 45) who are neither working nor classified as unemployed. Other definitions, including those used elsewhere in this publication, define retired people as anyone aged 55 and over who is not employed. The Scherer calculations are based solely on labour force participation, not on receipt of a pension. The age of withdrawal is therefore somewhat higher than in other definitions. For example, a pensioner working only a few hours a week or actively looking for such work would be considered as in the labour force, not as retired, for these calculations.

4. See Tables A.4 and A.5 in the Statistical Annex. They show the percentage of men and women in older age groups that are employed. Unlike the data on age of withdrawal from the labour force, these data exclude unemployed people, but they do include people who are not employed for reasons other than retirement (a particularly important factor for women). In the United States, Burtless and Quinn (2000) argue that there has been a trend towards later retirement since the mid-1980s, a trend that was caused by the ending in the period of growth in the generosity of social security and by shifts to defined-contribution occupational plans – more than by improvements in labour-market conditions.

5. These calculations are understated in the sense mentioned above that they refer to the age at which people completely left the labour force. They do not reflect the common notion of retirement as occurring when people leave a main career job and receive a pension. That is, the median age of withdrawal from the labour force is greater than the median age of withdrawal from full-time work.

6. The most interesting figure may be the very large number of people who indicated that they have not given any thought to their own retirement. It is, of course, younger people who have reflected least on retirement (only one-third of people aged 15-24 had), but one-fifth of people aged 55 and over also responded this way. Higher-income people are most likely to look forward to retirement. For sources of public opinion data used in this report, see Hicks (2001). His paper draws on several sources of internationally comparable data, including the Eurobarometer surveys in 1992 and 1999 with tables and some of the analysis taken from Alan Walker (1999) and from the International Social Survey Programme (ISSP). The ISSP data and analysis are, in turn, drawn from two papers by Smith (2000*a* and 2000*b*).

7. This discussion is based on an article by Rix (1999).

8. Hicks (2001) shows that the number who believe that people will retire later in the future has grown a little over the 1990s in the countries covered, but actually fell in Germany. The high Swedish figure is an exception that might reflect the reforms underway there. Data from the Finnish Old Age Barometer, 1994 suggest that expectations about working longer are lower in Finland than in most European countries. Looking at all the European countries (not only those in our study), there seem to be no obvious linkages between actual reforms to raise pensionable ages and the views that are expressed about working longer.

9. For example, an increase in female pension ages in the United Kingdom met little opposition. A larger increase in ages of eligibility for the New Zealand public pension was introduced relatively quickly without a long period of advance notice. Employment rates among older workers rose significantly, and public opposition was

less than anticipated. In other countries, however, proposed increases in pension eligibility ages have provoked strong opposition.

10. Other reforms can also play a role in increasing work – migration policies, policies to reduce unemployment or encourage more female participation – or increasing productivity at work. All these are important and positive, but their fiscal consequences, at least, on pensions may not be as large as often thought. For example, to the extent that pensions are linked to real earnings, higher productivity will also increase the future cost of pensions. See OECD (1998a) and Visco (2001a).

11. For example, the much-needed longitudinal data that are beginning to become available (from the health and retirement survey in the United States) are painting a picture of the determinants of retirement that is considerably more complex than is reflected in the traditional literature. There is a useful discussion in Gustman and Steinmeier (2001).

12. Better understanding is needed of the role of income and wealth effects and of how work incentives in pensions relate to alternative retirement routes such as unemployment and disability benefits, to labour demand for older workers, to the retirement decisions of spouses, to sickness, etc. Earlier studies by the OECD and others (Gruber and Wise, 1999; Blöndal and Scarpetta, 1998; OECD, 1998a) show that the benefit formula of old-age pension systems discourages work at older ages in many countries. The effects are potentially large. It has been estimated by Blöndal and Scarpetta, with respect to the situation prevailing in the early 1990s, that increasing the incentives to remain in the labour market could lead to an increase in the participation rate of older workers by about 8-9 percentage points in countries with particularly large financial penalties (Finland, Italy, the Netherlands). Subsequent reform especially in Italy, will have affected these numbers. Note, however, that the literature is not unanimous on the ultimate effects of increasing effective retirement ages, particularly as it relates to savings. See Visco (2001b) for a discussion. There is clearly a need for continued empirical study. Current work at the OECD is further exploring retirement incentives, as discussed in Annex II.

13. Here governments have a potentially large lever in their role as an employer and provider of occupational pensions to their own workers – often a significant portion of the labour force. However, these potential levers are not often used since governments tend to be reluctant to have their own employment practices too far out of step with those of private employers.

14. The World Bank has calculated a simplified case that illustrates this very clearly. It can be found on the Internet in their pension primer series (World Bank, 1999).

15. The Swedish reform also introduced a funded defined-contribution component into the system. Workers save 2.5% of wages in an individual account and are given a wide range of investment choices for this amount.

16. The earnings-related component of the old pension system was based on average earnings during the best 15 years of the career.

17. *Regeling inzake Vervroegde Uittreding* (VUT) schemes, which will be referred to here as the collective pre-retirement programme.

18. The new flexible pension schemes which are meant to replace the pre-retirement (VUT) schemes are actuarially adjusted.

19. The data were provided by the participating national authorities. For Germany, Italy, Japan and the United Kingdom data from 1997 are used instead of data from 1999. As the notes to the chart indicate, there are important gaps in the numbers; in several countries, existing data do not allow ready comparison of the beneficiaries of different programmes, for example because individuals may benefit from several different but related programmes or because of the decentralisation of programme delivery.

20. There is less substitutability across benefit streams for people aged 65 and over, as the majority relies almost solely on old-age pensions. In some countries, though, some older people receive social assistance. This is particularly important in the United Kingdom, where approximately 5% of the 65+ age group receive the benefit. This is approximately three percentage points higher than for the 55-64 age group.

21. For these two countries, only two observations exist over the period.

22. The preferential tax treatment of pre-retirement (VUT) schemes will be phased out over the next 10 years.

23. A useful discussion of the economics of retiring earlier is found in Disney and Whitehouse (1999).

24. Retirement decisions by individuals involve choices between work and leisure that are affected by factors such as current and expected earnings, the accumulation of financial assets and other resources to support leisure, the physical and mental demands of work, health considerations, the desire to leave inheritances and the availability of jobs. In the absence of institutional barriers, one might expect that these factors would result, on average, in more preference for leisure and less preference for full-time work as people become older – but with a wide range of individual preferences about the timing of retirement and the speed of the transition to full retirement. A similar variety of preferences might be expected from the employer's perspective. The decision to continue employing a person, or a group of people, would be based on factors such as the employee's skills, productivity and costs – including both wages and the additional costs associated with part-

time or non-standard work. Since a number of these factors are related to age, but often only weakly related, then one might also expect a modest decline in the demand for workers in older age groups, with much variation in the timing of retirement and working arrangements.

25. The 1992 Eurobarometer survey showed that, while a majority of people favoured a flexible retirement age, a significant minority preferred a fixed retirement age. In some EU countries (France, Spain, Luxembourg) there remains a strong feeling that pensioners should not be able to take on paid work. However, in the countries in this study, this is a common view only in Italy, and there has been a small reduction in this view over the 1990s, as is shown in Hicks (2001).

26. On the other hand, when workers are asked about their own wishes when they do reach retirement age, they have a stronger preference for part-time work. That clearly changes when they actually reach retirement age, perhaps because of the lack of suitable part-time work or because part-time work, at least with one's lifetime employer, may not make financial sense as a result of final salary formulas in many pensions.

27. Earlier, the OECD (OECD, 2000a) examined the increase in part-time work among men aged 60 to 64. These men were compared with the same cohort five years earlier (that is, people aged 55 to 59 in 1999). In only three countries in this study – Sweden, Japan and the United Kingdom – is there a substantial increase in the share of the older male population working part-time, that is, a switch to part-time status for some. In the Netherlands and Italy, there have been actual declines.

28. This is a "net" finding and does not necessarily indicate the absence of bridge jobs in other countries. It is possible, for example, that people are shifting from self-employment as a main career job to wage and salary status in their bridge jobs. This appears to be the case in the United States (Quinn, 1999). The United States has the lowest level of self-employment amongst older men in the nine countries studied and shows a fall over time in the importance of self-employment for this group.

29. Employers are obliged to top up earnings but receive a state subsidy if they fill the vacancy with an unemployed person. But the reduced work time does not have to be taken in the form of shorter weeks or months. Instead, employees can continue to work full-time for half of the time until they become entitled to an old-age pension and then not work at all for the remaining half of the time. In most cases, it is this "blocking" of time that is chosen (Oswald, 1999).

30. The new reforms in Japan will raise the partial pension age to 65-69.

31. The removal of the earnings test was a major change. The academic literature on the likely effects of earnings tests is not conclusive, particularly as it relates to the role of earnings tests on early retirement. Gruber and Orszag (2000) argue for caution before dropping the earnings test below the age of 65. They draw attention to the incompleteness of the evidence, but indicate that it has not been suggested that the earnings test has had a large effect on labour supply in the past, at least among men – but it has been associated with greater receipt of social security benefits.

32. Three OECD papers give a quite complete review: Blöndal and Scarpetta (1998), Casey (1998) and Swaim and Grey (1998).

33. It is difficult to measure productivity by age directly. Skills are one proxy. A "work ability" index developed in Finland can also be used as a proxy and, in a number of small-scale studies, it has been found that work-ability does fall with age in some occupations, particularly for people in their 50s, and that this is often related to factors such as reduced ability to undertake sustained hard physical labour. However, these studies have also found that remedial action in the workplace could be effective. See Ilmarinen (1999).

34. Note that basic skills such as literacy are more related to cohort than to age. When account is taken of a variety of demographic and economic variables, literacy skills show no more than a modest decline with age. These surveys of adult literacy cover a broad range of skills that are used in the workplace. They are available for most of the nine countries in this study. There is a fall in skill levels as people age, but other factors are more important, such as education and actual usage of skills. See OECD and Statistics Canada (2000).

35. The United Kingdom is an exception where older employed women have a lower educational attainment than those who are not employed.

36. The data in Chart 5.5 do not take into account the number of hours that each participant received. The German figures were excluded from the chart because definitions of training differ between Germany and the other countries. However, they too show a tailing-off among the older group. For a description of, and monitoring of, lifelong learning in countries, see OECD, 2001b.

37. *Education Policy Analysis* (OECD, 1998 and 2001), provides a thorough description of country-specific reforms.

38. In the United Kingdom, for example, a Secretary of State for Older Workers has been appointed, to oversee a plan containing 73 action points.

39. Neumark (2001) argues that recent American evidence suggests there is little ground for differential treatment of older workers based on their productivity or pay. If there are age-related factors at play, they are not large. Discrimination against older workers may well exist, and thus anti-discrimination legislation is justifiable. A

review of the recent evidence suggests that, in practice, anti-discrimination legislation has positive effects on balance, although the evidence is thin and does not at all point in the same direction.

40. In the United Kingdom different programmes for subsidised work exist. There is a programme that includes tax subsidies (credits) for firms that hire older workers. In Germany, subsidising the wage cost of older workers has been used as an important measure in the context of the structural adjustment of industry, in particular in the eastern part of the country.

41. A Ministerial statement in the Netherlands in March 2000 is representative of views found in many of the nine countries. The statement, which is directed to the legislature, presents the cabinet's view on older workers following a major independent review of the topic. It points out the need to increase employment rates among people aged 55 to 65 and the central role of the social partners in doing this, with the support of government policy. Action is needed on both the supply and demand side, and on retaining and re-integrating older workers. Many steps have already been taken to remove work disincentives found in early pensions, disability and unemployment benefit programmes. More consultation is needed with the social partners on age-awareness personnel policy, employability policy and working conditions policy. It also argues for a change in mentality on the part of employees about working later in life. (That may have started to happen as a result of economic conditions and the removal of some financial incentives.) Thus, sustained action is needed on many fronts, including financial incentives. In other words, the Dutch statement suggests that the market will adjust, imperfectly, as financial incentives to early retirement are removed. However, that adjustment must be supported by sustained discussion, monitoring and action on the part of employers, workers' organisations and a number of government agencies on a range of issues – including informational and promotional activities directed to older workers, as well as good "workplace-for-all-ages" practices. [*Bevordering arbeidsdeelname ouderen* (Promoting the participation of older workers in the labour process), The Hague, 14 March 2000.]

42. Gauthier and Smeeding (2001). The time-use data on which these findings are based have many limitations, but they are significantly better than alternative sources of information on unpaid work and voluntary activities that simply ask whether people engage in such activities without inquiring about actual allocations of time to these activities.

Chapter 6
RESPONSES TO THE CHALLENGE OF BALANCED RESOURCES IN RETIREMENT

6.1. Introduction

A retirement income system based on different components enables a better balancing of risks, facilitates burden-sharing between different generations and offers more flexibility both in the adjustment of systems to changing economic and demographic conditions and in the individual worker's retirement decisions. This chapter examines likely future changes in the balance of elements that comprise the retirement system – earnings and pensions, pay-as-you-go and advance-funded elements, defined-benefit and defined-contribution, public and private. It then examines the diversification strategies of the nine countries.

Section 6.2 opens with a discussion of trends in the balance of system elements and describes the rationale for, and problems of, a more diversified system. A new balance also changes the risks faced by different groups. There are clear political constraints on moving quickly towards greater balance. Public opinion is often negative about changes to existing arrangements. However, there is also a belief that existing approaches are unsustainable and that change, if not welcome, is inevitable.

Section 6.3 outlines possible actions that could be taken. Reforms that are intended to strengthen the role of earnings in the incomes of older people were discussed in Chapter 5, with the result that most of this chapter is devoted to the structure of public pensions and, especially, public policy support for a stronger system of private pensions.

Section 6.4 reviews reforms that have resulted in greater diversification of financing methods within the public system. The main part of the chapter, however, addresses the ways in which private pension arrangements could play a larger role. The present situation is reviewed in Section 6.5, which points out the large differences in coverage that exist in both occupational and individual plans. Broader coverage of individual plans requires that high administrative costs be tackled. In many countries, people who change jobs lose out with respect to occupational pensions. Section 6.6 examines improvements in vesting and portability arrangements that have been made. However, this remains a key area of weakness in several countries. There are many potential risks in private pensions, including those related to insolvency, fraud or unethical behaviour – as well as the normal ups and downs of financial markets. Section 6.7 describes action that has been taken to improve financial security while Section 6.8 addresses the issue of public information.

6.2. A changing balance: its rationale and likely public reaction to change

Chart 2.5 in Chapter 2 shows the changing mix of the main income sources of older people in recent decades. Working income played a much larger role in the household income of people aged 65 and over in earlier decades. It has since fallen as a result of earlier retirement (in the period before the 1990s) and reductions in joint households. Capital incomes have, on the other hand, risen over time with the growth of private pensions. In Canada, the Netherlands and the United Kingdom, these two trends have been of about equal magnitude (thereby leaving the share of social transfers about the same). In Finland, Italy and Japan, however, the drop in working income was compensated for by an increase in net social transfers. In Germany and the United States, both transfers and capital income played a smaller compensating role.

Public expenditure: likely to grow in total, but not on a per capita basis

Chart 6.1 compares public expenditure trends in various categories[1] as a percentage of GDP:

- Canada, the United States and Japan are similar in having relatively small public expenditure, mainly in the form of pensions (old-age cash benefits), and with relatively flat expenditure patterns – although expenditure in Japan has increased slightly since 1992.
- Germany, the United Kingdom and the Netherlands also have fairly flat expenditure trends for pensions, but with a larger role for other elements such as disability and services for older people. Note that disability "pensions" cover a younger population as well.

Recent reforms have tended to reduce pension benefits on a per capita basis especially in Italy and, to a lesser extent, Japan, as was shown in Table 4.1 in Chapter 4. However, because of demographic trends, many more people will be eligible for pensions, and the table also shows large increases in total public pension spending. Future pressures for reform are likely to continue to be in the direction of reducing the rate of growth of public spending.

The share of working income and private pensions: likely to increase

Chapter 5 discussed the recent stability in the employment rates of older workers and new evidence on later withdrawal from the labour force. This suggests that the decline in the share of earnings in the retirement income data may come to an end, or even be reversed, in future decades.

Trends in the assets held by pension funds provide a signal of future income from private pensions. Table 6.1 shows that assets are equivalent to over 80% of GDP in the United States, the Netherlands and the United Kingdom and almost 50% in Canada. They have been growing most in these same countries. In these countries, it would be reasonable to expect to see significant future growth in the share of income from private pensions.

The rationale for more balance: reducing public spending and diversifying risk

Reducing the public role in the retirement income system (or, in most countries, not allowing it to increase as much as projected) means that the share of other elements – mainly earnings and private pensions and savings – must rise unless older people are to become worse off. The pressures to reduce the public share are partly fiscal, as noted. However, they are also based, at least to some extent, on social policy grounds.

Chart 6.2 shows that, in most countries, around 40 to 50% of total public social expenditure is devoted to old-age cash benefits.[2] (Note that education expenditure is not included in these numbers and that disability benefits also go to younger people.) In Italy, the proportion going to pensions is somewhat higher than in the other countries and exceeds 60% in recent years. Finland and Sweden also provide significant services to older people. Indeed, if health expenditure is included (and about a third of all health spending is directed to older people), then most social spending goes to people when they are in their older years. One concern is that even higher future spending on older people as a result of population ageing may crowd out other social expenditure, including interventions at other stages of people's lives.[3] Large public systems, in particular pay-as-you-go systems with relatively high replacement rates, require high contribution rates that may not leave much space for additional contributions to other schemes.

Furthermore, there are intrinsic merits to a more balanced system. A system composed of a number of separate, sustainable elements diversifies risk. The premise[4] is that a retirement system composed of several main elements, with several methods of financing and benefit calculation, will minimise unforeseeable threats to any one of those elements.

Box 6.1 outlines the main risks associated with each of the main elements of the system.[5] Some of them are large. The risks associated with the sustainability of public pension contributions in light of population ageing have been, clearly, a major driver of reform in many countries. However,

Responses to the Challenge of Balanced Resources in Retirement

Chart 6.1. **Public social expenditure related to the retirement-age population**
Percentage of GDP, 1980 to 1997

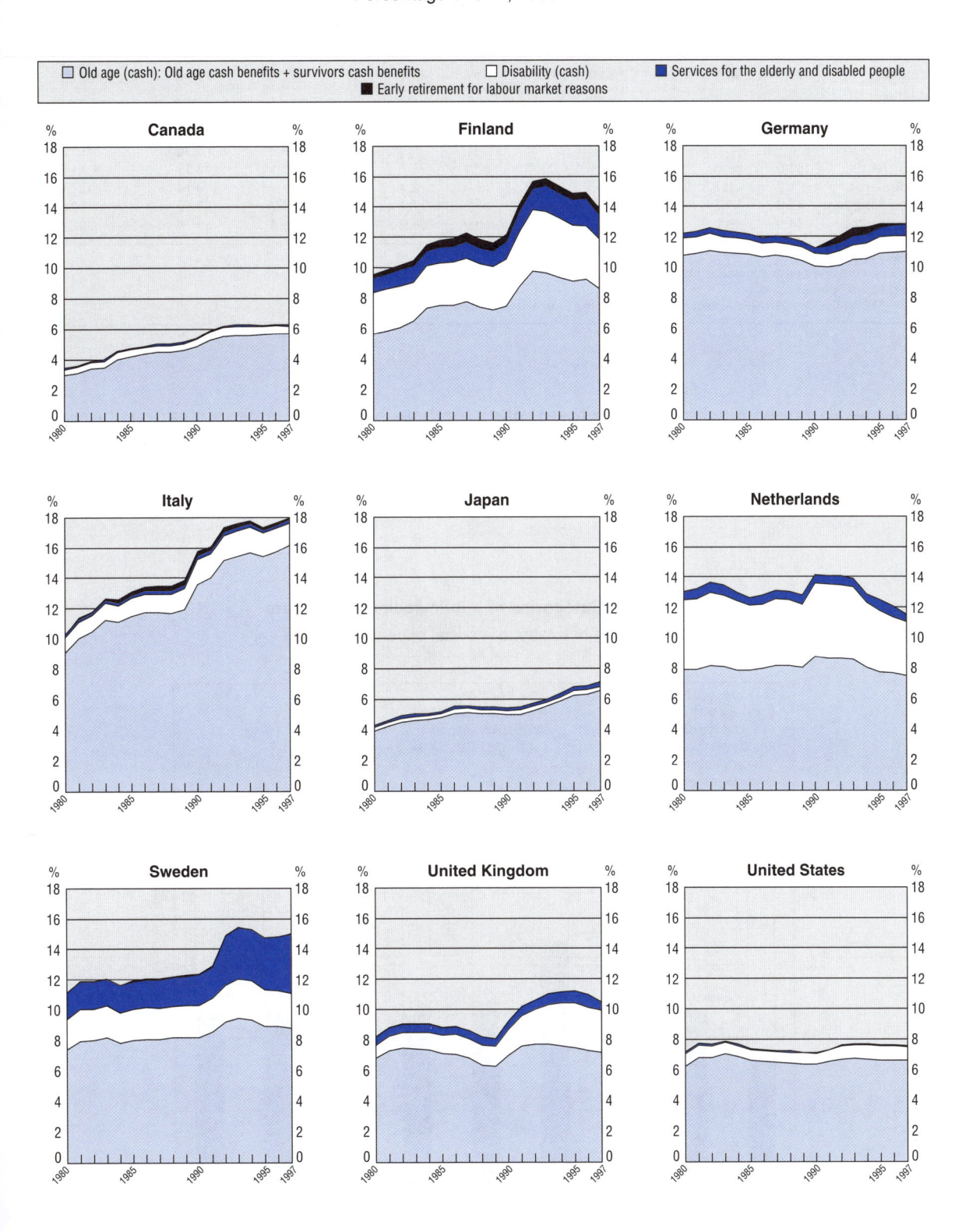

☐ Old age (cash): Old age cash benefits + survivors cash benefits   ☐ Disability (cash)   ■ Services for the elderly and disabled people
■ Early retirement for labour market reasons

Source: OECD Social Expenditure Database (2000).

Ageing and Income

Table 6.1. **Financial assets of pension funds**[a]
Percentage of GDP, 1990 to 1998

	1990	1991	1992	1993	1994	1995	1996	1997	1998	Annual average growth	1997-1998 period growth
Canada	28.8	30.7	31.3	34.0	35.9	38.6	40.7	43.3	47.7	2.36	0.10
Finland	..	..	..	..	..	..	..	..	..	..	..
Germany	3.1	3.3	2.9	2.5	2.7	2.7	2.8	2.9	3.3	0.03	0.14
Italy	3.5	4.3	3.1	3.4	3.5	3.6	3.2	3.0	3.2	−0.04	0.07
Japan	..	..	..	..	..	..	..	14.6	18.9	4.30	0.29
Netherlands	81.0	83.6	76.0	83.1	87.0	88.4	93.1	101.1	106.1	0.57	−0.15
Sweden[b]	1.7	1.7	1.6	2.0	2.2	2.4	2.4	2.7	..	0.14	0.13
United Kingdom	55.0	59.2	52.7	72.5	64.8	68.6	77.4	83.1	83.7	3.59	0.01
United States	44.9	48.9	50.0	52.9	52.6	60.0	66.9	76.9	86.4	5.19	0.12

.. Data not available.
a) Autonomous and non-autonomous pension funds.
b) 1996 to 1997 period growth.
Source: OECD (2000), *Institutional Investors*; Netherlands figures updated by national authorities.

there has also been much recent attention, particularly as a result of large fluctuations in capital markets, on the risks associated with advance-funded elements. And, as described in Chapter 5, public concern about the risks associated with earnings – particularly concern about the lack of suitable work for older people – is still strong.

Chart 6.2. **Categories of public social expenditure**
Percentage of total public social expenditure, 1997

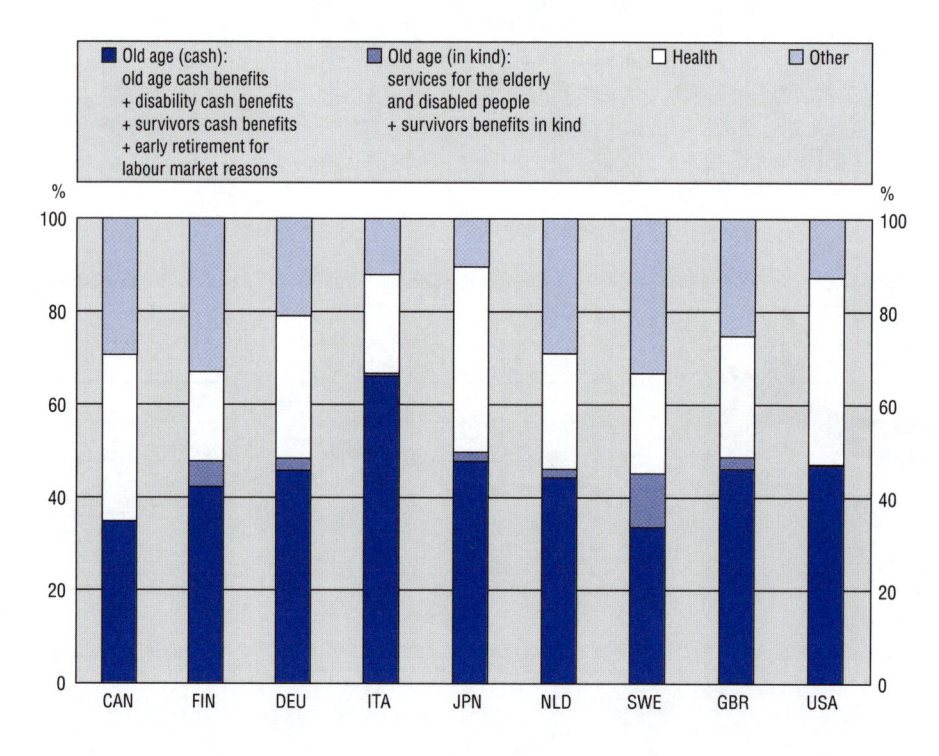

Source: OECD Social Expenditure Database (2000).

Box 6.1. Risks and risk diversification

Risks of pay-as-you go public pensions

Pay-as-you-go defined-benefit plans can be put at risk by demographic changes that may result in pension promises that cannot be met in the long term. In the absence of reform, population ageing could result in contribution rates that are too high to be sustained. It has been argued that the political risk might take the form of inter-generational tension, although evidence for this based on past experience, at least, is weak.

In the nine countries, changes to public pension promises have been frequent, but typically not large (at least in terms of their initial effects) and have mainly benefited older people. Exceptions have been larger changes related to retirement ages and the formula for up-rating benefits in payment. Potentially negative effects are typically managed by grandfathering arrangements. The main risks concern the future, as a result of the pressures of dependency ratios when the baby-boom generation retires.

Risks of advance-funded pensions

Advance-funded, defined-contribution schemes are a protection against the political risks above. However, they are more susceptible to the risks of unforeseen economic developments, including the ups and downs of financial markets. These have been high historically in the nine countries. The incidence of scandals in the selling of private pensions has been much more limited, but does exist, as described in Section 6.7. Advance-funded elements in the public system, including advance-funded reserves, run the risk of a too-close political involvement in the operation of financial markets.

Risks of assets

Financial and housing assets can play a large role in shielding people against unforeseen events, but they too are subject to risks of unforeseen economic developments. Housing assets are often hard to convert into income.

Risks of earnings

It would be much easier to adjust to changes in pension arrangements such as age-of-entitlement changes and the undershoots and overshoots that arise from the ups and downs of financial markets, if there were a real opportunity to adjust the length of working life in a flexible way.

Working longer, however, is not always possible and labour-market risks are often concentrated in vulnerable groups.

Risks of household living arrangements

Household living arrangements – pooling of income among household members – play a role in risk adjustment, as families de-merge and re-merge over the course of later life. These mechanisms are particularly important in Japan and Italy. Household living arrangements, as with all other elements of the system, have their own vulnerabilities, which can change over time. Falling family sizes and increased divorce rates are examples.

Risks of other social benefits

Benefits (such as social assistance, unemployment insurance or disability benefits) and services (such as those related to health and housing) provide a strong measure of risk-protection. Again these come with their own vulnerabilities. Disability benefits, for example, often play a large role before full retirement benefits are available but have been greatly affected by rule changes – typically widening of eligibility to include labour-market related factors and then a subsequent closing of those extensions.

Post-retirement risks

Post-retirement risks are growing in importance, as the durations of retirement become ever longer. The main problems centre on the role of annuities associated with defined-contribution arrangements and the escalation of pension benefits over the course of retirement in defined-benefit arrangements.

Sharing risks

When adjustments are needed because the expected benefits are not in the amount anticipated, defined-benefit pensions, transfers and services spread the risks associated among a large group. Defined-contribution pensions, earnings and assets concentrate responsibility for remedial action on the individual in question. This, in turn, can create new pressures on social programmes such as social assistance or disability benefits.

Box 6.1 also makes it clear that a changing balance among the elements can render some groups more vulnerable to risk and others less vulnerable. It is not possible for all individuals to have diversified retirement income packages. Low-income people often have only one source of income – social transfers. Chart 2.6 in Chapter 2 shows that this has been consistently the case in recent decades – except in Japan, but even there, reliance on these transfers grew over the past decade.

In summary, no single resource is ideal for dealing with all retirement risks: a system based on a mix of strong, sustainable components is the best approach. This need for balance has led countries to place emphasis on strengthening weak links in the system – underdeveloped annuities markets, high administrative costs in individual pensions, projected contributions to public pensions that may be too high to be sustained politically – and dealing with the consequences of weak labour-market attachments and broken households. The main responses are reviewed later in the chapter.

People accept, but do not welcome, re-balancing

Re-balancing means change, and some changes, particularly in pension arrangements, may be unpopular if implemented too quickly or without full regard for potentially vulnerable groups.[6] Countries have, therefore, placed much emphasis on public consultations, transitional measures and the timing of change, as will be discussed further in Chapter 8. There is a high level of public support for existing arrangements and principles in all the countries:

- Comparable public opinion surveys suggest strong support for the basic premise of pay-as-you-go pensions, namely, that workers have a duty through taxes and contributions to support a decent standard of living among older people.

- Most people continue to support both public pensions and employer-based occupational pensions. Support for other private arrangements (such as individual accounts) has grown a little since 1992, but the absolute level remains low – perhaps surprisingly low, given the attention paid to the role of privatisation during public debate in the 1990s.

- Support for the role of government in providing a "decent standard of living for older people" is high,[7] but the extent of that support varies considerably among the seven countries for which data are available (Table A.11 in the Statistical Annex). Less than half in the United States and Japan felt it was "definitely" a responsibility, while support was highest in Italy. Support has been falling slightly over time.

- In terms of the size of the public role, Table A.12 in the Statistical Annex shows a high level of support for a continuation of public support either at existing levels (Canada) or increased levels (other countries). Support for more public spending for pensions was reasonably stable over the decade from the mid-1980s to the mid-1990s in the four countries for which data are available: Germany (West), the United Kingdom, Italy and the United States.

- Support for more spending tends to rise with age in most countries and is highest among the retired. Canada and the United States are exceptions, where people of retirement age see less need for increased retirement spending than younger people. This may reflect greater satisfaction among older people with the adequacy of the retirement income systems in those countries – even though the public pension share in those countries is relatively low.

However, while people express support for existing arrangements, they are not confident about the future of those arrangements. People doubt whether actual public pension arrangements will be able to meet their goals. Most felt that people will get less pension for their contributions in the future, and the number who feel this has grown during the 1990s. Similarly, only a small number of people feel that, taken as a whole, older people will be better off than they are now – at least from public sources. This pessimism has generally grown since 1992.[8]

To some extent, this decline in confidence in the public system is a simple reflection of reality. Pensions and pension promises had become less generous during this period as a consequence of fiscally-driven reforms. For example, countries such as Italy, where reforms have been deepest, show high pessimism (despite a referendum that supported reform). However, closer examination (including that of other European countries that are not part of the nine-country study) shows that there is no obvious relationship between actual reforms and opinions. For example, pension levels are high in the Netherlands and Italy, and it may not be surprising that people do not expect that this level of support could be maintained. However, people in the United Kingdom are also pessimistic, despite the fact that pension spending levels there are relatively low.

This lack of confidence in the continuation of public arrangements means that while most people did not necessarily prefer to see more private pension arrangements, they expected them[9] (ranging from about 60% in Germany and Italy to 80% in the Netherlands, Sweden and the United Kingdom). In a 1999 Canadian survey, most people anticipated that private investments and individual retirement saving accounts would be their main sources of income in retirement. Over two-thirds of Canadians indicated that they, themselves, were saving for retirement and agreed there was a trend towards individual responsibility. A 1998 Japanese survey[10] indicated that 50% of the people expected to rely on a mix of public and private sources, and about 20% thought they would rely mainly on private savings or pensions.

Thus change may not be welcomed, but it is expected. The reaction to a particular proposal for change will, obviously, reflect the balance of winners and losers associated with that proposal. Often, since people who are already old are excluded from the effects of reform, they will have little to lose. However, potential reactions can only be assessed in light of the particular proposal and the conditions of the day. A common problem faced by countries in building support for needed change is the low levels of awareness of existing arrangements in many countries, as discussed in Section 6.8.

6.3. What can countries do?

In countries with large public systems, reducing the size of that system is a necessary step. One consequence of fiscally driven reform[11] is likely to be a more diversified system. Reducing public pension expenditure, however, is not sufficient for diversification. Increasing coverage of occupational and personal retirement arrangements has been associated with additional incentives for employers and individuals to establish such schemes, or even government action to make participation in occupational or personal pension schemes mandatory. The incentives most commonly used are tax-related incentives, such as deductions of contributions or refundable tax-credits. Some countries also offer rebates on public pension contributions if an employer or individual chooses to set up their own schemes, though such rebates usually imply forgoing a part of future public pension entitlements.

Another aspect of diversification relates to the mix of different financing methods, *i.e.* the combination of pay-as-you-go financing and advance-funded elements in the provision of retirement income. Advance-funding can be introduced both in public systems and, through regulatory requirements, in occupational pension schemes.

Some countries are also transferring certain types of benefit expenditure from the public pension systems to the general budget. Typically, such expenditure are related to pension benefits for which there is no strict link between benefits and contributions, for example, anti-low-income benefits, disability and early-retirement pensions. The result may a better-balanced system, with each of the programmes having a more clearly defined objective.

Further important elements that require policy action are the development, regulation and supervision of appropriate financial products for supplementary retirement savings as well as the establishment of a regulatory framework that ensures the security of private pension promises. This should include rules for vesting, portability and payment of pension benefits, as well as regulations to ensure the solvency of pension providers and the security of pension assets.

Finally, public information campaigns are important to raise awareness of pension issues among the population; workers need to be informed about the likely level of public pensions they can expect to receive in the future and about the necessity and options for supplementary pension arrangements. Public information is receiving new priority in many countries, and there is good potential for sharing experiences.

6.4. Diversifying financing mechanisms

One approach to diversification involves altering the balance between advance-funded and pay-as-you-go elements, and between defined-benefit and defined-contributions elements, within the public and the occupational system. Some of these have the effect of increasing the individual's control over the way their retirement savings are invested.

The big change – notional defined-contributions

Much the most dramatic and widely discussed of these reforms – the shift to notional defined-contributions in Italy and Sweden – was covered in Chapter 5. As noted in OECD (2000*a*), whether these reforms will result in systems that are fundamentally different from point-based systems (such as those in Germany), or whether the underlying mix of risks is greatly changed, remain much-debated issues. Yet there can be no doubt that these changes represent, at least, major breakthroughs in the way pensions are perceived. They have brought central issues, such as work incentives and individual choice, into the forefront of debate.

Increasing advance-funding in public schemes

Another approach has been to increase advance-funded reserves within existing pay-as-you-go public pensions. Canada and the Netherlands are using increased advance-funding in the present in order to contain contribution rate increases in the future. The United States and Japan already have reserves, making their public pension schemes partially funded.

Occupational schemes are partially or fully funded in most countries. But most countries accept lower funding levels or even pay-as-you-go financing for public-sector occupational schemes. In Germany, Italy and Japan, unfunded book reserve schemes are also common. In Germany, such schemes offer occupational pensions, and their reserves are reinvested in the sponsoring company. Fully-funded defined-contribution plans are currently not allowed in Germany or Japan, but discussions are underway to permit and license such products. In Japan, a bill allowing plans based on the US 401(k) model was passed in 2001.

In Italy, the mandatory severance pay scheme also requires companies to set aside capital that can be borrowed back by the company. These are not pension schemes, although the possibility is being debated of possible integration of this scheme with defined-contribution private pensions.

Diversifying control of advance-funded schemes

Canada is aiming at diversifying the investment of public pension reserves. In 1997, it was decided that an Investment Board should be created that would manage the investment of the earnings-related Canada Pension Plan reserves in a diversified portfolio at arm's length from the government. In Japan, an investment committee composed of insurance industry representatives and finance specialists was established, but responsibility for the investment of the public pension reserves is currently still with the government. The United States specifically rejected this approach in the guiding principles given to the 2001 reform commission referred to below.

Individual choice

Another approach has been to create individual advance-funded accounts within the public system that individuals can control themselves. Sweden has diverted 15% of the total contribution rate to a funded component of individual accounts, which will be invested according to individual worker's choices.

Changes have also taken place with respect to occupational pensions. The two main Swedish private-sector occupational pension funds have been restructured, introducing a defined-contribution component with individual choice over fund management.

In the United States, there has been recent public debate about scaling down the public pay-as-you-go system and creating funded individual accounts to supplement the public pension scheme. On May 2, President Bush announced the establishment of a commission to make specific recommendations regarding social security reform, with one of its guiding principles being that modernisation must include individually controlled, voluntary personal retirement accounts.[12]

6.5. Encouraging more occupational and personal provision

This section describes the coverage of occupational and personal plans. Incomplete coverage of private pensions is a central issue. As Table 6.2 shows, coverage of occupational plans is near 50% in four countries and approaches full coverage in three countries. Unfortunately, consistent data for personal pension plan coverage are not available.

Table 6.2. **Coverage of occupational pension plans**
Percentage of workforce

	Year	Coverage rate
Canada	1997	33
Finland	1998	100 (statutory plans)
		15 (voluntary plans)
Germany	1990	46
Italy	1998	5
Japan	2000	50
Netherlands	1996	91
Sweden	1997	90
United Kingdom	1995	46
United States	1995	45

Source: OECD Secretariat. See endnote 13 in text for further explanation.

Occupational plans

Governments have several policy options to encourage increased coverage of private pensions. Finland, the Netherlands and Sweden have gone the route of statutory or quasi-mandatory provision of occupational pension plans by employers or groups of employers. An alternative route is to continue with voluntary provision of occupational plans and increase coverage by several means. Another is to promote their provision by employers via tax benefits and simplified regulatory systems. Another avenue is to offer those who have no access to occupational plans alternative retirement savings vehicles that benefit from similar tax incentives as occupational plans. Of the nine countries, only Canada is currently taking this latter approach.

Private pension coverage differs significantly across the nine countries both in level and structure.[13] The three countries with the highest level of coverage of occupational pension plans are the Netherlands, Finland and Sweden, where these plans account for over 90% of the working population. The plans cover salaried workers in the public and private sector, and also most self-employed professionals:

- In Finland, occupational plans are compulsory, part of the social security system and managed in a public-private mix. There are also incentives for additional, voluntary provision by employers, which currently cover less than 15% of the workforce.
- In the Netherlands and Sweden, the high coverage is the result of collective bargaining between social partners at the national level (Sweden) and at the industry level (Netherlands). Collective bargaining makes the plans *de facto* compulsory for both employers and employees. In the

Netherlands, the collective agreements are sometimes extended by statute to non-members of employers' associations. New legislation permits individual employers to opt out of the operation of a compulsory industry-wide plan if, for example, the pension fund performs badly with respect to investment.

These high-coverage countries are also the most active in taking action to improve access to occupational pension plans. In the Netherlands, new policies have been introduced over the past few years to extend the occupational pension system to part-time workers, who now have the same eligibility rights as full-time employees, and to women, who are protected from discrimination in plan provision. As a result, coverage increased from 83 to 91% between the mid-1980s and the late 1990s.

Countries with coverage of from one-third to one-half of the workforce are Canada, Germany, Japan, the United Kingdom and the United States. In all these countries the provision of occupational pension plans is voluntary. In Japan and the United Kingdom, however, employer provision becomes mandatory if the employer decides to contract out of the public pension plan. The United Kingdom is a particular case, since employees are also allowed to opt out of occupational arrangements if they take up a personal pension plan. This policy, introduced in 1988, has contributed to a decline in coverage rates of occupational pensions.

Coverage of occupational pension plans is lowest in Italy. This can be explained largely by the absence of any tax advantages up to the mid-1990s and by generous public pension benefits and a deficient regulatory framework for private pensions. Prior to the introduction of new legislation and tax measures in the mid-1990s, occupational pension plans were reserved for a very small section of the workforce, located mainly in the financial sector. Because of future reductions in the replacement rates of public pensions, the fiscal incentives to build the occupational pensions are now receiving policy attention.

Personal pensions: growing rapidly from a small base

In all these countries, occupational pension coverage is much higher than coverage of personal pension plans. An exception is Canada, where personal pension plans are popular[14] and growing rapidly; some 55% of the population now have a plan.[15] Canadian plans benefit from similar tax advantages as occupational pension plans, and the public is extremely well informed about these. Each year, as part of the income tax process, Canadians receive a statement indicating exactly how much they can put aside in these tax-advantaged accounts in the following year.

The only other country where personal plans cover more than 10% of the workforce is the United Kingdom (23% in 1998, according to recent surveys). This is due to the possibility of substituting both the public earnings-related pension scheme and occupational plans by personal pension plans. The government's objective is to make private provision much more important in the future. The current mix is 60% public and 40% private. The goal is to reverse those proportions by the year 2050.

Membership in personal pension plans is growing rapidly in other countries, although the level of coverage is still quite small. In the United States, for example, over 6% of the workforce had an Individual Retirement Account in 1998. In Finland, membership was also near this level in 1998. The driving force behind the growth of personal plans has been the introduction of more advantageous tax treatment. Tax incentives and personal pension plans have been introduced most recently in Italy. After a first failed attempt to make individual pension arrangements mandatory, Germany too will likely offer refundable tax credits to encourage personal pension take-up. The United States is currently considering raising the contribution limit to personal pension plans.

Personal pensions: facing the challenge of high administrative costs

Experience with personal pensions and individual retirement accounts in many countries shows that one major obstacle to the growth of personal plans is their often high administrative cost. Indeed, they can be so high as to reduce workers' retirement capital substantially (see, for example, Murthi, Orszag and Orszag, 1999; James, Smalhout and Vittas, 2001; Whitehouse, 2000; and Queisser, 1998).

Transparency with respect to costs is particularly important. In most countries, personal retirement arrangements are offered by a wide range of banks, insurance companies and other financial service providers who apply an equally wide range of fees and transfer conditions to these products. But often people do not understand the implications of various fees and find it difficult to make cost comparisons.

The United Kingdom government has addressed this problem by introducing an alternative "stakeholder pension" in April 2001. All employers are obliged to provide workers access to this product unless they already either offer an occupational pension plan with immediate vesting or pay contributions into a personal plan for the worker. The stakeholder pension will be operated either by financial service providers or by non-profit organisations, including trade unions. They might be industry- or occupation-wide, and in all cases will provide easy opportunities for transfer. Contributions can be stopped and started without penalty, and charges will be capped at 1% of assets.[16]

Other governments have tried to solve the problem of administrative costs by modifying the organisational structure of pensions or by regulating the type of costs that can be charged. In Sweden, the new individual accounts are centrally managed by a public agency, but workers can choose individually the different funds and portfolios in which they want to invest. The agency acts as a clearing-house that communicates workers' choices to the providers and requires providers to grant certain rebates on costs, depending on fee level and fund size. By severing the direct contact between provider and worker, the intent is to keep marketing and administrative costs low. In the yet to be established personal pension pillar in Germany, for example, providers will be required to amortise administrative costs over a period of ten years; in this way, workers who switch providers will not be required to pay high up-front fees.

Overall coverage of private plans

While it is difficult to estimate the total coverage rate of the private pension system as a whole, the record is not good apart from Finland, the Netherlands and Sweden, where policies are in place to ensure a near 100% coverage rate through the occupational pension system. None of the other countries have achieved overall coverage rates greater than 70% of the workforce. Left out are the more vulnerable groups in society, such as young unskilled employees, those working part-time and under fixed-term contracts (often women), employees of small companies (which are less likely to provide occupational plans) and the self-employed.

Some governments have thus found that tax incentives introduced to promote the development of private pensions are largely benefiting the richer groups of society. An extreme example of the way differences in coverage rates between different social groups can adversely affect equity is the United States. Two-thirds of the benefits of current tax incentives for occupational and personal pensions accrue to those whose family incomes place them in the top fifth of the income scale. The bottom 40% of the income distribution enjoys only 2.1% of the total tax benefit.

In the United Kingdom, the most recent reforms to the pension system introduced a pension credit to ensure that retirement saving by low-income earners is not discouraged. Previously, pensioners who were entitled to the minimum income guarantee saw their benefit reduced in line with any retirement savings they had built up. In the future, retirement savings by low and modest income-earners above the level of the public pension will be rewarded through cash additions.

6.6. Job changing, vesting and portability

Changing jobs can result in lower occupational pension benefits. Using the United States and the United Kingdom as examples, Chapter 3 shows that, if a worker in the United Kingdom were to spend a full 40-year career in the model scheme, he or she would receive a pension of one-half (40 x 1.25%) of final, pre-retirement salary. People who spend 20 years in two schemes would get a quarter of final salary from the second scheme plus a quarter of their salary in the last year of the first job from the first scheme.[17] The relevant measure of earnings for the first scheme is their real salary, because this must now be up-rated in line with price inflation (to a 5% ceiling) in retirement. So if people's real earnings continue to grow in their second job, then the pension from their first scheme will be less than a quarter of "final" salary, *i.e.* their pay immediately before retirement. The degree of loss depends on how fast individual earnings grow.

Chart 6.3 illustrates this effect for a range of different earnings-growth assumptions and for a series of equal-length tenures in different plans. In the United States, if real earnings were to grow at 1%, the pension replacement rate falls from one-half of final salary for people who joined one scheme to 45% for people who spent equal time in two plans. The replacement rate falls with faster increases in earnings: to less than 40% with 3% earnings growth and just one-third with 6% earnings growth.

Chart 6.3. **Pension replacement rates by number of schemes joined and rate of individual earnings growth**
Percentage of final salary

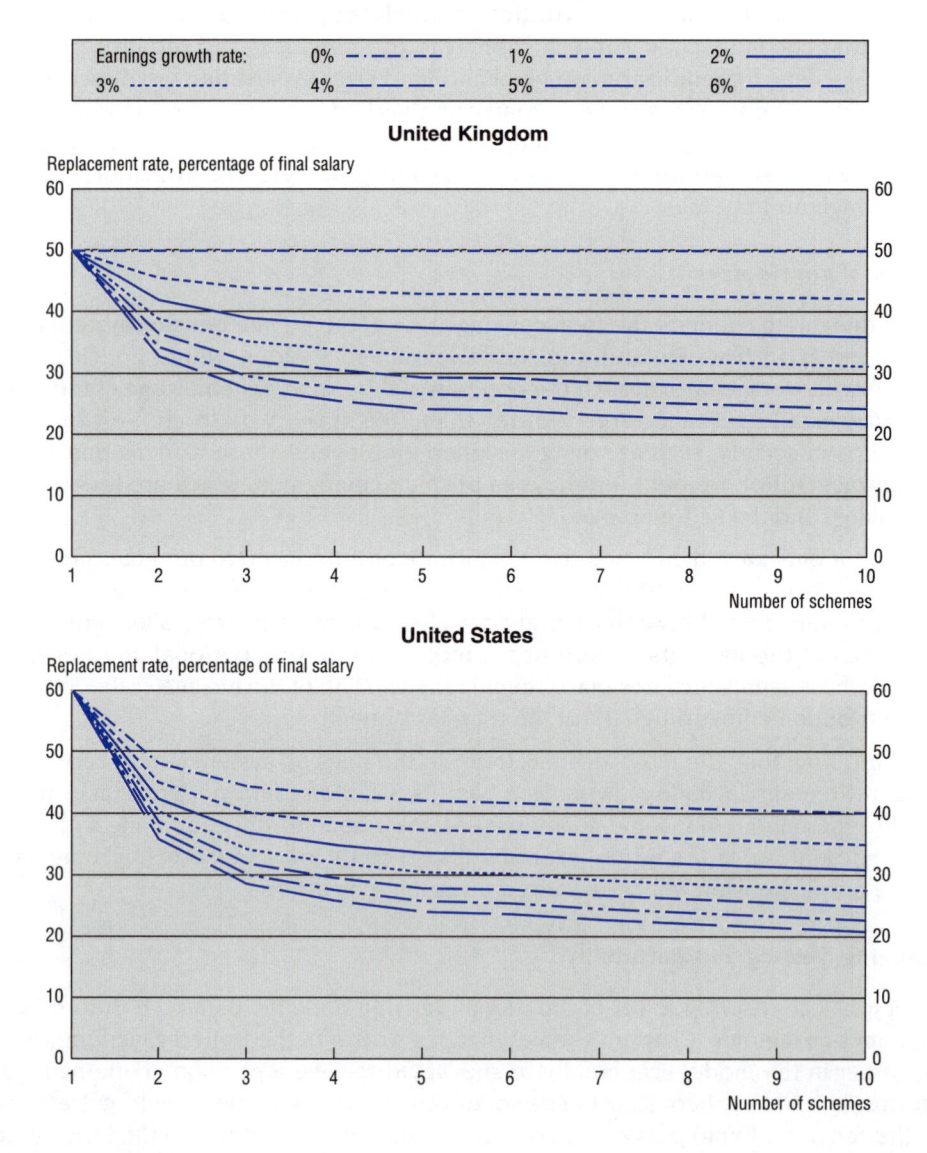

Source: OECD Secretariat calculations.

Working across the figure, the more schemes the individual joins, the lower the replacement rate at any positive rate of earnings growth. For example, if someone spent eight years each in five different plans, the replacement rate falls to under a third with 3% earnings growth and to less than a quarter with 6% earnings increases. Note that these are hypothetical, worst-case scenarios. In practice, there is the possibility of transferability across plans.

While the United Kingdom has introduced protection against price inflation in its occupational pension system both before and after retirement, regulatory attention in the United States has focused on the solvency of occupational pension schemes and on vesting rights. Pension benefits are almost never indexed, both after retirement and, for early leavers, between the point of leaving a job and the point of retirement. Early leavers' pensions are, as a result, much lower relative to their level in the United Kingdom.

The greater cost of moving jobs can be seen clearly by comparing the two panels. In the United States model scheme, a full career in an occupational scheme would give a replacement rate of 60%. But joining two schemes for 20 years each would cut this replacement rate to 45%, and five schemes for eight years each to just 37%. This assumes inflation of 2.5% a year: an episode of higher inflation would erode the value of preserved or deferred occupational pension rights more rapidly. This assumes individual real earnings grow at just 1% a year. With 3% real earnings growth, these figures are 40% and 30%, respectively. The pattern in Canada would be similar to the United States.

More generally, vesting and portability losses arise when a worker changes jobs but is not entitled to full preservation of his or her accrued rights in either the old or new plan. These losses can arise because the employee leaves a plan before a vesting period is completed (vesting losses), or because the accrued pension rights calculated do not take full account of wage and price dynamics until retirement (pension annuity losses). There have been many reforms aimed at reducing these losses. However, in many of the nine countries a worker who stays with a single employer for, say, 40 years will do significantly better than an employee who works for ten years for each of four employers – creating pension problems and disincentives to labour mobility.

Vesting losses can be reduced easily by introducing regulations that limit the maximum vesting period before which benefits begin to accrue. Finland, Italy, Japan[18] and Sweden have introduced immediate vesting. While social partners in the Netherlands are free to arrange their own vesting provisions, a recent agreement with the cabinet commits the social partners to accept immediate vesting to the extent possible. The United Kingdom requires vesting after two years of service with an employer, Canada after two to five years depending on the province and the United States after five years. Germany has the longest vesting period of the nine countries. Employees are entitled to benefits only if they stay with a company for at least 10 years and if they are older than 35 at the moment of leaving. However, this period will be cut to five years. In Japan, vesting losses are also a major problem for supplementary benefits under the Employee Pension Funds (EPF) and for lump-sum retirement schemes, which are not subject to any vesting rules. It is not uncommon for even employees' contributions to lack vesting protection under such schemes.

Few countries have attempted to limit pension annuity losses. Finland and the Netherlands have introduced clearing-house mechanisms, which ensure a relatively efficient transfer of accrued rights between different plans by requiring a high degree of homogeneity in defined-benefit formulae and funding levels. Sweden has no specific portability mechanisms but, as there are only four occupational plans (two each for private-sector and public-sector employees, respectively), portability losses are very limited. The other six countries have not introduced specific regulations on the portability of accrued rights to the new employer. In Japan, for example, a clearing-house system is also in place for substitutive EPF benefits. However, transferring to a new employer-sponsored pension plan is not possible; only annuities may be purchased. In Canada, the United Kingdom and the United States, early leavers can choose between transferring their accrued rights to occupational or personal pension plans. Portability losses (both vesting and pension annuity) are highest in Germany and Italy.

The main alternative to the portability of accrued rights to a new plan is deferring pension entitlements in the old plan. This option is generally less attractive than transferring rights to the new plan, because of the back-loading of defined-benefit formulae.[19] Moreover, few countries have introduced indexation mechanisms for deferred benefits. Although indexation to inflation is not required in Japan for substitutive EPF benefits, the indexed part of the pension is paid by the Employees' Pension Insurance. Indexation is required in the United Kingdom for all defined-benefit schemes (up to 5% per annum). Such protection equates the indexation treatment of private plans, both before and after retirement, with the public plans for which they substitute. In the Netherlands, deferred benefits must be indexed in the same way as normal retirement benefits, but there is no legal obligation to index benefit rights of early leavers before retirement. Nevertheless, more than 99% of the pensioners of a scheme that is executed by a pension fund have an indexed benefit.

6.7. Increasing the financial security of private arrangements

Placing greater reliance on occupational and personal pension arrangements for retirement income provision requires public policies to ensure that pension promises to workers are kept. The main areas for action are funding requirements to ensure the financial soundness of defined-benefit arrangements, investment regulations for pension assets, other regulations regarding the protection of assets and the functioning of pension plans, as well as an efficient and effective supervisory structure. A sound regulatory framework and good supervision are a prerequisite to encourage employers to provide occupational plans and to encourage individuals to save voluntarily for their retirement. Frequent changes of the rules, in particular if they affect the costs of running a pension plan through changes in tax treatment or onerous administrative requirements, can discourage employers from providing pension plans to their workers.

Protection against insolvency, mismanagement and fraud

There are two main aspects to the security of private pensions that require policy action: *i)* the protection of the pension plan against the financial insolvency of the plan provider or sponsor; and *ii)* the protection of the plan against mismanagement and fraud by the plan administrators.

Rules governing the funding of pension liabilities are the first regulatory barrier against insolvency of the plan sponsor or provider. All nine countries require pension plans for private-sector workers to be funded.[20] Public-sector workers, on the other hand, can have unfunded schemes in Finland, Germany, Italy, Japan, Sweden and the United Kingdom. These plans rely ultimately on the tax-payer to meet any contingencies.

Funding may be carried out via insurance policies, an option that is most attractive for small employers. Banks and collective investment providers can also manage defined-contribution occupational pension plans in some countries. Personal pension plans, meanwhile, are directly administered by financial institutions in all the countries surveyed. In the case of pension plans administered directly by insurance companies or other financial institutions, the regulatory and supervisory structure for these institutions is meant to ensure that contractual obligations can be met. But there have recently been a number of cases, for example in Japan, the United Kingdom and the United States, where insurance companies have had problems delivering on annuity and life insurance contracts with interest rate guarantees.

The main alternatives to direct insurance as funding vehicles for pension plans are the book reserve method and pension funds. Book reserves do not require the legal separation of assets from the sponsoring employer. Hence, they are attractive to employers as a cheap source of capital, but beneficiaries are directly exposed to insolvency risk. The only two countries that permit these plans (Germany and Sweden) require sponsors to be insured through a mutual credit insurance system. So far, these insurance schemes have been successful in preventing major losses for beneficiaries.

Pension funds are used predominantly in occupational pension plans in Canada, Japan, the Netherlands, the United Kingdom and the United States. They are also the only financing vehicles permitted for both occupational and personal pension plans in the new system introduced in Italy.

Current retirees from occupational pension plans in the nine countries, who benefit mainly from defined-benefit pensions, are protected against sponsor insolvency risk via various regulatory policies.

Minimum funding rules are in place in most countries. In Finland and Germany, pension funds are subject to the same solvency requirements as insurance companies. These are more stringent than those for pension funds in the other countries. In Italy, minimum funding rules are not relevant for the new plans, since they must be defined-contribution plans. Only Sweden has no minimum funding rules; all responsibility for funding occupational pension promises lies with the employers.

The supervision of funding levels is done via actuarial reports that assess pension liabilities. In recent years, reports in Japan, the United Kingdom and other countries have revealed a worrying degree of under-funding arising from underestimation of increases in longevity. Policies to improve the calculation of funding levels were put in place in Japan in 1997. They now focus on the ongoing approach (which takes into account the whole future funding strategy of the pension plan), rather than purely the winding-up approach (which takes into consideration only current funding levels), which is used in the other countries. In the United Kingdom, there is a major ongoing debate about changing the minimum funding requirements. In the Netherlands, too, debate has arisen about modernisation of minimum funding rules. Limits on self-investment are in place in all countries. The limits vary significantly, with Finland and Italy allowing the highest investment in the sponsoring company (30%). Given that plan sponsors are not required to insure their pension liabilities in these countries, the high level of self-investment presents a real threat to the security of pension promises.

An additional level of protection for beneficiaries of defined-benefit plans is provided in the United States and in the Canadian province of Ontario against the risk that the sponsoring company goes bankrupt. Insurance through the public Pension Benefit Guaranty Corporation and the Guarantee Fund is compulsory in the US and the province of Ontario, respectively, and is financed through premiums. The premium structure is similar in the two systems. It has been a source of concern because it bears no relation to the risk of company bankruptcy.

Another risk to private pension plans is mismanagement, unethical practice or fraud by the plan administrators. For pension plans directly administered by insurance companies or financial institutions, their respective regulatory and supervisory frameworks should in principle prevent such cases. However, the Maxwell case and the pension mis-selling scandal in the United Kingdom (see Boxes 6.2 and 6.3) point to holes in the regulation of certain aspects of these products, such as marketing, distribution, information disclosure and transparency. The United Kingdom has designed a new type of pension plan, the so-called stakeholder pension, that will address these issues.

Box 6.2. **The Maxwell case and its consequences**

The Maxwell case in the United Kingdom has by now become the textbook example of a pension fund raided by the plan sponsor under the blind eye of theoretically independent plan administrators (so-called trustees in the United Kingdom). During the mid-90s, a large portion of the Maxwell companies' pension fund assets were used by the fund managers, under the direction of the late Robert Maxwell, to prop up the share price of companies under his control, which in some cases were close to bankruptcy. When the companies became insolvent, the assets were lost. The money was only "recovered" as a result of voluntary contributions by the financial services industry that feared legislative retaliation.

In part as a result of this unfortunate episode, the United Kingdom introduced the 1995 Pensions Act, which included five forms of regulation to protect pension plan members against the risk of fraud and mismanagement: *a*) governance regulations, *b*) investment regulations, *c*) disclosure requirements, *d*) consumer redress mechanisms, and *e*) mandatory insurance against fraud by the plan administrators or plan sponsors. It is the only one of the nine countries to have introduced this last protection. The act also extended the responsibilities of trustees significantly, and made them more independent of plan sponsors.

> **Box 6.3. The pension mis-selling scandal in the United Kingdom**
>
> After the 1986 Social Security Act took effect, employees in companies with or without an occupational scheme were eligible to open a personal pension. Government advertising promoted the option widely. Given the abolition of life insurance premium relief from income tax in 1984, personal pensions proved an ideal new product for the financial services industry. Insurance companies, who are the main providers of personal pension schemes (PPS), moved quickly to take advantage of the sales opportunities.
>
> By 1993, press reports of individual cases of mis-selling to such high-profile groups as teachers and nurses led to the closer study of the sale of pension transfers. It became clear that the sale of a PPS did not always represent "best advice" to the customer as required by the Financial Services Act of 1986.
>
> It was where a person failed to join, or on occasion was persuaded to leave, an occupational pension system that the greatest disadvantage was suffered. Only in about one in eight cases does an employer contribute to an employee's personal pension, according to the results of the General Household Survey.
>
> Some employers also withdrew non-pension benefits from employees who opted out of the employer pension plan. Whitehouse has estimated that the cost of losing the employer's contribution for someone not joining their employer's scheme and taking a personal pension instead is worth 70% of the pension on average.
>
> In addition, although it was younger people who would benefit most from rebates, pensions were also sold to people over 45 who would have been better off staying in the state system.
>
> Some 700 000 cases of potential mis-selling over the period 1988 to 1994 have been identified. Of these, 400 000 have been settled with compensation paid by the personal pension provider. Compensation so far has totalled over £3 billion, an average of £7 500 per case (FSA Press Release, FSA/PN/022/2000). When the review is complete, it is expected that a further 1.3 million cases will be evaluated for potential mis-selling. The costs of this compensation will fall on company profits and on other insured people holding with-profit policies, which means that at least part of the cost is socialised after all.

Governance regulations for pension funds are also well developed in Canada and the United States. These countries, like the United Kingdom, require the appointment of a trustee to manage the fund's assets in the best interest of beneficiaries. Moreover, in the United States, plan sponsors must appoint an independent custodian. In both countries trustees bear personal liability for the management of pension fund assets and must insure this liability. In Italy, the governance issue has been solved by regulations that require pension assets to be managed by professional asset managers, and benefit payment to be administered by insurance companies. Hence, most aspects of the administration of pension funds and pension plans are completely insulated from the influence of employers. A similar method is applied to the Tax Qualified Plans in Japan.

Sweden is the only country where pension funds are not subject to any specific governance regulations. In practice, however, the powerful presence of trade unions in this country acts as a disciplining force on employers, and most pension funds are under the supervision of a committee in which employers and employees are represented on an equal basis.

Investment regulation in Canada, Italy, Japan, the Netherlands and the United States follows guidelines similar to those in the United Kingdom. All these countries follow a prudent-person approach, and impose few or no quantitative restrictions on investment. The prudent-person approach requires pension fund managers to invest assets in a prudent and sound manner. Japan eliminated its minimum and maximum investment limits in the mid-1990s and liberalised fund management, permitting in-house pension fund management for the first time. The second group of countries (Finland, Germany and Sweden) have opted for a comprehensive quantitative approach to investment regulation, setting restrictions on specific asset classes and securities. Finland and Germany impose relatively strict quantitative restrictions by asset class. Sweden also imposes important, but less stringent, restrictions by asset class. As is to be expected, allocation into higher return, higher risk asset classes, such as equities, is higher in the first group of countries, although there has been a move in this direction in Sweden as well.

6.8. Raising awareness of retirement income needs and opportunities

A critically important and, until recently, often neglected policy area is the provision of public information and communication on retirement income needs and opportunities to help individuals prepare for their retirement. Unless people know their entitlements under the public system, for example, they cannot adequately determine how much private savings are needed, or when they should plan to retire. A truly diversified system requires informed pensioners. Ideally, every worker should have clear, integrated information on what they have contributed to public and private pensions and what their likely pension benefits would be under various circumstances, such as different retirement ages or different economic circumstances.

Age factors, irregular employment records and lack of provision by employers may explain why some workers are left out of occupational pension schemes. Take-up of personal pensions by these vulnerable groups is low even in countries like the United Kingdom and the United States, which have comparatively well-developed personal pension systems and efficient capital markets. While the tax treatment of personal plans is less generous than that of occupational plans, the critical barrier to membership of personal plans appears to be insufficient understanding of retirement needs. In most countries, the general public is not well informed about pension rights and expected future benefit levels.

In the United Kingdom, for example, a recent survey (Office of Fair Trading, 1997) revealed that less than a third of those interviewed knew the criteria for entitlement to the basic pension or its actual value for single persons within a range of 7%. Less than half of those interviewed knew that the basic pension is price-indexed. These results appear surprising, given that individual choice of retirement arrangements has been an important feature of pension policy in the United Kingdom since the 1980s. In the United States, the 1998 retirement confidence survey found that only half of Americans know the difference between a stock and a bond, and only 16% understand the details of an Individual Retirement Account. More generally, the public opinion data described in Hicks (2001) suggest that citizens in their working years know very little about the details of their pensions or indeed about their likely income requirements during retirement.

All nine countries have as an objective to make their public systems more transparent by sending regular statements to the insured explaining current pension rights and projected benefit levels. The nine countries are at different stages in this process, and most have not actually implemented this new policy due to the administrative complexities of sending out statements to all members. In the United Kingdom, for example, it is planned to ultimately have a combined statement that informs beneficiaries of expected public and private pension benefits. Sweden is advanced in this process; the statements were sent out in 1999, and it was found that this not only led to a better understanding of pension issues but also to an increased interest in voluntary personal retirement savings products. Canada, as well, has begun a series of annual mailings of personal statements of contributions to the public earnings-related pension as well as estimates of future entitlements.[21]

In most countries, benefits and the management of private pension funds are much more transparent than those of the public systems. Disclosure to pension fund members plays an important role in Canada, the Netherlands and the United States, though it is not as developed as in the United Kingdom. A comprehensive disclosure system is also being developed in Italy. Disclosure to individual members is least encouraged in Finland, Germany, Japan and Sweden. Historically, this lack of transparency towards affiliates in some countries can be attributed to the fact that employers have offered defined-benefit plans in which they bore the main risks (investment and mortality). More recently, however, many countries have begun to develop defined-contribution plans in which employees bear investment risks. Adequate disclosure to employees and investors in these systems is essential to ensure that suitable choices are made.

The disclosure of defined-contribution plans raises different issues, depending on whether it is offered at the company level or directly through a financial intermediary. Company-managed defined-contribution plans are common in three countries (Canada, the United Kingdom and the United States) and are the only type of employer-sponsored plan in the incipient private pension system of Italy. Individual retirement savings instruments also involve employer decision-making in some countries (*e.g.* group Registered Retirement Savings Plans in Canada, 401(k) plans in the US and group personal pension plans in the United Kingdom). Different degrees of involvement of employers in defined-contribution plans exist. In 401(k) plans, for example, employers typically offer a limited choice of funds in which workers can invest. Such decisions can simplify investment choices for workers and lower fees.

Mechanisms for consumer redress with regard to private pension schemes, on the other hand, are not widespread in the nine countries. The United Kingdom introduced a channel for consumer redress in 1995, again as a response to the Maxwell incident. Individuals may now turn to the Pensions Ombudsman with any complaints about the administration of occupational pension plans. The only two countries that have consumer redress mechanisms as developed as those of the United Kingdom are the Netherlands and the United States. The Netherlands introduced a pension ombudsman in 1995. No legislation was needed, and decisions are enforced by goodwill and industry ethics. In the United States, the right to redress can be exercised through individual action in the federal courts to enforce benefit rights or by referring to the Department of Labor for any offence that affects the pension fund as a whole. Despite its legal force, formal redress through the courts is a rather expensive option for any single individual.

NOTES

1. The data, from the OECD's social expenditure database, reflect public social expenditure related to the retirement-age population. They cover cash benefits, including expenditure on old-age cash benefits, survivors' cash benefits, disability cash benefits, services for older people and disabled people, early retirement for labour-market reasons, and survivors' benefits in kind. Benefits in kind are important for older people but were excluded from the household income analysis because of limitations in data sources. Health expenditure, which relate to the whole population, are not included in this chart. The numbers differ somewhat from the projected estimates in Chapter 4. The differences are discussed in OECD (2001a).

2. Chart A.1 in the Statistical Annex compares recent retirement expenditure (as a percentage of GDP) with the ratio of retirees per employee. This gives a rough picture of the responsiveness of spending to changes in demographic and labour market pressures. Overall, the chart shows the expected general relationship between increased expenditure and relative number of retirees. However, the slope and positioning differ considerably among the nine countries, reflecting different levels of generosity of public pensions and the effects of recent reforms. The chart illustrates the fact that pension expenditure do not have to move in lock-step with external pressures, although they are closely related.

3. Gruber and Wise (2001) use OECD expenditure data to argue that, if the past is any guide, the burden of paying the high pension fiscal bills is likely to be met through reduced spending elsewhere, particularly on programmes for the non-elderly. More study would be needed, however, before any firm conclusions can be drawn about the extent to which past pension spending has actually crowded-out other kinds of social spending, including educational spending.

4. As set out in *Maintaining Prosperity in an Ageing Society* (OECD, 1998a, Chapter IV) and in statements of other organisations, including the International Labour Organisation (Gillion, 2000) and the World Bank (Holzmann, 2000).

5. See Thompson (1998) and Holzmann (2000) for a fuller discussion of the risks associated with various elements of the system. The fundamental risks that gave rise to pensions in the first place – uncertainty about the length of life, the risk of poverty in old age or sudden income drops at the end of a career – have, with some exceptions, been met by existing arrangements in the nine countries.

6. The analysis here is drawn from Hicks (2001), which in turn draws on data from many sources, particularly two sources of internationally-comparable public opinion data: the ISSP surveys (see Smith, 2000a, 2000b) and the Eurobarometer surveys (see Walker, 1999). The Hicks paper provides tables that compare attitudes in the countries.

7. Support is generally higher among women. In terms of labour force status, support is, perhaps unsurprisingly, highest among the retired. Support grows with age, although the gap is not large enough to signal any intergenerational rift. The gap between the views of older and younger people does not appear to be strongly related to actual programming arrangements. It was highest in Sweden and Canada, and lowest in the United States and Japan. While the American media often reports on intergenerational conflict – greedy old people being supported by a hard-pressed younger generation – a review of a large number of American surveys found that support for social security is high among all age groups. These data are analysed in Hicks (2001).

8. Walker reports that there are no large differences in these results by gender or by occupational or income group.

9. The 1999 Eurobarometer question asked people whether they expected that, in the future, most pensions would be funded by private arrangements with less state involvement.

10. Public Opinion Survey on Public Pension Scheme (1998), Prime Minister's Cabinet Secretariat.

11. While the fiscal theme is common, other factors have influenced the design of particular reforms as well, including fairness, individual choice and greater neutrality with respect to the retirement decision.

12. This is one of six guiding principles established for the commission. The entire list is: 1) Modernisation must not change social security benefits for retirees or near-retirees; 2) the entire social security surplus must be dedicated only to social security; 3) social security payroll taxes must not be increased; 4) the government must not invest social security funds in the stock market; 5) modernisation must preserve social security's

disability and survivors insurance programmes; 6) modernisation must include individually controlled, voluntary personal retirement accounts, which will augment social security.

13. Except in the case of Canada, where administrative data are available, the figures for pension plan coverage are based on survey data and are therefore only estimations. Furthermore, coverage data apply to individual workers at any point in time. They do not focus on households, and do not take into account past membership in a pension plan. The split between occupational and personal plans is further complicated by the fact that the countries use different definitions for occupational and personal pension plans.

14. In reality, 401(k) plans in the United States are similar in many respects to the personal plans in Canada, although they are classified as occupational plans.

15. The median amount of the pension is modest for the total of all families (equivalent to some 57% of the annual earnings of the average production worker in 1999) but is higher in the 55-to-64 age group (equivalent to 140%). There is considerable variation in the size of the holdings, as indicated by the much larger average size of the plan when expressed as a mean (where it is nearly 3 times the size of the annual earnings of the average production worker in the 55-64 age group). In 1999, group RRSPs accounted for some 12% of total individual assets, up sharply from 4% in 1984 (Statistics Canada, 2001).

16. The advent of the stakeholder pension has already led to downward pressure on personal pension plan fees.

17. Note that there is full transferability with no loss between many different public-sector schemes in the United Kingdom.

18. For the Employee Pension Funds, contracted-out substitutive plans only.

19. Pension rights accrue faster as the membership period of the plan increases.

20. Book reserve plans, which are prevalent in Germany and Sweden, are frequently considered as unfunded schemes. But, in a strict sense, they are funded, with all assets reinvested in the sponsoring company.

21. The Canadian mail-out programme, which was implemented in 2000, is the centrepiece of a more general effort to provide Canadians with information on the retirement income system.

Chapter 7

MAINTAINING ECONOMIC WELL-BEING AND PROTECTING THE VULNERABLE

7.1. Introduction

As shown in Chapter 2, the retirement income systems in all nine countries are by and large successful in meeting earnings replacement objectives for the majority of the older population. It is thus not surprising that there have been fewer reforms in this area than with respect to the two challenges previously discussed.

The overall success of the retirement income system in meeting income replacement objectives on average does not, of course, preclude the possibility of significant disadvantaged minorities of older people. Indeed, there has been more unevenness across countries in meeting low-income and distributional objectives than in meeting average replacement rate goals. However, in all cases, problems that once existed have been considerably reduced. In some cases – for instance, widows living alone, the largest group of older people with low incomes that can be identified in the data – the implications for pension policy are not always clear. Some of the income problems will resolve themselves with time, and priorities for policy action may be greater in other areas, such as long-term care and support for independent living in the community.

There are other groups that are at-risk as they enter retirement. These often include those who have lost employment and cannot find work for reasons of sickness or lack of relevant skills. The vulnerabilities are clear and policy action is needed, but it has proved to be a mistake to tackle these problems through the use of pensions, pre-retirement programmes and disability programmes. In order to raise output in the future, and to raise employment rates in order to help achieve this goal, it makes little long-term sense to use policies that needlessly exclude people from employment, training and other employment services.

In terms of tomorrow's vulnerable groups, those most likely to be at risk are people with intermittent or weak job attachments during their working years (and correspondingly weak contribution histories). A new, more diversified system of retirement income is emerging – one that typically includes a larger role for private pensions and earnings, and one where defined-contribution arrangements are more common. Monitoring is needed to ensure that success in meeting traditional earnings-replacement and anti-low-income goals is not undermined in a more diversified system.

Section 7.2 describes existing and potential future groups of older people that are, or could become, at risk. Section 7.3 outlines possible actions, as well as areas where immediate action may not be warranted. Reforms aimed at particular problems are reviewed, including contribution gaps, survivors and those with the lowest incomes in general (Sections 7.4, 7.5 and 7.6). More systemic issues of annuitisation and benefit escalation are examined in Sections 7.7 and 7.8. Another approach is to set, and monitor, targets for replacement rates (Section 7.9).

7.2. Key vulnerable groups

The oldest old, especially older women living alone: still the main area of vulnerability

Income studies have typically found that the oldest old, in particular widows and other single women living alone, have the lowest incomes among older people. Table 7.1 suggests that this is still the case in the nine countries.[1]

Table 7.1. **Percentage of the oldest old that are in the lowest income quintile**
Percentage of each category in the lowest income quintile of the adult population aged 18 and over
Mid-90s

	Age 18+	Age 75+			
	Entire population	All older old	Single women living alone	Women living with spouse only	Single persons living with others (and the person is not household head)
Canada	20.0	33.9	60.9	20.2	6.9
Finland	20.0	43.2	75.2	19.8	9.6
Germany	20.0	30.8	42.7	14.8	..
Italy	20.0	23.2	43.3	15.9	11.6
Japan	20.0	33.5	78.7	58.5	18.2
Netherlands	20.0	43.4	50.6	40.6	..
Sweden	20.0	31.6	38.1	21.6	..
United Kingdom	20.0	38.5	47.4	39.3	12.6
United States	20.0	34.9	56.4	22.8	18.8

.. Data not available.
Note: The reference unit in the Swedish income data is a "tax unit" rather than a "family" or "household". The data on Sweden are, therefore, less comparable.
Sources: OECD calculations based mainly on data from the Luxembourg Income Study. See Yamada and Casey (2001).

The table refers to people aged 75 and over who are in the lowest-income quintile of the adult population aged 18 and over. Take Canada as an example. The first column is merely a reminder that, by definition, 20% of the adult population makes up the lowest-income quintile. The remaining three columns describe people aged 75 and over, the "older old". In Canada, 34% of these older people have incomes that would put them in the lowest quintile. Within that older age group, the figure for single women living alone, at 61%, is much higher. The table shows that:

- Although low incomes are prevalent among all the older old, they are dramatically more prevalent among old women living alone.

- Where the husband is still alive, the incidence of low incomes is close to the average in six countries, but higher in the United Kingdom, the Netherlands and Japan.

Some single older women, including widows, do not live alone, but go back to live with adult children. The table also shows the percentage of older single people living in a multi-generational household [of which another person is the household head and whose (grouped) income is in the lowest decile]. Most, but not all, such people will be women.[2] The table shows, again not unexpectedly, that living in a multi-generational family substantially reduces the likelihood of a single old person having a low income provided it is assumed – and this is a strong assumption – that all incomes in such households are pooled.

Single older men living alone are in a situation analogous to widows in not benefiting from household economies of scale, but they are a small group and have somewhat more income than their female counterparts. Because of differences in marriage age and longevity, women are likely to have longer durations of time with low income.

Table 7.2 compares the situation of widows who are living alone with women of the same age living with a spouse. (The top panel shows data for women aged 65 to 74 and the bottom panel provides data for those aged 75 and over.) This comparison gives an indication of how income composition might change after the death of a husband and how this, in turn, affects the disposable income of the widow. Note, as always, that this is only a general indication, since the data do not track particular individuals over time. (Indeed, evidence from panel data suggests that widows who are relatively worse off tend to have had lower incomes before the death of their spouse.)

Table 7.2. **Disposable income of widows living alone compared with that of couples**
Ratio of income of widows to couples in two-person households, by income category and age, mid-90s

	Total difference	Working income per capita	Public pension per capita[a]	Private pension per capita[a]	Other public benefits per capita[a,b]	Tax and contributions per capita[a]	Other income items	Household economies of scale
				Pure couple[c] to widow (65-74)				
Canada[d]	−31.8	−7.1	12.1	−12.7	3.0	6.9	−4.7	**−29.3**
Finland	−30.0	−2.9	−2.3	−0.1	0.5	6.7	−2.7	**−29.3**
Germany	−7.1	0.5	27.4	2.5	−0.1	−1.8	−6.4	**−29.3**
Italy[e]	−22.6	−1.9	18.8	−2.3	−1.3	..	−6.6	**−29.3**
Japan	−37.5	−21.5	−1.8	0.7	0.8	8.4	5.3	**−29.3**
Netherlands	−18.6	−6.2	31.4	−13.5	1.0	1.8	−3.9	**−29.3**
Sweden[f]	−22.1	−3.8	−1.6	−7.3	17.3	8.0	−5.5	**−29.3**
United Kingdom	−28.6	−5.7	12.6	−10.7	9.2	4.1	−8.8	**−29.3**
United States	−33.0	−6.9	4.8	−7.5	0.9	2.3	2.6	**−29.3**
				Pure couple[c] to widow (75+)				
Canada[d]	−28.9	−1.6	11.9	−13.7	3.0	6.5	−5.7	**−29.3**
Finland	−28.7	0.5	−9.1	0.0	1.5	9.4	−1.7	**−29.3**
Germany	−25.2	0.0	2.5	−1.4	0.3	−1.0	3.6	**−29.3**
Italy[e]	−19.8	−0.4	19.0	−1.8	−1.4	..	−5.8	**−29.3**
Japan	−33.1	−15.1	7.3	0.0	2.9	10.5	−9.4	**−29.2**
Netherlands	−12.5	−0.1	29.7	−3.7	1.9	−3.9	−7.1	**−29.3**
Sweden[f]	−12.8	−1.5	−9.9	−5.1	29.6	9.7	−6.3	**−29.3**
United Kingdom	−22.3	−1.1	8.4	−12.8	13.9	2.4	−3.9	**−29.3**
United States	−37.0	−6.9	3.0	−9.2	1.2	4.4	−0.2	**−29.3**

.. Data not available.
a) These components are not only "own income". The numbers are calculated from household-level income divided by household size (one or two).
b) "Other public benefits" include means-tested benefits.
c) Couple without children.
d) For Canada, "Widow" also includes "Separated" and "Divorced".
e) Variables for tax and social security contributions are not available in the Italian data.
f) For Sweden, "Widow" cannot be identified at all, and therefore the calculation is based on "single female living alone".
Sources: OECD calculations based mainly on data from the Luxembourg Income Study. See Yamada and Casey (2001).

The widows in both age groups had lower incomes than the women living with a spouse, and the table compares the sources of those differences. Take Canada as an example of how to read this table. The first row says that Canadian widows aged 65 to 74 who lived alone had 31.8% less disposable income than a couple of the same age (on a per capita basis), after making the necessary adjustments for equivalence. The figure of 31.8% resulted from less working income (−7.1%), greater public pensions (+12.1%), etc.

- The main cause of the lower living standards is the absence of household economies of scale (29% in all countries, an amount that is a mechanical result of the equivalence scale that is used).
- In Japan, the loss of working income is also important. (Recall that, in Japan, working income is an important source of income during retirement, through work both by those aged 65 and over and by others in the household.)
- In countries where private pensions are important, such as Canada, the Netherlands, the United Kingdom (and to a much lesser extent Sweden and the United States), the loss of income from this source was also important. Separate OECD calculations (not shown) confirm that the levels of private pensions on a per capita basis are lower for widows than for couples.
- Working in the other direction, public pensions (including survivors' benefits) were higher for the widows in Canada, Germany, Italy, the Netherlands and the United Kingdom. Separate OECD calculations (not shown) confirm that the average benefit levels of public pensions for widows are

higher than for couples (on a per capita basis) except in Finland and Japan. (They are also higher than for divorced women of the same age in countries where this calculation was possible.)

- Means-tested benefits are an important source of compensation for income loss associated with widowhood in Sweden and the United Kingdom.
- The effects of the tax system are mixed but, in general, there is less tax burden on widows than on couples.

Some early retirees may be at risk

Some groups of early retirees may also be vulnerable. These are typically thought to be people who had to leave work early because of factors such as permanent lay-off, sickness, lack of skills or lack of access to pensions or to comparably generous social benefits. Table 7.3 provides a breakout of men aged 60 to 64 by work and benefit status. (There were too few women in these categories to allow analysis.)

The table shows that, in this age group, early retirees (non-workers with a pension) in Canada, Germany and Japan were over-represented in the lowest-income quintile. There was also over-representation of low income among people who had no work and, in addition, had no pension or unemployment benefits. Many of these people rely on other means of support, notably means-tested benefits.

A review of national studies[3] suggests that problems of entering retirement at-risk of low income are concentrated among certain groups of the pre-retirement population. While there are variations from country to country, the following groups are often the most vulnerable: people with work-limiting health problems, minority groups (such as African-Americans and Hispanics in the United States and various immigrant/refugee groups in many countries), very early retirees, never-married women, divorced women, persons without employer pensions, migrants not entitled to full public pensions and those with low-educational attainment.

Tomorrow's vulnerable groups

Tomorrow's vulnerabilities will depend on the future economic situation, particularly on employment growth and on the outcome of reforms being implemented today. Three problems can be anticipated.

Table 7.3. **Percentage of men aged 60 to 64 in the lowest income quintile**
Percentage of each category in the lowest income quintile of the adult population aged 18 and over
Mid-90s

	People age 18+	Men, aged 60-64				
	Entire population	Normal employees (workers without pensions)	Early retirees (non-workers with pension)	Working pensioners	Unemployed	Non-workers without pension and unemployment compensations
Canada	20	9.5	27.8	17.3	30.3	51.1
Finland	20	17.9	14.9	..	..	..
Germany	20	7.4	30.5	..	..	51.0
Italy	20	15.9	10.2	..	..	42.1
Japan	20	21.2	25.7	13.6	..	..
Netherlands	20	..	4.8	..	..	45.7
Sweden	20	9.8	8.1	3.6	..	..
United Kingdom	20	7.6	15.9	..	..	..
United States	20	9.4	21.3	8.1	..	52.5

.. Data not available. The cell has samples (unweighted) of less than 50.
Sources: OECD calculations based mainly on data from the Luxembourg Income Study. See Yamada and Casey (2001).

The first is the impact of changes in living arrangements, particularly the extent to which divorces and family breakdowns will result in a new class of single older people living alone. As the situation with respect to widows improves with time, this new group may fill their place. However, the effects are complex (including the effects of higher labour force participation and the re-forming of new households) and cannot be forecast easily. At the least, the fairness of existing pension rules in cases of family breakdown should be reviewed. In Japan and Italy, the changing trends in household de-merging and re-merging discussed in Chapter 2 should be monitored closely.

The second issue is the consequences of changes in pension arrangements. These include i) a growth of defined-contribution arrangements,[4] ii) the greater linkage of life-time benefits and contributions in public pensions, iii) increasing overall reliance on work and earnings in light of an uneven distribution of opportunities to work longer, and iv) increasing reliance on private pensions that can have greater risk and cost. On balance, it would seem that these changes, if they occur, would increase the vulnerability of people with intermittent and weak labour-market attachments and of people who do not have full pension coverage, as is sometimes the case for the self-employed and those who work part-time.

The third issue is potential relative deprivation. The original design of most public pensions assumed a one-earner family as the norm.[5] Today, a new norm may be emerging. This would be a population that consists mainly of two-earner couples who enter older age with two public pensions, two or more private pensions and possibly continued earnings. Any large shift in this direction might undermine the relative position of remaining one-earner couples or single people.[6] Certainly, issues of pension splitting in the case of divorce and of individual versus household-based characteristics of pensions will require review in light of these trends.

Dealing with the effects of more defined-contribution arrangements

Of these potential threats, most policy attention has focussed on those associated with growing defined-contribution arrangements. In public pension plans, an increased reliance on defined-contribution mechanisms entails a higher risk of inadequate retirement income for some groups of the population, *i.e.* workers who move in and out of dependent employment, workers under non-standard employment contracts and workers who are long-term unemployed. Workers with broken contribution careers could end up receiving very low benefits. Some recent reforms may have contributed to greater vulnerability.[7] However, most countries do have safety-net provisions targeted either specifically to poor pensioners or to the lowest-income groups in general, which aim to prevent old-age destitution.

The situation is different for occupational and personal retirement plans, where the move to more defined-contribution schemes offers both improvements and the following potential concerns in terms of adequacy:

- Vesting losses can be as high as in defined-benefit plans (see discussion in Chapter 6).
- Fees paid by plan members can significantly reduce pension benefits.[8]
- There is a risk of myopic behaviour by plan members, unless adequate preservation and annuitisation regulations are in place.[9]
- Misinformed consumers can make inappropriate choices of investment and plan provider (again see the discussion in Chapter 6).
- Adverse selection in the provision of annuities can make these products too expensive for "good" risks (*i.e.* people who do not expect to live long lives).

The problem is obviously less pressing in countries that provide a universal pension based on residency, such as Sweden, Finland, Canada and the Netherlands, than in those countries that rely on contributory and earnings-related benefits. But these universal basic schemes offer low benefits and are complemented by employer-based supplementary pensions, from which workers with broken careers are unlikely to receive significant benefits. Not only may these persons be excluded from occupational plans but they will also incur vesting losses if they change employment frequently. As discussed in Chapter 6, most countries are taking steps to encourage private pension provision, but not with a particular focus on workers with broken contribution careers. Only the Netherlands has been very active in this area by making benefit portability a legal right for participants in a scheme.

7.3. What can countries do?

Actions that can be taken

The remainder of this chapter describes some of the more common approaches to reform that the nine countries have followed in addressing problems of vulnerability, both existing and potential – in addition to the steps already discussed in Chapter 6. One approach is to concentrate on particular areas of vulnerability: broken careers, the protection of dependants and survivors and other measures to protect those with the lowest incomes. Another set of responses lies in addressing some systemic weaknesses such as the annuitisation and escalation of benefits. Additional steps can be taken with respect to the coverage and adequacy of private pensions. Target replacement rates can be set.

Actions that need not be taken

Before moving to a discussion of reforms, it is useful to note that the existence of a problem, or a potential problem, does not necessarily mean that remedial action within the retirement income system is urgent, or even needed. For example, to some extent the situation of widows is likely to improve over time as pension schemes mature and as new cohorts of women enter old age. Future cohorts of older women are more likely to have been employed in their working years and to have private pensions. For some, remaining alone rather than living with children is a preference that outweighs income issues.

As well, the main policy challenges concerning living standards for widows, and other older people living alone, would appear to be less related to income *per se* than to housing, long-term care and services that support independent living in the community. The economic position of the oldest old cannot be easily compared without taking into account arrangements such as comprehensive long-term care insurance in Germany and Japan.

Measurement techniques may exaggerate the need for policy action. If retirement income is not linked to current wages, the income of the old will fall, by definition, in relation to the income of working people – assuming continuing real growth in productivity and wages. That is currently the case for many private pensions (which are up-rated either not at all or only to prices), and to public pensions, which are often up-rated in line with prices only. This issue becomes important because of the very long duration of retirement – with many years separating the oldest old from current workers. Traditional income measures compare the income of any one group with that of the whole population. As a consequence, they implicitly suggest that a problem may exist if, for example, the incomes of the oldest old are below those of the working-age population. Yet this is a matter of substantive policy choice. Provided that low-income goals are met, it is not self-evident whether the policy goal should be to maintain living standards in relation to the older person's past living standards, or in relation to the living standard of their children's generation, or some combination of the two.

Similar questions arise with respect to the groups discussed above for whom there may be greater problems in the future of entering retirement at risk. There is no doubt about their vulnerability. However, implications for retirement income policies are less clear. Many of the groups that are vulnerable in the pre-retirement or early-retirement period are those that are at a disadvantage over the course of their lives. Many have faced weak labour-market attachment or low earnings throughout life.[10]

Retirement policy cannot, therefore, address the source of vulnerability in many of these cases. However, in the past, some countries have often used retirement income to provide support for those people in their 50s and early 60s for whom the possibility of work seemed to be remote. Adequate incomes were provided in a way that treated people with dignity. Even today, a case is sometimes made against policies that promote later retirement on the grounds that this would delay the provision of much-needed support to these vulnerable groups.

In hindsight, and given today's heavy policy emphasis on raising employment/population ratios in many countries, there was an over-use of early-retirement and disability pensions as a substitute for labour-market measures, often as a consequence of judicial rulings. As discussed in Chapter 5, much effort in recent years has been devoted to eliminating some pathways to early retirement and reducing access to others – for example, by attempting to reduce the role of labour-market factors in determining eligibility for disability benefits. If an important feature of overall public policy is to encourage employment, then policies aimed at removing people from the labour force (and from employment-related benefits and services) become suspect – especially programmes that may create added incentives towards earlier retirement.

7.4. Protecting people with gaps in their working history

There are many different approaches to the protection of people who have gaps in their working history or who have not worked. Pension designs differ as they relate to the treatment of dependants. Another feature that helps people with incomplete career histories is a universal, basic pension scheme based solely (or mainly) on a residency test. Examples are Canada's old-age security and the basic scheme in the Netherlands. Similarly, income- or means-tested schemes, where they are assessed individually, ensure that all pensioners receive a minimum income in their own right, whatever their work record. Examples include the systems of Finland and Sweden.

In earnings-related schemes, there is great tension between the goal of protecting people with contribution gaps and the insurance aspects of the scheme. This is particularly obvious in the "notional accounts" systems in Italy and Sweden. A main objective of the recent reform was to enhance the "actuarial fairness" of the pension scheme. But if benefits are related more closely to contributions, the scope for protecting people with low lifetime levels of contributions is reduced.[11] Nevertheless, periods of sickness, maternity, military service and unemployment are credited in Italy. Sweden allows for "imaginary" contributions for periods spent out of the labour force for people with caring responsibilities and for unemployment, sickness, education, *etc.*

The United Kingdom follows a similar approach in its public basic pension. Under home-responsibilities protection, periods spent out of work caring for children in full-time education or for elderly relatives are credited. People can earn a full entitlement to the basic pension with just 20 years' actual contributions. Although the United Kingdom's basic scheme is in theory contributory, the scale of the credits for periods not working makes it closer to the universal, residency-tested scheme of, for example, Canada.

Japan allows people to accrue the basic pension at one-third of the normal rate during specifically exempt periods. Germany allows for credited periods (A*nrechnungszeiten*) to cover particular episodes of sickness, rehabilitation, unemployment and further education. Since 1992, both parents can claim credits for the first three years after the birth of a child should they so choose.

Some earnings-related schemes offer some protection to people with broken work histories by having a redistributive benefit formula. This does not involve a credit for periods spent out of the labour force, but rather pays a proportionally higher pension to lower earners it protects. For example, in Germany women who work part-time for a number of years and workers earning under half the average can have their pensionable pay increased. The United States pays a much higher replacement rate on earnings up to 37% of average. Canada and the United States exclude some of the lowest earning years from the lifetime average – 15% of the total number of years and five years, respectively – which has a similar effect.

Another way to protect pensions in the event of contribution gaps is to ignore periods of low or zero earnings, for given contingencies, in the calculation of earnings-related benefits. For example, in Canada, periods of low or zero earnings incurred while raising a child under the age of seven are dropped for the purpose of calculating average earnings on which benefits are based. Periods of zero earnings while in receipt of a disability pension are similarly dropped for purposes of calculating a retirement pension.

The remaining earnings-related schemes, however, have no specific provisions for contribution gaps. These include Finland[12] and Japan, plus the occupational schemes in the Netherlands and Sweden.

In the past, women often left paid work to raise children. Women are now spending increasing time in the labour force and earning their own pension rights, especially if they are not married. The policy focus, therefore, is more on actions that improve pension credits for time spent bringing up children and help women to acquire their own pension rights, even if they are temporarily or permanently outside the labour force. Germany, for example, has recently doubled the pension credits during a period of 10 years for women who work part-time due to child-rearing. Further, under the proposed personal pension scheme, non-working wives would be entitled to a fully refundable tax credit to build up their own retirement savings. In the new pension systems in Italy and Sweden, child-rearing will also earn credits in the individual account.

7.5. Providing for survivors

Older widows, as described above, tend to have low incomes, in part because they have had no or a very weak labour-market attachment over their lives and are living alone. Most countries regard this problem as a legacy of the past, which can be solved through anti-low-income benefits targeted to the affected persons, and which thus does not require structural reforms.

The public systems in all nine countries do provide survivors' benefits to surviving spouses and children and, in Italy, to surviving parents as well. Several countries have been changing the rules for survivors' pensions in recent years, again mostly to take better account of years spent bringing up children. But at the same time, moves have been made to concentrate benefits on low-income widows. Sweden, for example, changed its traditional survivors' pension in 1990 to a gender-neutral benefit that is paid only for six months after the death of the partner. This change was made because of the high level of female labour force participation and the fact that fewer and fewer women are economically dependent on their partners. Widows with dependent children receive the benefit over a prolonged period.

Germany has frozen the maximum allowed income from earnings, assets and other sources beyond which widows' benefits are withdrawn; the rationale for this step is that most women do work and earn additional income on top of their survivors' benefits. Changes have also been made in the treatment of acquired pension rights between partners. Since the beginning of 2001, German couples can opt for splitting rights between the two partners; the rights distributed in such a way count as each person's own acquired rights and are not reduced in case of divorce and remarriage. In 1994, the Netherlands introduced this mechanism for occupational pensions in the event of divorce or the dissolution of the marriage during retirement.

In occupational schemes, survivors' protection is less well regulated, but many defined-benefit schemes offer some survivors' benefits. This is true particularly in those countries where occupational pension plans are an important element of the retirement income system or where opting-out of the public system is allowed, *e.g.* in Finland, the Netherlands, the United Kingdom and Japan. In the United States, private defined-benefit plans which provide benefits as an annuity are required to offer the beneficiary a survivor's pension that is worth between half and a full pension. The price of this additional benefit can be lower benefits while the beneficiary is alive. The option can be refused only if both the insured person and the dependent give written consent. Survivors' benefits are less common in defined-contribution schemes. Protection in such plans does not come automatically but depends on the terms and coverage of the contract according to which the accumulated balance is annuitised. These factors are in addition to the basic problem of women having lower-paying jobs and living longer once retired.

7.6. Other action aimed at low-income groups

Low incomes can be the result of many factors in addition to incomplete working histories and dependent relationships. All countries have anti-low-income programmes available to pensioners. In countries where basic pensions are based on residency regardless of individual contributions, such as the Netherlands, Canada, Sweden and Finland, the pension itself protects against very low incomes. The other countries rely on combinations of a minimum pension guarantee within the public pension system, social assistance and other means-tested minimum income guarantees to help the low-income older population. Table A.8 in the Statistical Annex shows the percentage of older people that are in receipt of means-tested benefits and the size of that means-tested benefit as a percentage of the beneficiaries' disposable income. It also shows corresponding data for older people in receipt of private pensions.

In the United Kingdom, several characteristics of the system increase the low-income risk for older people. Eligibility for the basic state pension is not based on residence but on wage-related contributions. Persons who earn less than the minimum ceiling – again these are mostly women – are excluded from the system altogether. As they are the least likely to be covered by any other private pension arrangements, their risk of falling into old age with low incomes is the greatest. The substantial decline in replacement rates associated with indexation to prices, discussed below, has resulted in an increasing number of pensioners in the United Kingdom receiving means-tested income support and supplementary benefits such as housing allowances.

The old system in the United Kingdom also penalised personal efforts to save, since any personal retirement savings led to a one-for-one withdrawal of income support. In 2001, the capital limits in the minimum income guarantee will be increased to reduce the disincentive to save. Also, the means-testing process will be changed from weekly assessment to annual assessment, which should lower the administrative burden and perhaps encourage better take-up of the benefit.

The share of pensioners with means-tested benefits (in addition to those built into the pension system itself) is also high in the United States. The average level of public pensions is lower than in continental European countries and there is less widespread coverage of occupational pensions (compared with, say, the Netherlands, Sweden or the United Kingdom). A little over 10% of all old-age pensioners in the United States receive the means-tested supplement. One-third of these beneficiaries also have a pension from the public pension system; their eligibility thus results from a combination of low earnings and incomplete contribution careers.

An additional low-income risk for pensioners in the United States arises from health care expenditure. Unlike in the other countries in this study, in which there exists some form of public, or quasi-public health insurance system, individuals are required to make their own health insurance arrangements. The only people to have automatic, publicly provided insurance coverage are those with very low incomes. Those who are over the age of 65, or are in receipt of disability benefits, are served by the "Medicare" system. Medicare covers acute care costs, but it does not cover primary care costs or long-term residential care costs. To cover primary care costs, older people are dependent either on continuation of any insurance provided by a previous employer – which they are sometimes able to buy at the lower "group" premium the latter enjoys – or on their own insurance, or they have to meet expenses directly out-of-pocket.[13] To cover residential care costs, older people have to rely upon their own resources and can only access public assistance when they have depleted their own assets sufficiently to have become eligible for "Medicaid".[14]

Low numbers of social assistance recipients, however, do not necessarily mean that there is no need for anti-low-income benefits. Some countries have a means-testing process that may discourage potential beneficiaries from applying for the benefit. Under the social assistance scheme in Germany, the municipalities can recover the cost of assistance from the immediate family, if they are sufficiently affluent. This process means that older persons may prefer not to take up benefits rather than have their children asked for assistance. The government is therefore planning to drop the family recourse for people of pension age. This will put an additional burden on the pension system. As social assistance is administered and financed at the municipal level, the pension system will have to provide the additional funds that are currently paid by the municipalities and families.

In Japan, a low take-up rate for social assistance[15] suggests that there could be potential room for improvement in the way public assistance is used to tackle very low incomes. Although non-employed persons, who are not insured in the basic pension scheme, should be covered by the national pension scheme, there are problems of non-compliance and default, particularly among the self-employed, students, non-regular workers and, to a lesser degree, spouses of employed persons. The Japanese social assistance programme provides benefits only if the family is unable to support the affected persons; therefore, the same danger of failure to take up benefits exists. There is discussion in Japan today about changing this mechanism.

The old Italian system has a minimum means-tested social pension for older people, but there are still several groups at a higher risk of poverty. One group are pensioners in the southern part of the country, where unemployment rates are high. Young unemployed people tend to stay in their parents' home due to high unemployment, especially in the south. In the absence of an unemployment insurance system, the pension benefit has to serve as income for the whole family.

7.7. Adequacy of annuitised benefits

Members of defined-benefit plans generally receive pensions in the form of an annuity. This ensures that people do not make myopic use of their pension, or miscalculate their needs in old-age. Exceptions to this policy include the Tax Qualified Plans in Japan[16] and some occupational plans in the United States, which pay out lump-sums rather than monthly pensions. In the United States, it has been estimated that up to 12% of full-time participants in defined-benefit plans received benefits in lump-sum form (Bureau of Labor Statistics' Employee Benefit Survey for 1997).

Annuitisation is less widespread in defined-contribution plans. In Italy, up to half of the balance in an occupational or personal defined-contribution plan may be withdrawn as a lump-sum at retirement. In Canada and the United States, the whole accumulated balance of such plans may be withdrawn in a lump-sum at retirement. Such freedom is controversial because some workers, especially those with low incomes or with limited public pension benefits, risk outliving their own resources if they mismanage their assets or live substantially longer than expected. The presence of safety nets and government pension guarantees can also be an incentive for some workers to consume their balance more quickly than would be socially desirable.

Finally, concerns over the adequacy of defined-contribution pensions arise in the annuities market due to problems of adverse selection. These problems arise from the fact that individuals may have more information than insurance companies about their longevity risk. The introduction of some degree of compulsory annuitisation may mitigate adverse selection problems.

All these concerns have led some countries to require some degree of annuitisation. In the United Kingdom, the accumulated balance of both occupational and personal pension plans must be annuitised before the age of 75 (there is a facility to take out a tax-free lump-sum of 25% of the fund). The new funded individual accounts component in Sweden stipulates mandatory annuitisation for all account holders. The recently proposed pension reform in Germany stipulates that benefits may not be received any earlier than age 60. At the beginning of the benefits phase, a minimum percentage of capital must be set aside for a life annuity.

7.8. Protection of pension benefits against inflation

Indexation mechanisms play an important role for the economic well-being of pensioners. Depending on the type of benefit scheme, indexation affects both the valuation of pension rights and the value of the benefits in payment. In flat-rate pension systems, whether they are based on residency or on a certain period of contribution, indexation of pension rights is not an issue. For these systems, only the indexation of benefits in payment matters. In earnings-related pension schemes, however, both the valuation of pension rights acquired during past years and the adjustment of pensions in payment are important.

Indexation of public pensions in payment

In their reforms directed towards achieving fiscally sustainable pensions, many countries have introduced changes to the way pension benefits in payment are up-rated (*i.e.* escalated). This can affect the position of the oldest old relative to the working-age population. Price indexation can lead to substantial reductions of replacement rates when wages grow faster than the consumer price index. As this has been the case in the United Kingdom, the replacement rate provided by the public system has been declining steadily, from 22% in 1981 to less than 17% in 1998. According to the projections of the Government Actuary, the replacement rate will fall below 10% around 2030 (Government Actuary's Department, 1999). Thus, while the United Kingdom does not have a problem of financial sustainability in its public pension system, it does have a higher risk than other countries of pensioners living in low income. To address this problem, the United Kingdom introduced a minimum income guarantee for pensioners in 1999. This guarantee is higher than the basic state pension and is indexed to earnings.

Several countries have used indexation as a tool to temporarily or permanently reduce pension expenditure. In the Dutch flat-rate pension scheme, for example, public pensions are adjusted twice a year to the net minimum wage, which in turn depends on the evolution of the wage set in collective labour agreements. There is an escape clause in the law, which enables the government to freeze pensions due to unfavourable economic conditions. This clause was applied in the early 1990s, but the link between the minimum wage and the pension level was restored in 1996.

In Germany, pensions in payment are usually indexed to wages net of taxes and social security contributions; in order to limit contribution rate increases, temporary price indexation of benefits was introduced in 1999. Japan recently moved from net wage indexation of pensions in payment in its earnings-related pension scheme to price indexation.[17] Newly awarded pensions, however, will continue to be adjusted to net wages.

The Italian pension reform in 1995 also changed the indexation mechanism. Pensions are adjusted annually to inflation, but indexation is not linear. Smaller pensions are fully adjusted to inflation, pensions up to three times the minimum pension by 90%, and all others by 75%. In 1998, the government decided to suspend increases for all pensions above a threshold to achieve savings.

Finland also changed its adjustment mechanism for pensions in payment. In 1996, the indexation of benefits in payment was changed from 50:50 to an 80% weight for inflation and 20% for wage growth.

In Sweden, a more complicated mechanism was introduced. In the new system, the transformation of each worker's notional balance is based on annual growth of 1.6%, which will be taken into account in benefit indexation. If wage growth is exactly 1.6%, benefits will be adjusted to inflation. If it is lower than the supposed level, it will be adjusted less than inflation. This mechanism is also applied to all pensions paid by the old system.

Indexation of occupational pensions

Protection of occupational benefits against inflation is widely available in four of the nine countries. Benefit indexation is required by law in Finland, where privately managed pensions are part of the statutory social security system, and by labour contract in Sweden. In the Netherlands, it is not required, but is offered by most plans; 70% of occupational plan members are enrolled in schemes with wage indexation. In Finland, the reference in the statutory plans is a weighted average of the increase in the consumer price index and wages. In the United Kingdom, all post-1997 pension benefits must be indexed to inflation up to 5%.

The degree of protection against inflation is lower in the other five countries. Both in Canada and the United States, most public-sector occupational plans are price-indexed. Other plan sponsors have granted *ad hoc* increases in pensions during periods of high inflation (such as the 1970s). In Japan, plans that have opted out of the public system must reach an annual return of 4-5% from which benefit adjustment is paid, but there is no formal requirement of plans to index benefits. Non-substitutive benefits from Employee Pension Funds and benefits from the Tax Qualified Plans can be provided in the form of lump-sums. In Germany, protection against inflation is compulsory; employers must adjust benefits with prices every three years. This can be suspended if the sponsoring company does not have the means to provide the adjustment but the suspension needs to be made up for later as the situation improves.

Indexation of pension rights

Finland changed not the calculation of indexation but the definition of the base for pension rights. By defining pensionable wages as gross wages net of the employee's pension contributions, pension outlays were reduced. Benefit rights are adjusted annually to the change of a composite index with weights of 50% for inflation and 50% for wage growth.

Sweden introduced a new mechanism to index pension rights during the contribution phase. Generally, pension rights are adjusted to per capita wage growth. But since pension rights and benefits can grow faster than the contribution base, *i.e.* the sum of covered wages, the government has built in an automatic balancing mechanism. If expected future income and existing reserve capital is less than expected future pension liabilities, pension rights will be adjusted by less than wage growth.

7.9. Setting target replacement rates in diversified systems

In a more diversified system, it will be important to consider and ensure the integration, adequacy and security of the different components of the package as a whole.[18] Without information on total pension replacement income, it will be difficult for citizens to plan for their retirement. Nor will it be easy to assess the performance of the system as a whole.

One approach is to ensure that the public and mandatory or quasi-mandatory private elements are integrated at the level of design, with an agreed replacement rate for the combined total. Occupational defined-benefit plans already tend to be integrated with public pensions in most countries. The highest degree of integration is found in Finland and the Netherlands. This is partly a result of wage and benefit bargaining mechanisms, as well as tax rules, which limit deductibility to a combined maximum benefit from the public and private systems. Supplementary registered pension plans sponsored by employers in Finland have a target replacement rate for all pension benefits of 60%.[19] Dutch plans base their benefits on a 70% replacement rate for the overall pension benefit. In Sweden too, occupational pension benefits have been highly integrated with the public system in the past. Current retirees benefit from a fully integrated pension benefit that targets a replacement rate of around 65%. But under the reformed system workers will receive part of their compensation from a defined-contribution scheme.

Another approach is to integrate public earnings-related benefits with occupational plans at the company level (so that from the perspective of employees they are part of a unified package), but without setting a national target replacement rate. This is common in Canada. In the United States and the United Kingdom, about half of defined-benefit scheme members have benefits integrated with social security. In Japan, there is a high degree of integration only for occupational plans that have opted-out of the public earnings-related system. These plans have to provide a benefit that must be at least 130% of the public pension for which they substitute. For non-substitutive benefits and other plans, there is little if any integration. Benefits in these plans are in fact often paid out in the form of lump-sums at retirement.

Integration is lowest in Germany and Italy, the two countries in which public pensions currently play the largest role. Historically in these countries neither governments nor employees have given systematic consideration to private pensions. As the process of reform of the public system progresses, some degree of integration will become necessary for fiscal reasons. In Germany, the proposed new personal pension arrangements are supposed to replace part of the public benefit, so integration is implicit in this proposal. But targeting integrated benefits will not be easy with defined-contribution plans as it is difficult to assess the effects of administrative costs and the volatility of asset returns on retirement income. The same is true for Italy where the new plans, both occupational and individual, are defined-contribution plans only.

NOTES

1. Note again that these are relative comparisons. In absolute terms, expressed in US dollars and adjusting for purchasing power parities, the disposable income of single older women living alone ranged from USD 9 000 to 14 000 across the nine countries. This is significantly higher than the comparable figure for the bottom quintile of the population taken as whole (see Yamada and Casey, 2001).

2. Note that sample numbers are quite large in the two countries in which multi-generational families are important – Japan and Italy. Sample numbers are often small in other countries, and the results should be treated with some caution.

3. Particularly interesting are studies that use newly available longitudinal data. See Kingston and Arsenault (2000), from which the examples in the text were, in part, based.

4. See the discussion in Chapter 6. This is likely to come either as a result of the substitution of some public and occupational pension plans by personal pension plans, or by the transformation of existing occupational defined-benefit plans into defined-contribution or hybrid plans. In the United States, many employers have transformed their defined-benefit pension plans into cash-balance or 401(k) plans. 401(k) plans have been especially popular for various reasons, including their portability, the tax deductibility of employee contributions, and the limited fiduciary responsibilities for employers (they must ensure that plan members have a sufficiently broad menu of investment choices). Two of the nine countries, Italy and Sweden, converted their public pension schemes to notional defined-contribution plans, and in a number of other countries there are already close links between contributions and benefits.

5. Although not in Finland and Sweden. More generally, especially in some of the Nordic countries, the "new" norm of two-earner couples entering retirement is well advanced.

6. The reverse issue might also arise, of course, of a minority who receive very large incomes in retirement. This is an issue that has been evoked in media reports of an alleged generational conflict involving hard-pressed young workers who are required to support a growing number of rich leisured retirees. Chart A.7 in the Statistical Annex suggests that this is not a current problem, however. It looks at a "middle-upper" income rate which works in precisely the same way as the low-income cut-off – except that it identifies the relatively well-to-do rather than those with the lowest incomes. The main message is the following: about 10% of older people are relatively rich in most countries. In the United States and Italy, this share rises to over 15%. There are somewhat fewer rich people among those aged 75 and over, except in Japan where co-residence raises the economic well-being of older people to some extent. Compared with the whole population, there are relatively few rich older people. Concerns about potentially overly-advantaged as well as disadvantaged groups are more about possible future directions than present realities. Note, however, that if housing and subsidised services are taken into account, many older couples have consumption levels that are somewhat higher than those for the population as a whole.

7. For example, in Germany, the pension credits given to long-term unemployed persons were recently scaled down substantially; since structural unemployment in some regions is high, this measure was likely to create a new group of poor pensioners in the future. On the other hand, Germany has also recently reduced the threshold for mandatory insurance in the public pension scheme. Now even very low-paid jobs must be insured, but benefit entitlement is also very low, unless the beneficiary makes additional voluntary contributions.

8. Statutory restrictions on fees, such as those imposed in the new Swedish system of individual accounts and those set for the United Kingdom's stakeholder pensions, can limit the damage done to pension benefits, but only if they do not affect the efficiency of asset management. Fee regulations can, for example, mitigate the problems of excessive marketing costs and lack of transparency from which personal pension plans generally suffer. They can also simplify choices for investors to the extent that fee structures become comparable across providers. For a longer discussion of fees and policy responses, see Chapter 6.

9. Defined-contribution plans, because they allow for individual choice, also increase the risk of myopic behaviour by pension plan members. In the United Kingdom, the risk of early consumption of benefits is eliminated by a prohibition on cashing out of defined-contribution pensions before retirement. The United States has followed a different route: savings from occupational defined-contribution plans and from Individual

Retirement Accounts that are not rolled-over into other qualified plans are subject to a 10% penalty, in addition to normal taxation. This penalty acts as a powerful disincentive to early consumption of pension benefits. The situation is very different for defined-contribution plans in Canada, where workers changing jobs are able to commute their accumulated balance. Individual retirement savings can also be liquidated without additional penalties beyond normal taxation. In Italy, workers changing jobs are able to transfer their total accrued contributions into another pension fund or can ask for their accumulated balance if they lose their status as a worker.

10. There are, of course, cases where the vulnerability in question does arise as a consequence of retirement policies and requires solutions within the retirement income system. The situation of migrants to the country who have not met the residential or full contribution requirements for pensions appears to be the main example. However, data are not available that would allow an assessment of the extent of this particular problem in the nine countries. Canadian data, for example, suggest that, on average, the income of most older immigrants is similar to that of other older people. What they lose in public and private pensions is compensated for by more income from work (see Baldwin and Laliberté, 1999).

11. See Disney (2000) for an extensive discussion of the tension between redistribution and actuarial fairness.

12. Although if an absence from work (*e.g.* for maternity leave) lasts less than one year, the worker will be covered.

13. In 1995, according to an EBRI survey, of those full-time employees in medium and large firms who had health insurance on their jobs, 46% received health coverage if they retired before 65 and 41% were covered from the age of 65. However, the proportion of the workforce employed by firms which offer retiree health protection is shrinking, and many employers now require retired employees to pay a greater share of the premium.

14. Other authors have suggested the figure for the US to be even higher. According to the US Senate Committee on Ageing, older persons pay 28% of the cost of their care from their own resources, much of this being for skilled nursing and mental health services. Two-thirds of prescription drug expenses are met out-of-pocket (see Binstock, 1998).

15. The take-up rate of Japanese public assistance is around 10% (90% of potential beneficiaries do not or cannot receive public assistance) according to Wada and Kimura (1998). This low take-up rate can be explained by: 1) a strict means test (older people usually have some kinds of financial wealth) and 2) reluctance to apply for assistance and therefore publicly signal that children are unwilling or unable to provide support.

16. The current regulation requires TQPs to pay a minimum of a five-year annuity; special TQPs, which were introduced in 1993, must provide lifelong annuities, however.

17. Japan recently experienced a decline in the Consumer Price Index. However, on an exceptional basis, the government and parliament decided to maintain the current notional value of pensions, rather than downscaling them.

18. Unfortunately, the information on policies concerning occupational and personal pensions is not systematically collected in most countries. It is only possible to sketch a few trends that will have an influence on the private pensions component of the income package. The adequacy of private pension benefits can be investigated more easily in those countries where defined-benefit plans dominate. Finland, Germany and Japan (a defined-contribution proposal was submitted to the Japanese Parliament in November 2000) permit only defined-benefit, while the new pension plans in Italy have to be defined-contribution plans; elsewhere both plan types are allowed. But defined-contribution plans are important only in Canada, the United Kingdom and the United States. In Sweden, the occupational pension plans were recently transformed into a mixed defined-benefit and defined-contribution system, but for the next twenty years retirees will be receiving only defined-benefit pensions.

19. However, these supplementary pension plans have now been closed as the statutory pension schemes have matured and already provide a replacement rate of 60%.

Chapter 8

CONCLUSION – LESSONS ABOUT REFORM STRATEGIES

8.1. Introduction

This concluding chapter describes practical approaches to dealing with the dilemmas and problems outlined in Chapter 1 and illustrated throughout the paper.

First is the difficulty, discussed at length in preceding chapters, of introducing needed reforms to a system that has been successful in meeting its primary goals.

Second is the related need for coherent policy action on several fronts, involving many different actors and constituencies. For example, responses to the work-retirement challenge may involve action affecting both public and private pensions, alternative retirement paths such as disability or unemployment benefits, and work-related measures. There are few mechanisms to support policy-making that encompasses so many jurisdictions. The experience of the nine countries does, however, provide some lessons.

Third is a lack of full consensus on the right mix of steps to be taken. There are often large discrepancies between what people say and what they do. The basic problem is a lack of empirical understanding of how the retirement income systems actually work and what policy levers are likely to have the greatest effect. The data that are currently available are strong enough to indicate sensible directions for future reform. However, over the longer-run, richer data will be needed to sustain the effectiveness of reforms that are designed to meet a variety of often-conflicting social and economic goals.

Section 8.2 summarises the scope of reform strategies and reviews mechanisms for consultation and policy formation that have been developed in the nine countries. Section 8.3 describes priorities for filling information gaps.

8.2. Strategic frameworks for policy development and consensus-building

A framework is needed to encourage coherence among policies that support:

- A transition from full-time work to retirement that occurs later, on average, than at present and that provides greater opportunities for more flexible and gradual pathways to full retirement. There should be a realistic possibility for many people to have a continued attachment to the labour force, and an active life in society, well into later life. However, highest priority should be addressed to later retirement for those who now retire well before age 65.

- A diversified system of income support for older people during retirement (and the transition to retirement), with several significant and sustainable elements. This would include a significant role for public and private pensions, for defined-benefit and defined-contribution arrangements and for advance-funded and pay-as-you-go elements. It would include a greater role for earnings and greater coherence of retirement income policies with related financial market, labour-market and taxation policies.

- The continued provision of an adequate material standard of living for people in a more diverse system, consistent with a dignified life in retirement and during the transition to retirement. This would include special attention to vulnerable people for whom large private retirement savings, or employment in their older years, may not be a realistic possibility.

Such ambitious goals could only be met gradually and through policy action on many fronts, involving many government and non-governmental bodies. No single consultation or policy-development mechanism could co-ordinate all the activities that would be needed. However, the nine countries have had a wide range of experience with a variety of mechanisms for building public understanding and engagement and viable political support across these topics.

Some mechanisms for providing coherence

One key lesson from the experience of the nine countries is that successful reform requires a mix of both special[1] and ongoing consultation mechanisms:

- In some countries (Japan, Sweden, Canada), reform has been facilitated by strategic initiatives that resulted in statements of general goals and principles related to ageing or retirement. These have reduced the ideological content of subsequent debate (for details see Tambouri, 1999). Japan may have gone furthest at the level of general principles.

- Ongoing means include budget consultation processes, continuing mechanisms for consulting with social partners, and the regular reports of research councils and policy advisory boards, which have often been adapted to the needs of reforms related to retirement and the transition to retirement. In some countries, there are ongoing advisory bodies that monitor and periodically review pension policy (the United States and Germany). In the Netherlands, the government sometimes reaches an agreement with the social partners instead of introducing legislation.

- Consultations around particular themes are common. In Finland, a special group that includes all the social partners has been set up by the government to examine the future development of social protection expenditure.

- In many cases, Prime Minister's offices or cabinet offices have played a central role, reflecting the priority of the issues but also the reality that reform overlaps the boundaries of several ministries.

- In most countries, consultations have been organised around major analytic studies such as white papers (the United Kingdom, Japan, Sweden and Canada). In a few cases, such studies did not exist (Italy in 1992), or consultation was weak (the United Kingdom in the mid-1980s). These latter reforms did not work well.

A review of many documents associated with such consultations suggests that debate might be facilitated by greater reference to the experience of other countries in similar circumstances. There could also be more sharing of best practices related to analytic techniques and the presentation of materials. Much of the content of the various planning and consultative documents is quite similar in all nine countries – including the scale of the demographic, labour-market and fiscal challenges, the tools used in developing projections and scenarios and the formulation of goals, objectives and principles. Study of recent documents of other countries might well be helpful in finding effective ways of presenting these findings.

The role of the social partners

The actors involved in these consultations have varied across countries. Given the long time periods involved, some countries strive for co-operation among political parties in order to provide continuity. Examples are Sweden, Italy and the United States. In some countries, the government of the day plays the lead (the United Kingdom and Germany, recently, and Canada[2]). The role of unions and employer organisations has been quite different. This experience suggests that some involvement of social partners is critical to successful reform, but that complete consensus among partners is not always necessary:[3]

- In some countries where consensus is highly valued and social partners traditionally play a large role, their role was, in fact, reduced in recent reforms – as in Germany (in 1997, but not in 2001 when a bipartisan approach is being used). Nor were unions a central player in the Swedish reforms. In still other countries, unions are only one among many participants (the United States, the United Kingdom and Canada), where their participation is sometimes limited to receipt of information or the right to make submissions when consultation is sought.

- In some countries pension reforms and legislation are realised on the basis of tripartite agreements between the social partners and state authorities – reflecting, in the case of Finland, a priority on extensive political and societal co-operation and national consensus which requires that the parties involved consider the system legitimate and agree on the need to participate in its development.

- By and large, members of well-organised groups such as unions tend to be among the biggest losers in the short- and medium-term and can oppose reform because of fears of loss of current "acquired rights" – unless they are convinced that the system is in danger. In this case, they may play an active role in planning reform. For example, in Italy, unions played a central role in convincing the public of the necessity for reform in the longer-run. A positive vote for reform in a referendum of union members was a key factor in successful reform.[4] However, it has been argued that one price of this union support is an extremely gradual transition to the new system.

Will the growing number of older voters make a difference?

Chapters 6 and 7 showed that there are sensitivities in public opinion that need to be taken into account in framing reform agendas, but that, equally, there is nothing in public opinion today that would present impossible barriers to the development of an informed consensus. People may not welcome change in the mix of retirement income resources, but they do expect it. They may not welcome having to work longer, but the main concern is likely to centre on the availability of suitable jobs for older people – a topic that can and should be part of the broader reform agenda.

This is a relatively optimistic assessment of today's public opinion. Looking to the future, there will be a demographically-based shift in the balance of political influence toward older people, who may share a strong common interest as pensioners. Older people vote in above-average numbers. They are playing a more active political role (see Walker and Naegele, 1999) in most of the European countries in this study – through lobbying (United Kingdom), in unions (Italy), in political parties (Germany) and even in forming older peoples' political parties (Netherlands). This kind of more active participation is well established in the United States; for example, the American Association of Retired People (AARP) is the largest lobby group in the world. What does this mean for mechanisms of policy-development and consensus-building?

The evidence suggests that the effect of the growing numbers of older voters on retirement policy debates may not be as large or direct as might be thought. The impact of their common interest in pensions is moderated, since large reforms tend to have grandfathering arrangements that often leave present pensioners under the existing system. As well, the growing numbers of older voters may not shape future retirement income policy debates in any direct or substantial fashion. People's behaviours and views are affected by many factors in addition to age, including work attachment, education, income, gender and ethnic status. The AARP (see Rix, 1999), for example, points to the heterogeneity of older people in their organisation. A recent OECD review of public opinion surveys[5] found that most views on pension-related issues do not, in fact, vary consistently by age.

The OECD study just referred to also found that public attitudes were, at core, based on a better understanding of the actual policy issues than appears on the surface. While awareness of the details of pension designs is, for example, quite poor in most countries, basic attitudes are realistic. There are good empirical reasons why people like existing arrangements (they have worked well, as shown in this paper), why people lack confidence in their sustainability (they are under serious demographic pressure), and why people are suspicious of later retirement (jobs for older workers were difficult to find in most countries in much of the 1990s). This suggests that, if debate is sensibly framed and if good empirical evidence is available, discussions about pension reform need not be as polarised as is often feared. The remaining sections will briefly describe some general steps that would help in framing reform agendas and in providing needed empirical information.

Finding better terminology and broadening the scope of policy agendas

A general problem has been the absence of a common language that would facilitate the sharing of experience among the various bodies concerned with policy development and consultation. In part, this reflects the lack of comprehensive empirical evidence on many topics, as described in the next section. However, there is even a lack of consistent terminology to describe administrative arrangements. The language of a "three-tier" or "four-pillar" system (for example, first-tier public pensions, second-tier occupational pensions and third-tier private pensions or savings) is widely used in most of the nine countries. However, that taxonomy misses many important elements of the system, such as earnings, disability and other benefits. Moreover, as explained in Section 3.2, this terminology is increasingly unhelpful even in describing the pension elements of the system.[6]

Communications might be improved by specifically framing policy agendas more broadly to include all the resources available to older people and by avoiding the practice of slotting a programme, in its entirety and forever, into one of three of four pre-determined tiers. It seems preferable to identify the various elements of the whole system by their actual names – such as social security benefits, old-age income tax deductions, occupational pensions, people's own earnings or a guaranteed income supplement – and then to simply describe these using taxonomies that make sense given the nature of the policy discussion at hand.[7]

The most common recent attempt to broaden the scope of policy debate among the nine countries was the use of an "active ageing" theme, although its substantive content[8] has varied from country to country. In principle, active ageing places emphasis on the role of employment in the retirement income system and on life-course perspectives in policies that affect older people. This is similar to the shift some decades ago towards active labour-market programming in employment policy, the shift towards deinstitutionalisation in health and long-term care policies and the shift in education policy towards the theme of lifelong learning. The concept has the potential to allow policy questions to be posed in a constructive way. Does it make economic sense to have a shrinking portion of the population producing goods and services? Does it make sense to collectively support institutional arrangements that result in growing periods in the last third of life being spent passively? Are there higher priorities for using scarce collective resources? Does it make sense to support incentives that concentrate leisure in the last part of life? However, little of this potential for shaping a broader debate has materialised. In practice, active ageing has been used in a more limited sense and has not yet played a significant role in shaping retirement income debates.

8.3. Information to sustain effective reform

The "resources of older people" policy agenda being discussed here is significantly different from the agendas[9] of even the recent past. New agendas typically need to be supported by significantly different data and applied research. And, indeed, there are data gaps in supporting policy analysis over the shorter and longer-term.

Data gaps in supporting shorter-term policy analysis

There are reasonably good data and empirical tools to support much shorter-term analysis. Models exist in all nine countries that allow the calculation of first-order effects of changes in pensions and often other programmes – who wins and loses in the several years after the change is introduced and the likely consequences for budgets and other programming calculations. Although there are weaknesses – for example, data and modelling often cannot deal with the simultaneous effects of changes in several components of the system – they are steadily improving.

Nevertheless, there are important gaps. The lack of data on private pension arrangements was described in Chapter 6. In most of the countries, empirical information on how people consume, save and spend their time as they grow older is still very patchy, as are data on constraints on their use of time, including health constraints. When richer data sets are available, they often indicate that many of the assumptions that underlie policy are wrong. For example, more sophisticated data tend to show that age may not be as important as it appears from the less sophisticated data sets that are more common today. It is often found, for example, that factors such as educational level, income, health and household living arrangements are more important in explaining people's skills and behaviour than physical age *per se*.

It is not only a question of data gaps. Fuller use could also be made of information that is readily available today. For example, some of the information and techniques used in the present report are not commonly found in national studies. These include converting labour-force surveys to a lifetime basis, quasi-cohort analysis and the use of data that are internationally comparable, such as comparative income, public opinion and time-use statistics.

Data to support longer-term policy analysis have the highest priority

The need for information to support very long-term time frames has been well recognised and has already attracted considerable research and development. Compared with other policy areas, data to support long-run analysis are important, because pensions make promises whose full effects can only be seen in the distant future – 50 or more years away. Fiscal projections, and the actuarial forecasts that are associated with pension administration, have typically been the main source of empirical information supporting recent pension reforms. There are good reasons for this. They provide an important discipline to policy-making by reducing the risk of introducing policies that could become unsustainable financially. If they come from a credible source, they help debate from being side-tracked into arguments over numbers. Projection techniques have been improving over the years.[10] For example, the international comparisons of age-related fiscal projections reported in Chapter 4 were not possible until recently.

Less attention has been given to data that could help understand the effects of policy over a 5 to 15 year time frame. Yet this is the critical period for much retirement income policy. It is during this period that most of the baby-boom generation will retire and that the main effects of reforms introduced today (including the effects of the transitional arrangements associated with many larger reforms) will be felt. The experience of the nine countries suggests that the maximum shelf-life of retirement programmes is also within this time range – with programmes either being replaced by new ones or being transformed by a series of incremental changes.

A recent OECD publication (OECD, 2000*a*) has illustrated the kind of information that is needed. Taking the example of the transition to retirement, it concluded that what is missing is comparative information about the pathways from work to retirement. This would include the institutional characteristics of those pathways, the characteristics of people who follow those pathways (including work, time use, health, income and assets), how the paths interact and the potential effects of policy interventions. Ideally, one would want data that could track the experiences of people as they moved through their working and retirement years and how trends changed over time.

Large-scale longitudinal surveys and sophisticated microsimulation models capable of integrating administrative and survey data are examples of new tools that are needed. A review of the experience of the nine countries indicates that a start has been made in developing these data in several countries:

- The Health and Retirement Survey in the United States is a good example of a longitudinal survey that will eventually fill many of the most critical gaps. The results from even the early waves of that survey are reshaping understanding of the retirement process. A similar survey has been announced in the United Kingdom.

- Many countries are developing increasingly sophisticated microsimulation models that can provide insights into the future of retirement and retirement income systems. The Canadian development of lifepath microsimulation modelling, which uses survey and administrative data to simulate people over the course of their lives, is one example. Another is the MINT model being developed in the United States, which uses panel data to examine the likely characteristics of future social security recipients.

Now is the time to develop the empirical base that can sustain reform

In one form or another, the new data and techniques that are needed either already exist or are in the process of development in various countries. There is therefore an opportunity to share the lessons that have been learned. It is, indeed, particularly important that major new data sets be designed, from the outset, to be internationally comparable. The value added from the ability to make international comparisons is high.

These observations suggest that, when countries develop strategic processes for retirement-related policy reform, they should place a high priority on developing the data and applied research that will be needed to develop consensus and political support and to sustain reform in the future.[11] Ideally, the basic longitudinal surveys and lifepath microsimulation analytic tools should be developed over the next several years (and development does take considerable time). If this happens, the tools will be in place to track the early baby-boom generation as they move into their retirement years. This will provide an empirical base to fine-tune policy, which will almost certainly be needed, as those entering retirement in 10 years time will have characteristics that are quite different from today's retirees. Existing data are strong enough to allow an understanding of the need for reform and the main directions for reform. However, in most of the nine countries, they will not be strong enough to effectively support policies over the medium-term. There is simply no substitute for a solid base of longitudinal data that can track people over the course of their working years and into later life, and for an analytic and research capacity that is strong enough to convert that data into practical lessons for policy.

NOTES

1. A useful review of some of these can be found in Reynaud (2000).

2. In Canada, the situation is dominated by close co-operation between federal and provincial governments on the earnings-related but not the basic pension. The Canada Pension Plan (CPP) is a joint programme in nine provinces, and a very similar province-only programme (QPP) exists in Quebec. The basic pension is federal. This means that it is simpler to structure separate consultations for these two programmes. Yet, as noted, the interaction between the two has been an important factor in the success of the Canadian system. Canada has committed to undertake public consultations on any changes to the CPP.

3. More generally, the "multi-directional and multi-dimensional" nature of social partnership, and its cyclical dimension, makes it very hard to draw simple conclusions about the role of social partnership – or to find lessons that can be easily transferred to other countries (Casey and Gold, 2000).

4. An interesting description of the process can be found in Baccaro (2000). The paper concentrates on what went on inside the unions to produce this support for reform. (Note that Italian unions include pensioners as members and they voted overwhelmingly for reform, much more so than active members. Because of grandfathering, they had little to lose from the reforms.)

5. Hicks (OECD, 2001). There are differences by age, but they do not point to any growing cleavage along the lines of age. Age-differences in attitudes do not appear to be systematically related to the actual retirement ages or pension arrangements in a country.

6. A perhaps less serious problem is that the language of fixed tiers may suggest that these are ideal arrangements towards which actual systems should evolve. There is no sign that the countries in this study are moving towards any single model, nor any suggestion that doing so would be appropriate. If anything, the opposite appears to be happening. There are common goals, but quite different ways of pursuing those goals. The World Bank and the International Labour Organisation have used the concept of ideal pension models with three or four tiers. However, they too stress the importance of flexibility and a multi-pillared approach rather than working towards any pre-defined model, especially in countries with mature systems, such as those studied here. A review of the positions of the ILO, World Bank and OECD can be found in Queisser (2000). The Geneva Association has long performed a useful role through its emphasis on employment as the "fourth pillar" of the system. However, for the reasons given, it might be better to drop concepts of a fixed number of pillars in the OECD world.

7. For example, in a fiscal discussion, the various elements of the system could be described using the public versus private dichotomy. If the subject of the discussion were risk, then the elements of the system could be analysed using, among others, the defined-benefit versus defined-contribution terminology. In some applications, the advanced-funded versus pay-as-you-go taxonomy is likely to be the most useful – with the advance-funded elements coming from any of the three traditional tiers (advance-funded public reserves, advance-funded occupational plans and individual savings accounts). In other words, there appears to be no necessity for trying to force an entire programme into a single slot for all time and for all applications.

8. Active ageing reforms were assessed in OECD (2000*a*), which described recent reforms in the 29 OECD countries. Sometimes the phrase is used in a comprehensive fashion to encompass both the social and economic policy implications of people's social and economic behaviour as they grow older, including with regards to the labour force. In other cases, it is used in a more limited context to refer to volunteer activities or health, including older people's physical well-being.

9. Past policy has tended to make a sharp distinction between work and retirement. It has created a sharp boundary between pensions and the many other resources that support people during the transition to retirement and through later years. Policy has not usually examined the economic and social contributions of older people, and their economic and social well-being, in an integrated way. It is only quite recently that there has been a major interest in the determinants of retirement decisions and how these might be influenced by policy.

10. Official projections, even those based on relatively stable demographic patterns, have been notoriously inaccurate in hindsight. In 1996, the Canadian authorities issued a document to open public consultations on

possible reforms to the Canada Pension Plan (CPP) that started with an example that illustrates both the use of projections for planning and consultation, and the limits of any analysis that attempts to address the very long run. The example showed that, in 1966 when the plan was first introduced, the projected contribution rate in 2030 was 5.5% of contributory earnings. Some 30 years later, in 1996, the projected costs for 2030 were 14.2% of contributory earnings – a seemingly staggering increase in the estimated costs. (Subsequent reforms have reduced the contributory rate in 2030 to 9.9%.) The revisions primarily came about as a result of assumptions used in measurement – mainly in projecting the demographic and economic situation, but also the incidence and duration of disability. These factors alone caused the CPP contribution rate to increase by 6.3 points – more than the originally projected total contribution rate of 5.5. Real changes to the programme had a much smaller effect – resulting in only a 2.4 point increase.

11. A much-anticipated report (National Academy of Sciences, forthcoming) on information to support ageing policy research is scheduled for publication. Prepared by scientists who have deep familiarity with the new American longitudinal data, it should help frame national statistical agendas in this area.

BIBLIOGRAPHY

AMERICAN ASSOCIATION OF RETIRED PEOPLE (1999),
"Baby-boomers Envision Their Retirement: An AARP Segmentation Analysis", Roper Starch, *http://research.aarp.org/econ/boomer_seg_toc.html*.

BACCARO, L. (2000),
"Negotiating Pension Reform with Unions: The Italian Experience in European Perspective", Paper presented at the 12th International Conference of Europeanists, Chicago, IL, 30 March-2 April.

BALDWIN, B. and P. LALIBERTÉ (1999),
"Income of Older Canadians: Amounts and Sources, 1773-1996", Research Paper 15, Canadian Labour Congress.

BANCA D'ITALIA (2000),
Fiscal Sustainability: Essays Presented at the Bank of Italy Workshop held in Perugia, 20-22 January.

BINSTOCK, R.H. (1998),
Health Care Costs and the Elderly, Century Foundation, New York.

BLÖNDAL, S. and S. SCARPETTA (1998),
"The Retirement Decision in OECD Countries", AWP 1.4, OECD, *http://www.oecd.org* (see theme "Ageing Society").

BÖRSCH-SUPAN, A. (1998),
"Retirement Income: Level, Risk and Substitution among Income Components", Ageing Working Paper No. 3.7, OECD, *http://www.oecd.org* (see theme "Ageing Society").

BURTLESS, G. and J. QUINN (2000),
"Retirement Trends and Policies to Encourage Work Among Older Americans", in P. Budetti, R. Burkhauser, J. Gregory and A. Hunt (eds.), *Ensuring Health and Income Security for an Ageing Workforce*, The W.E. Upjohn Institute for Employment Research, Kalamazoo, pp. 375-415.

CASEY, B. (1998),
"Incentives and Disincentives to Early and Late Retirement", OECD AWP 3.3, *http://www.oecd.org* (see theme "Ageing Society").

CASEY, B. and M. GOLD (2000),
"Social Partnership and Economic Performance", Edward Elgar Publishing Ltd.

CPB Netherlands Bureau for Economic Policy Analysis (2000),
"Ageing in the Netherlands", The Hague, August.

DANG, T-T., P. ANTOLIN and H. OXLEY (forthcoming),
"The Fiscal Implications of Ageing: Projections of Age-related Spending", OECD Economics Department Working Papers, Paris.

DISNEY, R.F. (2000),
"Notional Accounts as a Pension Reform Strategy: An Evaluation", Pension Reform Primer Series, Social Protection Discussion Paper No. 9928, World Bank, Washington, D.C.

DISNEY, R.F. and E.R. WHITEHOUSE (1999),
"Pension Plans and Retirement Decisions", Social Protection Discussion Paper No. 9924, World Bank, Washington, DC.

DISNEY, R., M. MIRA D'ERCOLE and P. SCHERER (1998),
"Resources During Retirement", *http://www.oecd.org* (see theme "Ageing Society").

GAUTHIER, A.H. and T. SMEEDING (2000),
"Time Use at Older Ages: Cross-national Differences", *http://www.oecd.org* (see theme "Ageing Society").

GAUTHIER, A.H. and T. SMEEDING (2001),
"Historical Trends in the Patterns of Time Use of Older Adults", *http://www.oecd.org* (see theme "Ageing Society").

GILLION, C. (2000),
"The Development and Reform of Social Security Pensions: The Approach of the International Labour Office", International Social Security Review, 1/2000, Vol. 53.

GILLION, C., J. TURNER, C. BAILEY and D. LATULIPPE (2000),
Social Security Pensions: Development and Reform, International Labour Office, Geneva.

GOULD, R. and L. SAURAMA (1999),
"The Finnish Case of Ageing and Work", mimeo, The Central Pension Security Institute, Helsinki.

GRUBER, J. and D.A. WISE (1999),
"Social Security and Retirement around the World", University of Chicago Press, Chicago.

GRUBER, J. and P. ORSZAG (2000),
"Does the Social Security Earnings Test Affect Labour Supply and Benefit Receipt?", CRR WP 2000-07.

GRUBER, J. and D.A. WISE (2001),
"An International Perspective on Policies for an Ageing Society", NBER Working Paper 8103, *http://www.nber.org/papers/w8103*.

GUSTMAN, A.L. and T.L. STEINMEIER (2001),
"Retirement and Wealth", NBER Working Paper Series No. 8229, *http//:www.nber.org/papers/w8229*.

HICKS, P. (2001),
"Public Support for Retirement Income Reform", OECD, *http://www.oecd.org* (see theme "Ageing Society").

HOLZMANN, R. (2000),
"The World Bank Approach to Pension Reform", International Social Security Review, 1/2000, Vol. 53.

HOLZMANN, R. and J. STIGLITZ (2001),
New Ideas about Old Age Security, World Bank, Washington.

ILMARINEN, J. (1999),
"Ageing Workers in the European Union", Finnish Institute of Occupational Health.

JACKSON, W.A. (1998),
"The Political Economy of Population Ageing", Edward Elgar Publishing Ltd.

JACOBS, L.R. and R.Y. SHAPIRO (1998),
"Myths and Misunderstandings about Public Opinion. Towards Social Security: Knowledge, Support and Reformism", *http://www.polisci.umn.edu/faculty/ljacobs/myths/index.html*.

JAMES, E., J. SMALHOUT and D. VITTAS (2001),
"Administrative Costs and the Organization of Individual Account Systems: A Comparative Perspective", in Holzmann and Stiglitz (2001).

JOHNSON, P.G. (1998),
Older Getting Wiser, Institute of Chartered Accountants in Australia, Sydney.

KINGSTON, E.R. and Y. ARSENAULT (2000),
"The Diversity of Risk among Age 62 Retired Worker Beneficiaries", CRP WP 2000-8, Centre for Retirement Research, *http://www.bc.edu/crr*.

LATULIPPE, D. and J. TURNER (2000),
"Partial Retirement and Pension Policy in Industrialized Countries", *International Labour Review*, Vol. 139, No. 2.

MCHALE, J. (1999),
"The Risk of Social Security Benefit Rule Changes: Some International Evidence", Working Paper No. 7031, National Bureau of Economic Research, Cambridge, Mass.

MURTHI, M., J.M. ORSZAG and P.R. ORSZAG (2001),
"Administrative Costs under a Decentralized Approach to Individual Accounts: Lessons from the United Kingdom", in Holzmann and Stiglitz (2001).

MYLES, J. (forthcoming),
"The Maturation of Canada's Retirement Income System: Income Levels, Income Inequality and Low Income Among the Elderly", in *Canadian Journal on Aging*.

NATIONAL ACADEMY OF SCIENCES (forthcoming),
"Preparing for an Aging World: The Case for Cross-National Research".

NEUMARK, D. (2001),
"Antidiscrimination Legislation in the United States", NBER Working Paper 8152, National Bureau of Economic Research Working Paper, Cambridge, *http://papers.nber.org/papers/W8152*.

OECD (1998a),
Maintaining Prosperity in an Ageing Society, Paris.

OECD (1998b),
Education Policy Analysis, Paris.

OECD (2000a),
Reforms for an Ageing Society, Paris.

OECD (2000b),
    Economic Survey – Finland, Paris.
OECD (2000c),
    Taxing Wages: 1999/2000, Paris.
OECD (2000d),
    OECD Economic Survey – Italy, Paris.
OECD (2000e),
    Private Pension Systems and Policy Issues, Private Pensions Series No. 1, Paris.
OECD (2000f),
    Private Pensions Systems: Administrative Costs and Reforms, Private Pensions Series No. 2, Paris.
OECD (2001a),
    Economic Outlook, No. 69, June, Paris.
OECD (2001b),
    Education Policy Analysis, Paris.
OECD (2001c), OECD 2000 Private Pensions Conference, Private Pensions Series No. 3, Paris.
OECD and STATISTICS CANADA (2000),
    Literacy in the Information Age, Paris and Ottawa.
OSWALD, C. (1999),
    "Altersteilzeit: Nur Frühpensionierung mit Vorlaaufzeit?", Zeitschrift für Sozialreform, Vol. 45, No. 3, pp. 199-221.
PRIME MINISTER'S CABINET SECRETARIAT, JAPAN (1998),
    Public Opinion Survey on Public Pension Scheme.
QUEISSER, M. (1998),
    The Second-generation Pension Reforms in Latin America, OECD Development Centre Studies, Paris.
QUEISSER, M. (2000),
    "Pension Reform and International Organisations: From Conflict to Convergence", International Social Security Review, 2/2000, Vol. 53.
QUINN, J.F. (1999),
    "Retirement Patterns and Bridge Jobs in the 1990s", EBRI Issue Brief, No. 206, Employee Benefit Research Institute, Washington.
RAINWATER, L. and T.M. SMEEDING (1997),
    "Demography or Income Packaging: What Explains the Income Distribution of The Netherlands?", LIS Working Paper, No. 169.
REYNAUD, E. (2000),
    "Social Dialogue and Pension Reform", ILO.
RIX, S. (1999),
    "Social Security Reform: Rethinking Retirement Age Policy – A Look at Raising Social Security's Retirement Age", AARP Public Policy Institute, Washington, http://research.aarp.org/econ/ib40_age_policy.html.
SCHERER, P. (2001),
    "Age of Withdrawal from the Labour Force in OECD Countries", OECD, http://www.oecd.org (see theme "Ageing Society").
SMITH, T.W. (2000a),
    "A Cross-national Comparison on Attitudes towards Work by Age and Labor Force Status", National Opinion Research Center, University of Chicago, http://www.oecd.org (see theme "Ageing Society").
SMITH, T.W. (2000b),
    "Public Support for Government Benefits for the Elderly Across Countries and Time", National Opinion Research Center, University of Chicago, http://www.oecd.org (see theme "Ageing Society").
STATISTICS CANADA (2001),
    "The Assets and Debts of Canadians: An Overview of the Results of the Survey of Financial Security".
SWAIM, P. and A. GREY (1998),
    "Work-force ageing", OECD AWP 4.3, http://www.oecd.org (see theme "Ageing Society").
TAMBOURI, G. (1999),
    "Motivation, Purpose and Process in Pension Reform", International Social Security Review, No. 52.
THOMPSON, L. (1998),
    "Older and Wiser: The Economics of Public Pensions", The Urban Institute Press, Washington.
US Bureau of Labor (1997),
    Employee Benefit Survey.

UK Government Actuary's Department (1999),
"National Insurance Fund – Long-term Financial Estimates", Report by the Government Actuary on the Quinquennial Review for the period ending 5 April 1995 under Section 166 of the Social Security Administration Act 1992 (Cm 4406), The Stationary Office.

UK Office of Fair Trading (1997),
"The Director General's Inquiry into Pensions", Vol. 2, Research undertaken by the OFT for the Pensions Inquiry Consumer Survey.

VISCO, I. (2001a),
"Paying for Pensions: How Important is Economic Growth?", Paper presented to the CSIS Conference, "Managing the global ageing initiative", Zurich 22-24 January, http://www.csis.org/gai/Zurich/speeches/visco.pdf.

VISCO, I. (2001b),
"Ageing Populations: Economic Issues and Policy Challenges", Paper presented to Kiel Week Conference, Kiel, 18-19 June.

WADA, Y. and M. KIMURA (1998),
"Poverty in Post-war Japan: Estimates based on Household Consumption Data", *The Quarterly of Social Security Research (Kikan Shakai Hosho Kenkyu)*, Vol. 34, No. 1, pp. 90-102 (in Japanese).

WALKER, A. (1999),
"Attitudes to Population Ageing in Europe: A Comparison of the 1992 and 1999 Eurobarometer Surveys", http://www.shef.ac.uk/uni/academic/R-Z/socst/staff/staff_page_elements/a_walker/attitudes.pdf.

WALKER, A. and G. NAEGELE (1999),
"The Politics of Old Age in Europe", OU Press, Buckingham.

WHITEHOUSE, E. (2000),
"Administrative Charges for Funded Pensions: An International Comparison and Assessment", Pension Reform Primer Series, Social Protection Discussion Paper No. 0016.

WHITEHOUSE, E. (2001),
"Modelling the Rules of Public and Occupational Pensions in Nine OECD Countries", http://www.oecd.org (see theme "Ageing Society").

WORLD BANK (1995),
Averting the Old-age Crisis: Policies to Protect the Old and Promote Growth, Oxford University Press, Oxford.

WORLD BANK (1999),
"Can Pension Reform Reverse the Trend to Earlier Retirement", Pension Reform Primer Series, World Bank, Washington, http://www.worldbank.org/pensions.

YAMADA, A. (2001),
"The Evolving Retirement Income Package: Trends in Adequacy and Equality in Nine OECD Countries", OECD, http://www.oecd.org (see theme "Ageing Society").

YAMADA, A. and B.H. CASEY (2001),
"Getting Older, Getting Poorer? A Study of the Earnings, Pensions, Assets and Living Arrangements of Older People in Nine Countries", OECD, http://www.oecd.org (see theme "Ageing Society").

ANNEXES

Annex I

MAIN FEATURES OF THE RETIREMENT INCOME SYSTEMS IN THE NINE COUNTRIES

	Pensions and public transfers that apply to people aged 65 and over	*Typical patterns among people under age 65*
Canada	Flat-rate public pension, topped-up with an income-tested supplement, plus earnings-related public pension. Occupational and individual private pensions play a large role.	Work begins to decrease after age 60. Compared with other countries, there are more pensioners who also work and more people on unemployment benefits. Regular (non-working) pensioners become the norm only after age 65.
Finland	Basic pension guarantee, tested against pension incomes only, statutory earnings-related pillar with public/private management at occupational level plus some individual private plans.	Early-retirement, disability and special unemployment pensions for older workers are important for early exit from the labour market. Work drops off after age 55 and by age 60-64 almost everyone is a regular (non-working) pensioner.
Germany	Public earnings-related pension system with some redistributive elements, supported by municipally-financed and administered general social assistance. Some private occupational and personal plans, supported by means-tested social assistance (for a very small number of older people).	Early-retirement and disability programmes are important. Work drops off after age 60 and the majority of people are regular (non-working) pensioners by age 60-64.
Italy	Old system: public earnings-related defined-benefit system with minimum pension, some occupational and few personal pension schemes. New system: notional defined-contribution pension without minimum pension, supported by social assistance. Only defined-contribution occupational and personal pension schemes.	Early retirement was important under the old system. Until the mid-1990s seniority pensions were a common pathway to retirement at early ages. Work started dropping off after age 50 and steadily after age 55. A significant number of people are regular (non-working) pensioners by age 55-59, and a considerable majority are in this category by age 60-64. New system: early retirement possible starting at age 57 but with actuarial adjustment of benefits.
Japan	Contributory public basic pension with lower-earners exempt from contributions, separate basic scheme for non-employed persons, earnings-related scheme with possibility of opting-out for employers plus retirement lump-sum schemes and occupational pensions, supported by (nationally-financed but locally-administered) means-tested social assistance.	Early-retirement and disability programmes are unimportant. Indeed, work does not start to drop off until after 60, and combinations of work and pension are much more common than in the other countries.
Netherlands	Flat-rate public pension based on residence plus quasi-compulsory private occupational plans, most of which are defined-benefit.	Disability arrangements and special unemployment schemes have been important – much more so than in other countries. Regular public pensions start at the age of 65 and cannot be advanced. Work starts to drop off after age 55 (but with somewhat later retirement in recent years).
Sweden	Old system: flat-rate public pension plus earnings-related pension, plus occupational plans. New system: notional defined-contribution pension with a minimum pension guarantee for residents, mandatory funded individual accounts component, plus quasi-mandatory occupational pensions.	Disability benefits and partial pensions are important. Work starts to drop off after age 60 and combinations of work and pension are more common than in other countries. However, partial pension arrangements, which are partly responsible, are being phased out. Regular pensioners (not working) become the norm only after age 65.

© OECD 2001

	Pensions and public transfers that apply to people aged 65 and over	*Typical patterns among people under age 65*
United Kingdom	Flat-rate contributory basic pension plus public earnings-related pension with possibility of contracting-out to occupational or personal pensions. Supported by a national means-tested minimum income guarantee.	Disability benefits have been an important early-retirement route. Work starts falling off gradually after age 50, but mainly after 60. Combining work and receipt of a pension is relatively common. About half of those aged 60-64 are regular pensioners.
United States	Earnings-related public pension with redistributive component, minimum pension guarantee for persons with full contribution careers. Supported by federally-financed and administered means-tested social assistance for people of pension age; occupational and personal pensions are important.	Work begins to fall off gradually after the age of 55, but only significantly after the age of 60. There are more people combining work and pensions than average (including after age 65). Regular (non-working) pensioners are a minority among those aged 60-64.

Annex II
RETIREMENT INCENTIVES

The proportion of earnings "replaced" by the pension benefit, the "replacement rate", is the standard measure to assess incentives to retire. Chapter 3 of this report discusses the structure of the pension systems in the nine countries by showing how the replacement rate varies with income. However, the modelling in that chapter assumes that all persons do in fact retire at the "standard" retirement age for the country in question.

In most pension systems that are based on contributions, the pension payable will increase ("accrue") for additional years of work. This means that anyone retiring before the "standard" age will normally receive a lower pension. However, the fact that the pension increases with years of work does not necessarily mean that the system does not encourage early retirement.

In analysing the incentives to retire offered by the pension system, another measure is also relevant. This is accumulated pension wealth. Pension wealth is the equivalent of the sum required today to purchase the stream of income accorded by the pension system from the day the pension is drawn until death. In other words, it is the net present value of all the future pension payments that the eligible person can expect to receive. Clearly, pension wealth is affected not only by the size of the pension, but also by the point of retirement, since that determines over how many years the income stream is paid.

For each additional year worked without drawing a pension, two countervailing factors will affect pension wealth. One factor is that deferring the pension one year *reduces* total pension wealth by the amount that would have been received during that year, to which should be added the cost of pension contributions payable during that same year. The other factor is the affect of accrual: if the replacement rate is higher after an additional year of work, this will increase pension payments for all the years the pension is received, thus *increasing* pension wealth.

A pension scheme is "actuarially neutral" if these two effects exactly balance each other: the loss in pension wealth due to not receiving a pension and paying an extra year's contributions equals the (present) value of the stream of increased benefits. However, most pension systems are not neutral in this sense. If benefits increase at too slow a rate (or if contribution rates are high), pension wealth will fall if retirement is deferred another year. One way to interpret this is that a person who nonetheless does work another year pays an implicit tax equal to the loss of pension wealth. For instance, taking the case of a 64-year-old in Finland, for whom the loss of pension wealth would be 60 per cent of earnings. If that person works another year, his or her overall reward will be only 40 per cent of the wages received.

Occupational pension schemes have similar characteristics: that is, their structure can provide a strong incentive to cease work and start to receive a pension at a relatively early age. Not taking retirement can easily result in a loss of pension wealth. However, this could be overcome by leaving the pensioned job and taking a new job, even if that job pays a substantially lower wage. For a fuller understanding of whether someone would respond to a fall in pension wealth by retiring, it would be important to look at whether the person was likely to obtain income from an alternative source, at the level of that alternative income, and at the length of time he or she would enjoy it. In countries such as Japan, where employment opportunities are available for older workers, it is common to combine receipt of a public pension with low wage employment.

All other things being equal, defined-contribution pension systems contain no incentives to retire early or late: they are actuarially neutral by definition. Pension contributions are used to build up a savings account upon which interest is earned (or, if invested in equities, in which dividends are paid and where the value of the equities themselves is presumed to rise). The sum accumulated is used at retirement to buy an annuity. It is the same as pension wealth, and the annuity is the stream of pension payments from retirement until death.

Defined-benefit systems are often not actuarial neutral even though many make reductions if the pension is taken early and/or enhancements if it is taken late. Table A gives examples of such reductions and enhancements.

Furthermore, many defined-benefit pension systems contain special provisions that permit benefits to be taken early under certain conditions, in particular in case of long-term unemployment or disability. In these circumstances, the pension is normally not subject to any actuarial reduction. However, assuming that early liquidation means that no more contributions are made and fewer years are accrued, the affected person might still receive lower benefits. In the case of disability-induced early retirement, this is not common, as frequently at least some, if not all, lost years

© OECD 2001

Table A. **Retirement age and "actuarial" reduction and enhancement**

	System	Statutory retirement age[a]	Actuarial reduction rate for early retirement (%)	Actuarial enhancement rate for later retirement (%)
Canada	Current	65	6	6
Finland	Current	65	4.8	12
Germany	Current	65	3.6	6
Italy	Old	65/60	No reduction with at least 35 years contributions; reduced by accrual rate otherwise	Only extra years' accrual
	New (Dini)	57 to 65	Retirement permitted at 57, but with "full" actuarial adjustment	No adjustment after 65
Japan	Current	65	Earnings related at 60 and special unreduced equivalent of basic pension if not working at all	12% until 67 26% from 67 onwards
	New	65	No pension payable before 65	8.4 until 67 16.8 from 67 onwards
Netherlands	Current	65	No early liquidation possible for public or occupational pension	No enhancement for late retirement
Sweden	New	65	6	8
United Kingdom	Current	65/60	No early liquidation possible for public pension	8
United States	Current	65	6.7	5
	New	67	6.7	8

a) Data for retirement age refer respectively to men and women. For Italy, 57 to 65 refer to both genders.
Source: OECD Secretariat.

are credited. In some countries, special early pensions for long-term unemployed people or disabled people are paid for out of schemes that are separate from the old-age pension system. However, such schemes are, effectively, integrated with the old-age system so that, at normal pension age, the affected person makes the transition from one benefit to another. In such cases, there is a positive replacement rate, and pension wealth can be understood as the net present value of the stream of income from both the old-age pension system and the pre-pension system.

In the analysis that follows, alternative income sources are not considered. However, to give a degree of standardisation to the analysis, account is taken not only of income and wealth associated with the public old-age pension system in the nine countries, but also of complementary, occupational pensions where these both provide recipients with a substantial share of retirement income and are available to a majority of the older working population. Table B shows, for each of the nine countries, the various parts of the systems that are examined.

Table B. **Parts of the pension system considered**

Canada	Basic (OAS) and supplementary (CPP/QPP) state pension
Finland	Basic and earnings-related state pension
Germany	State earnings-related pension
Italy	State earnings-related pension
Japan	Basic and earnings-related state pension
Netherlands	State pension plus defined-benefit occupational pension
Sweden	Earnings/contributions related state pension
United Kingdom	State basic and earnings-related pension
United States	Social security age pension

Source: OECD Secretariat.

Illustrations

In order to show the extent to which the systems do or do not provide incentives to retire early or late, the situation of a full-career worker – one who had started making contributions at the earliest possible age, generally 20 – has been taken. The situation of that person at each year from the age of 55 to 69 is then analysed. The analysis shows the effect of working one additional year a) on replacement income and b) on pension wealth.

Because most public pension systems contain some element of progressivity, separate calculations are necessary for people with different levels of earnings. At low levels, benefits will be determined by a "social minimum", so that they do not increase with an additional year of work; in this case, the replacement rate and pension wealth will fall with each year of deferment. At high levels, a "ceiling" on the benefit may have been reached, so that once again the replacement rate and pension wealth will fall with each year of deferment. For any given age, there is likely therefore to be a "reverse U" relation between current income and the loss of pension wealth from working one year longer.

An illustrative representation of the calculations is provided in Chart A. The chart can be understood as follows. The heavy line shows the pension replacement rate. Note that it is zero until the age at which a reduced pension can be drawn – here 62 – is reached. Deferring the pension after 62 will lead to a higher benefit being paid, both because more years are accrued and because, for each year between 62 and 65 the pension is increased as the early retirement "penalty" is reduced. After age 65 the replacement rate continues to rise (in this example, there is no age ceiling on accruals) but at a lower rate.

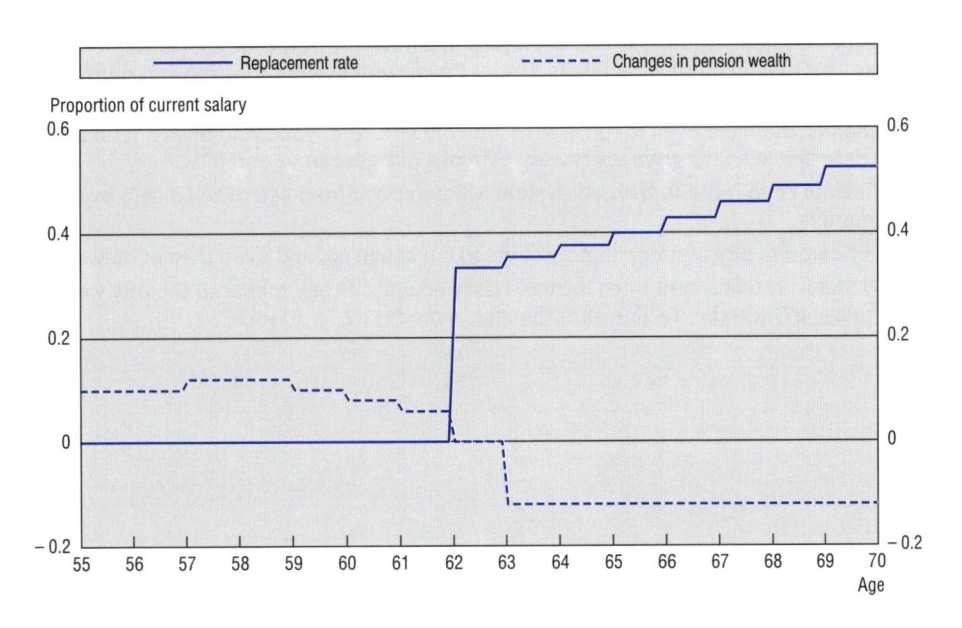

Chart A. **Replacement rate and changes in pension wealth**

Source: OECD Secretariat calculations.

The dotted line shows the change in pension wealth measured as a proportion of current income. In the initial years, an additional year of working adds to pension wealth. The amount of that increase varies over time. It becomes larger when the person reaches 57 and then becomes smaller again upon reaching 59. At age 63 there is no further increase in pension wealth, and each year of working after that age results in a fall in pension wealth. This is depicted by the dotted line passing below the horizontal axis. In this example, the early retirement penalty is not sufficient to make the reduction "actuarially neutral". If the system were fully neutral, once the age of entitlement to benefits (62) had been reached the dotted line would remain on the horizontal axis, since the age of retirement would have no impact on pension wealth.

The examples that follow show replacement rates and pension wealth changes resulting from working an additional year. For each country there are three sets of graphs for varying proportions of earnings of the average production worker (half, one and 2.5). Since taxation systems are usually progressive and therefore impact differently on different income levels, the calculations are presented on a net basis, that is, they show the combined effects of the benefit schedule and the tax system on replacement rates and pension wealth. In doing so, they assume that no income other than pension income is received.

Implications of the results

In Chart B, the greater the divergence of the "change in pension wealth" from the horizontal axis, the greater the incentive not to retire (if the line is above the axis) or to retire (if the line is below the axis). In general, because of the impact of the flat-rate component of pension systems (see Chapter 3) the incentive to retire early is greatest for those with low incomes.

The chart illustrates the trade-off between high income security (*i.e.* high replacement rates) and the incentive to retire: if replacement rates are high at young ages, it is mathematically impossible for them to increase fast enough to preclude retirement incentives – unless they are allowed to increase close to (or above) 100% of current salary.

- In Canada, replacement rates remain broadly constant from 65 onwards, which means the implied tax on an additional year's work increases for each additional year. This implied tax is higher for low-income people because they have greater replacement rates.
- In Finland, replacement rates increase only slightly beyond 60, to reach a maximum at around 63 (when the maximum accrual is reached). Pension wealth falls at this age too. Low-income people have strong incentives to retire earlier.
- In Germany, pension wealth starts to fall one or two years after the age (63) when the pension can be drawn.
- In Italy, the "full" actuarial reduction envisioned in the new system does not appear to fully compensate for tax effects, and pension wealth will start to fall at 57 (on a before-tax basis, not shown, this fall only occurs at age 59 or 60).
- In Japan, the new system (shown) will concentrate incentives to retire at 65: pension wealth continues to increase up to that age for all income levels. Under the current system (not shown), pension wealth starts to decline at 60-61, except for low-income earners.
- In the Netherlands, the incentives to retire at 60 are very strong: anyone who does not take up the pension at that age will experience an effective tax rate on earnings of between 62 and 80%.
- In Sweden, incentives to retire in the new system will be strong from age 61 to 62, and overwhelmingly so for low-income earners.
- In the United Kingdom, pension wealth only starts to fall at age 66, and even then at only a moderate rate.
- In the United States, replacement rates increase fast enough with age for social security wealth to continue to increase up to age 67, and the decline after that age is moderate.

Annex II

Chart B. **Replacement rates and changes in pension wealth for working an extra year**
Panel A. Earnings level = 50% APW

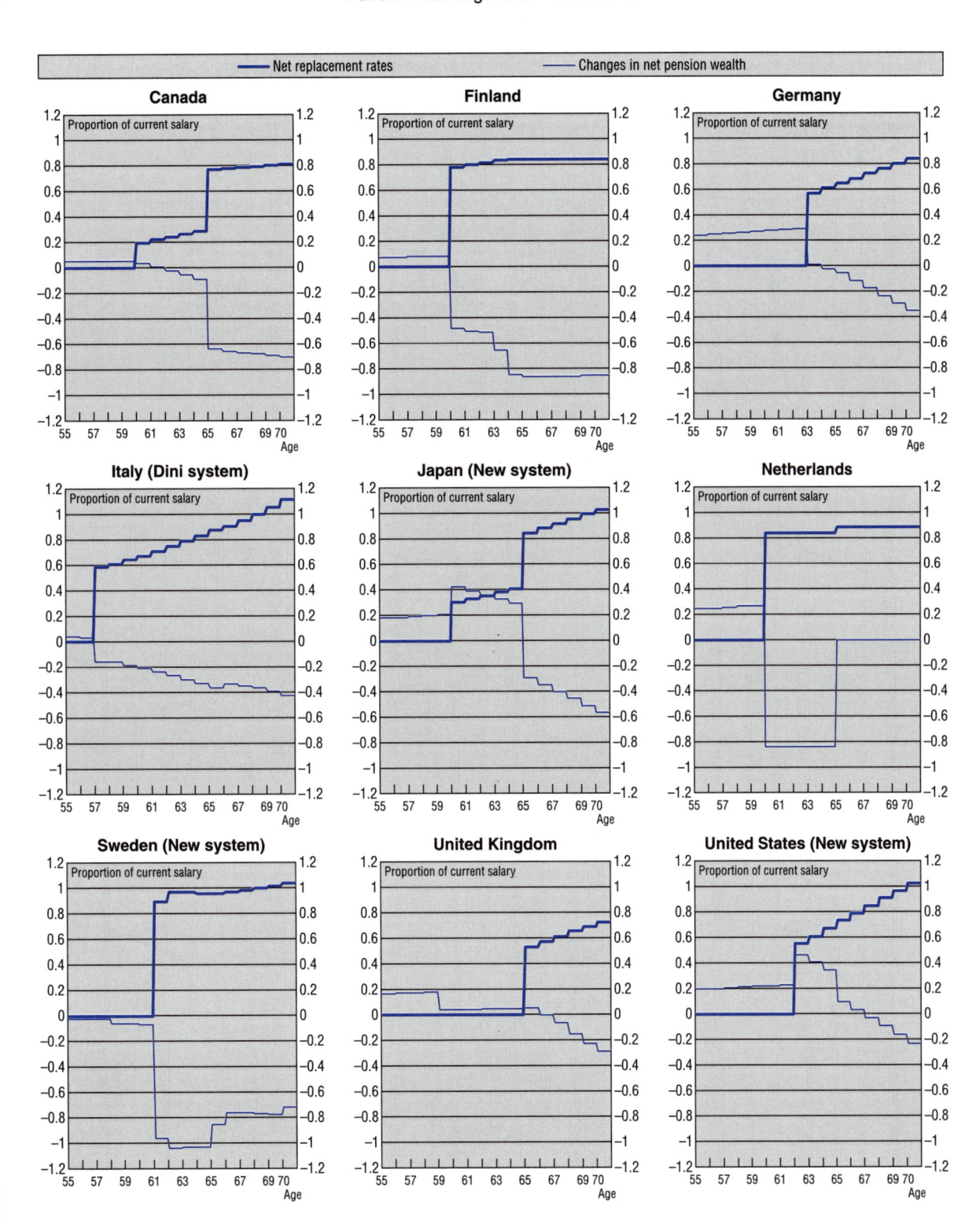

Source: OECD Secretariat calculations.

Ageing and Income

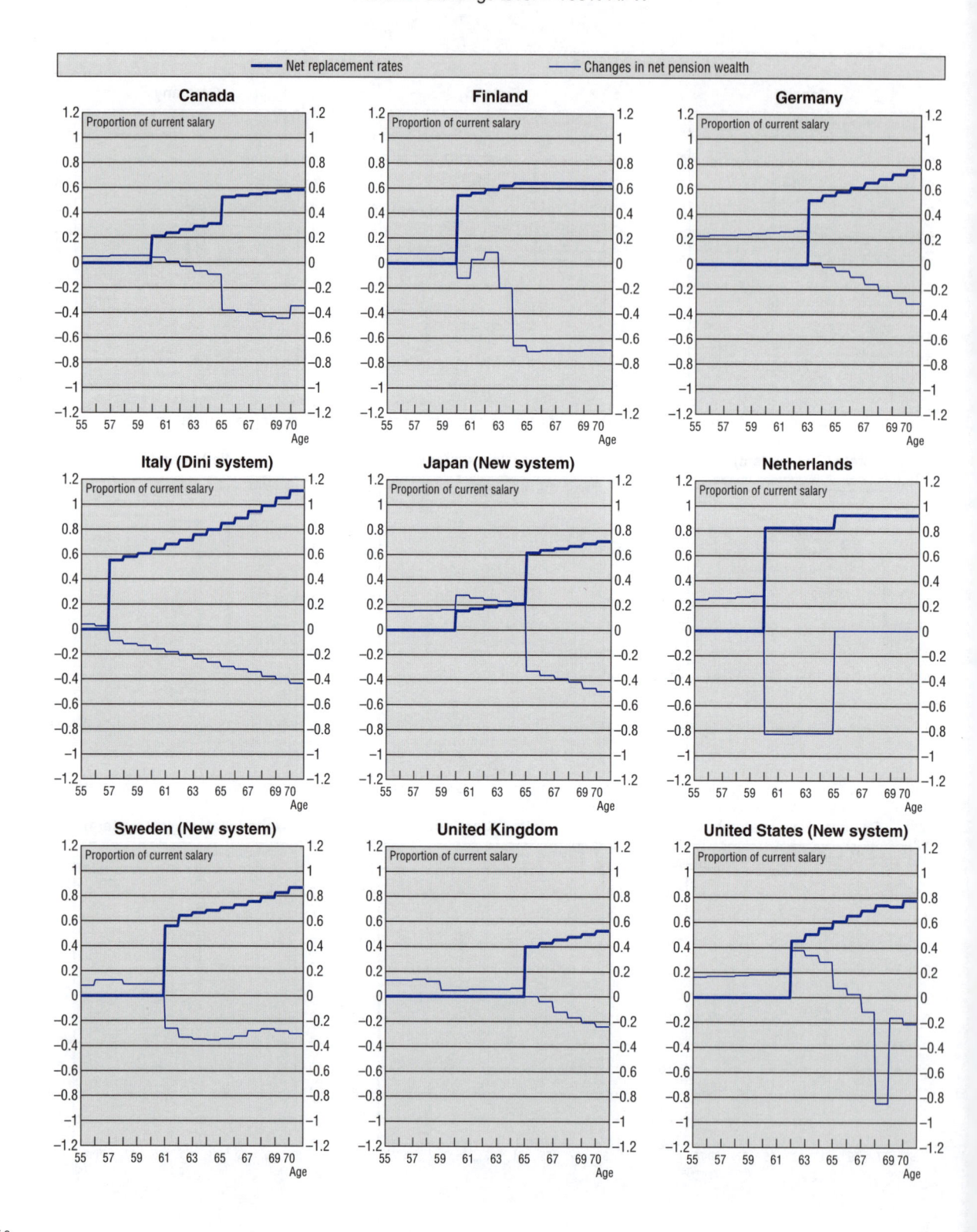

Chart B. **Replacement rates and changes in pension wealth for working an extra year** *(cont.)*
Panel B. Earnings level = 100% APW

— Net replacement rates   — Changes in net pension wealth

Source: OECD Secretariat calculations.

Annex II

Chart B. **Replacement rates and changes in pension wealth for working an extra year** *(cont.)*
Panel C. Earnings level = 200% APW

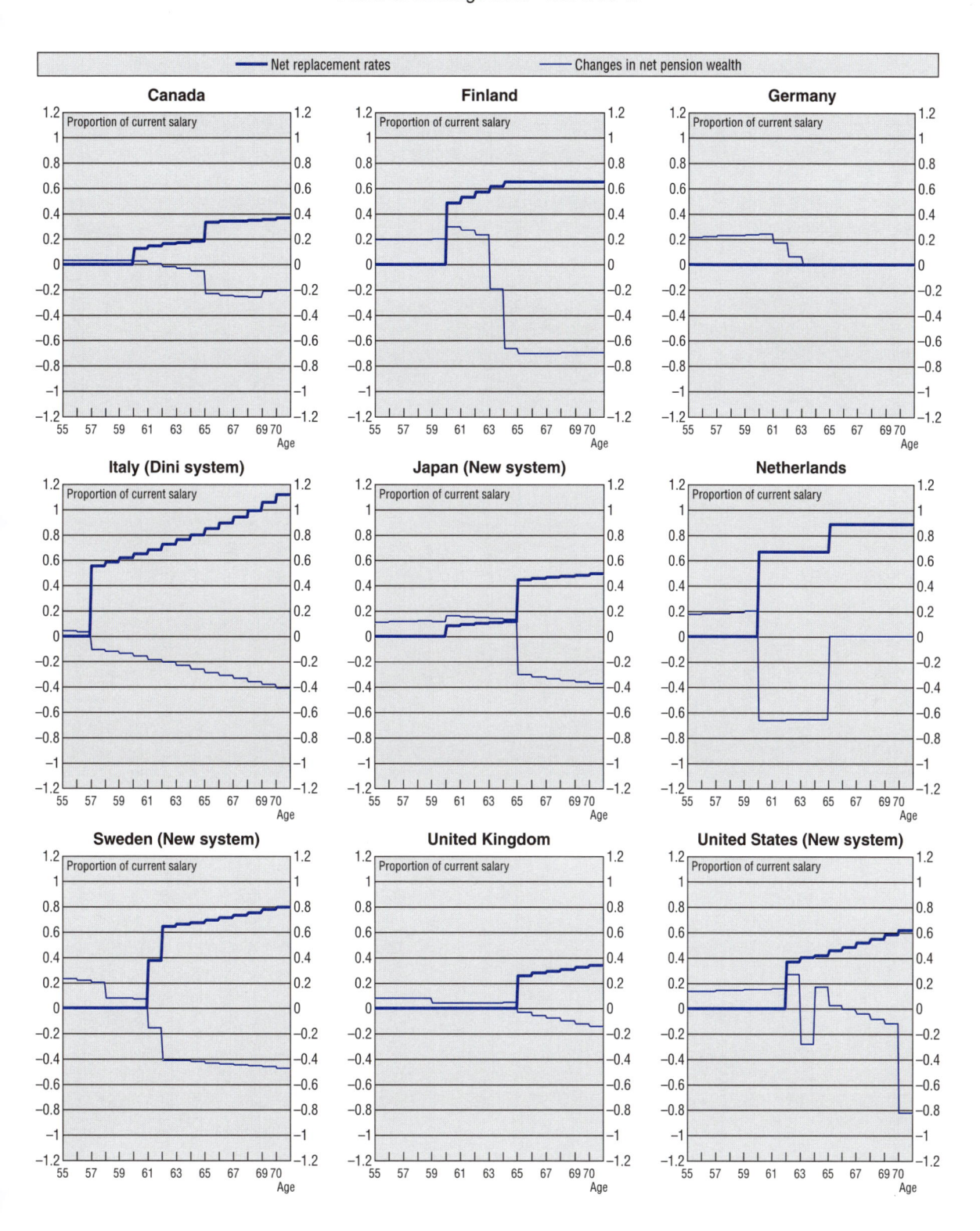

— Net replacement rates   — Changes in net pension wealth

Source: OECD Secretariat calculations.

© OECD 2001

Annex III
STATISTICAL ANNEX

Table A.1. **Selected demographic estimates and projections, 2000 and 2030**

	Life expectancy at birth		Percentage of the population aged 65 and over	Percentage of the population aged 80+	Traditional old age dependency ratio[a]
	Men	Women			
Canada					
2000	76.3	82.1	12.8	3.1	18.7
2030	79.0	84.7	22.6	5.9	37.3
Finland					
2000	73.5	81.0	14.9	3.4	22.2
2030	78.2	84.6	25.3	7.7	43.5
Germany					
2000	74.3	80.5	16.4	3.6	24.0
2030	77.7	83.3	26.1	6.8	43.3
Italy					
2000	75.4	81.5	18.2	4.0	26.9
2030	78.4	84.1	29.1	8.5	49.1
Japan					
2000	77.0	83.1	17.1	3.7	25.0
2030	79.4	85.5	27.3	10.2	46.0
Netherlands					
2000	75.3	80.9	13.8	3.3	20.2
2030	78.1	83.7	25.6	6.9	43.0
Sweden					
2000	76.7	81.2	17.4	5.0	27.1
2030	80.0	84.5	25.5	8.4	43.4
United Kingdom					
2000	74.9	80.2	16.0	4.2	24.6
2030	78.0	83.2	23.1	6.5	38.3
United States					
2000	73.8	80.3	12.5	3.3	19.0
2030	77.5	83.2	20.6	5.1	33.6
Unweighted average					
2000	75.2	81.2	15.4	3.7	23.1
2030	78.5	84.1	25.0	7.4	42.0

a) Ratio of population aged 65 and over to population aged 16 to 64.
Source: OECD Secretariat estimates.

Table A.2. **Life expectancy at ages 60 and 65, 1998**[a]

	At age 60 Men	At age 60 Women	At age 65 Men	At age 65 Women
Canada	20.0	24.2	16.3	20.1
Finland	18.6	23.5	15.2	19.3
Germany	19.0	23.3	15.3	19.0
Italy	19.6	24.3	15.8	20.2
Japan	21.0	26.4	17.1	22.0
Netherlands	18.5	23.0	14.7	18.8
Sweden	20.1	24.3	16.5	19.9
United Kingdom	18.8	22.6	15.0	18.5
United States	19.6	23.1	16.0	19.1
Unweighted average	19.5	23.9	15.8	19.7

a) 1997 for Canada, Italy and the United Kingdom.
Source: OECD Health Data.

Table A.3. **Selected employment indicators, 2000 and three scenarios[a] in 2030**

	Percentage growth in employment compared with 2000		Percentage of the population that is employed	Ratio of retirees to employees	Number of employees for each retiree
	Men	Women			
Canada					
2000	–	–	48.7	34.7	2.9
2030 – S1	20.9	23.9	50.2	49.7	2.0
2030 – S2	9.0	12.6	45.5	61.5	1.6
2030 – S3	2.0	1.4	41.8	71.4	1.4
Finland					
2000	–	–	45.7	48.2	2.1
2030 – S1	2.6	3.0	45.9	65.5	1.5
2030 – S2	–7.7	–6.4	41.5	78.9	1.3
2030 – S3	–12.6	–15.8	38.4	89.0	1.1
Germany					
2000	–	–	46.1	51.1	2.0
2030 – S1	3.1	7.2	48.6	60.3	1.7
2030 – S2	–9.7	–2.5	43.3	76.1	1.3
2030 – S3	–15.6	–12.3	39.8	87.6	1.1
Italy					
2000	–	–	36.3	71.7	1.4
2030 – S1	–5.5	16.2	39.7	87.2	1.1
2030 – S2	–15.1	5.6	35.9	103.8	1.0
2030 – S3	–21.0	–4.9	32.9	118.3	0.8
Japan					
2000	–	–	51.3	36.1	2.8
2030 – S1	–4.2	3.8	55.0	42.3	2.4
2030 – S2	–13.0	–5.6	50.0	53.6	1.9
2030 – S3	–18.9	–15.0	45.9	63.9	1.6
Netherlands					
2000	–	–	49.4	41.2	2.4
2030 – S1	7.9	29.3	51.6	53.9	1.9
2030 – S2	–3.7	17.6	46.4	66.9	1.5
2030 – S3	–9.1	5.8	42.9	76.3	1.3
Sweden					
2000	–	–	47.6	43.3	2.3
2030 – S1	7.5	13.0	50.2	48.9	2.0
2030 – S2	–0.4	2.7	46.1	58.4	1.7
2030 – S3	–4.6	–7.6	42.9	66.2	1.5
United Kingdom					
2000	–	–	47.4	42.0	2.4
2030 – S1	2.6	20.0	49.2	50.4	2.0
2030 – S2	–5.6	9.1	45.0	60.3	1.7
2030 – S3	–10.0	–1.8	41.8	68.3	1.5
United States					
2000	–	–	49.3	30.7	3.3
2030 – S1	21.7	34.1	51.2	39.8	2.5
2030 – S2	14.4	21.9	47.4	47.1	2.1
2030 – S3	9.2	9.7	44.0	54.2	1.8
Unweighted average					
2000	–	–	46.8	44.3	2.4
2030 – S1	6.3	16.7	49.1	55.3	1.9
2030 – S2	–3.5	6.1	44.6	67.4	1.6
2030 – S3	–9.0	–4.5	41.1	77.2	1.4

a) See Section 5.2 in Chapter 5 for definitions of scenarios.
Source: OECD Secretariat estimates.

Table A.4. Employment/population ratios for older men
Percentages, 1983-1999

	Age	1983	1984	1985	1986	1987	1988	1989	1990	1991	1992	1993	1994	1995	1996	1997	1998	1999	Variation (in percentage points) 1992/1983	1999/1993
Canada	55 to 59	74	74	74	73	73	73	73	72	69	67	66	65	66	66	66	66	67	−7	2
	60 to 64	55	54	51	51	48	48	48	48	44	43	42	42	40	40	42	41	44	−12	1
Finland	55 to 59	61	60	59	60	57	56	58	62	58	52	49	48	46	50	50	51	54	−9	5
	60 to 64	39	36	36	34	31	29	29	30	29	25	22	21	22	23	23	23	23	−14	1
Germany	55 to 59	74	72	71	72	71	70	69	70	71	67	64	64	64	64	64	65	65	−7	1
	60 to 64	37	33	32	32	32	32	32	32	28	28	27	26	26	26	27	27	28	−9	1
Italy	55 to 59	71	69	68	67	68	66	64	66	66	61	62	59	55	55	52	51	52	−10	−10
	60 to 64	36	37	37	37	36	36	34	34	36	31	31	30	29	28	30	30	29	−5	−2
Japan	55 to 59	87	87	87	87	87	89	89	90	92	92	92	92	91	92	92	91	91	4	−2
	60 to 64	70	69	67	67	66	66	67	69	71	71	71	70	69	68	68	67	66	1	−4
Netherlands	55 to 59	65	..	64	..	62	63	64	64	61	61	60	59	58	59	62	65	67	−4	7
	60 to 64	34	..	29	..	28	25	22	22	22	21	21	21	20	20	21	24	27	−13	6
Sweden[a]	55 to 59	..	..	..	..	84	84	86	86	84	82	78	76	76	77	76	78	81	−2	3
	60 to 64	..	..	..	..	63	63	62	62	63	58	53	51	51	53	50	50	49	−4	−4
United Kingdom	55 to 59	76	74	75	73	71	73	73	75	74	69	66	67	66	68	69	69	70	−6	4
	60 to 64	52	51	50	49	49	49	50	49	49	47	45	45	45	45	48	46	47	−5	2
United States	55 to 59	76	76	76	75	77	77	77	77	75	75	74	74	75	75	76	76	76	−1	2
	60 to 64	54	53	53	53	53	52	53	54	52	51	51	50	51	52	53	54	53	−2	2
	65 to 69	25	24	24	24	25	25	25	25	24	25	24	26	26	26	27	27	28	0	3

.. Data not available.
a) 2000 instead of 1999. Variations are calculated on years 1992/1987 and 2000/1993.
Sources: National Labour Force Survey: Canada, Germany, Finland, Japan, Sweden and the United States; European Labour Force Survey: Italy, the Netherlands and the United Kingdom.

Table A.5. Employment/population ratios for older women
Percentages, 1983-1999

	Age	1983	1984	1985	1986	1987	1988	1989	1990	1991	1992	1993	1994	1995	1996	1997	1998	1999	Variation (in percentage points) 1992/1983	1999/1993
Canada	55 to 59	36	36	39	39	40	41	42	43	42	44	43	44	44	45	44	47	48	7	5
	60 to 64	23	23	22	22	23	23	21	23	22	22	22	23	22	21	23	24	25	-2	2
Finland	55 to 59	57	56	55	52	52	53	56	59	57	54	52	50	50	49	49	50	56	-3	5
	60 to 64	30	30	30	25	22	22	23	21	21	19	16	13	16	17	16	16	20	-11	4
Germany	55 to 59	37	35	34	34	34	34	34	35	37	36	37	37	40	42	43	44	44	0	8
	60 to 64	11	10	10	10	10	9	10	10	9	9	9	9	10	11	11	11	11	-2	3
Italy	55 to 59	19	19	19	20	19	20	19	19	21	17	19	19	19	20	21	22	22	-2	3
	60 to 64	9	11	10	9	10	10	9	10	10	8	8	8	7	8	8	7	8	-1	-1
Japan	55 to 59	50	50	50	49	50	50	51	53	55	55	56	55	56	57	57	57	57	5	1
	60 to 64	39	37	38	38	38	38	39	39	40	40	39	39	39	38	39	39	38	1	-1
Netherlands	55 to 59	17	..	18	..	21	22	21	23	22	25	26	27	28	29	32	30	32	8	6
	60 to 64	8	..	7	..	8	7	8	8	7	6	7	7	8	9	7	9	10	-1	3
Sweden[a]	55 to 59	..	..	..	..	77	78	77	78	78	77	75	75	73	74	75	75	76	0	1
	60 to 64	..	..	..	..	48	49	49	52	53	50	47	43	45	46	44	43	43	2	-4
United Kingdom	55 to 59	47	48	49	49	49	49	51	52	51	52	51	52	53	52	50	53	54	5	3
	60 to 64	20	20	18	18	18	19	22	22	23	23	24	25	25	25	26	23	24	3	1
United States	55 to 59	46	48	48	49	50	52	53	54	54	54	55	57	57	58	59	60	60	8	5
	60 to 64	32	32	32	32	32	33	35	35	34	35	36	36	37	37	39	38	38	3	2
	65 to 69	14	14	13	14	14	15	16	16	16	16	16	17	17	16	17	17	18	1	2

.. Data not available.
a) 2000 instead of 1999. Variations are calculated on years 1992/1987 and 2000/1993.
Sources: National Labour Force Survey: Canada, Germany, Finland, Japan, Sweden and the United States; European Labour Force Survey: Italy, the Netherlands and the United Kingdom.

Table A.6. **Self-employed, older age groups**
Percentages, 1999

	Men			Women		
	55-59	60-64	65+	55-59	60-64	65+
Finland						
% of employees	25.6	37.9	71.4	11.7	17.9	..
% of population	14.3	9.1	1.7	6.3	3.8	..
Germany						
% of employees	17.3	28.2	52.7	8.2	15.8	24.4
% of population	12.5	8.0	2.3	4.0	1.9	0.4
Italy						
% of employees	42.5	54.2	73.8	28.1	38.2	45.4
% of population	22.7	15.3	4.0	6.5	2.8	0.7
Netherlands						
% of employees	20.1	42.1	72.5	14.4	18.9	76.9
% of population	13.3	11.2	3.3	4.6	1.9	0.8
Sweden						
% of employees	17.7	25.5	60.9	7.5	6.3	..
% of population	13.3	12.7	4.2	5.4	2.7	..
United Kingdom						
% of employees	21.5	25.6	44.4	8.6	10.2	22.3
% of population	14.3	11.8	3.3	4.5	2.5	0.7

.. Data not currently available. Data for men aged 60-64 in Canada, Japan, and the United States are analysed in OECD (2000a).
Sources: Eurostat, national labour force surveys, and UN demographic database.

Table A.7. Disposable income of older age groups
Percentage of various working age groups, mid-70s, mid-80s and mid-90s[a]

	Canada mid-70s	Canada mid-80s	Canada mid-90s	Finland mid-70s	Finland mid-80s	Finland mid-90s	Germany mid-70s	Germany mid-80s	Germany mid-90s	Italy mid-70s	Italy mid-80s	Italy mid-90s	Japan mid-70s	Japan mid-80s	Japan mid-90s	Netherlands mid-70s	Netherlands mid-80s	Netherlands mid-90s	Sweden mid-70s	Sweden mid-80s	Sweden mid-90s	United Kingdom mid-70s	United Kingdom mid-80s	United Kingdom mid-90s	United States mid-70s	United States mid-80s	United States mid-90s
													Age 65-74 to....														
All ages	55	91	98	74	81	85	..	85	93	..	82	86	..	91	89	92	93	90	77	87	95	73	74	80	90	99	98
18-25	63	89	99	69	83	97	..	86	97	..	77	82	..	85	86	84	89	93	93	117	160	62	65	72	87	100	106
26-40	49	88	98	67	78	84	..	83	93	..	77	81	..	95	90	93	91	86	70	83	96	73	70	75	86	95	97
41-50	51	78	87	68	70	76	..	75	78	..	78	78	..	85	82	86	85	79	65	74	80	62	60	65	77	84	84
51-65	69	82	87	80	78	79	..	78	84	..	76	79	..	82	80	81	83	81	71	76	76	67	70	74	76	82	80
													Age 75+ to....														
All ages	49	84	94	70	74	78	..	81	78	..	78	82	..	92	87	93	84	79	60	68	78	71	72	74	78	84	82
18-25	56	83	95	66	76	89	..	82	81	..	73	79	..	86	84	84	80	82	72	92	130	60	64	67	75	86	88
26-40	44	82	94	64	72	77	..	79	78	..	73	78	..	96	88	93	82	76	54	65	78	70	69	70	75	81	80
41-50	46	72	83	65	64	69	..	72	65	..	74	75	..	86	80	86	77	69	50	58	65	59	58	60	67	72	69
51-65	62	76	83	76	72	72	..	74	71	..	72	75	..	83	78	82	75	71	55	60	62	65	69	69	66	70	66

.. Data not available.
a) Disposable income of people aged 65-74 (or people aged 75 and over) divided by disposable income of x-y years old.
Source: Calculations from the OECD questionnaire on distribution of household incomes (1999).

Table A.8. **Recipients of means-tested benefits, private pension beneficiaries and amount of benefits, older age groups**
Percentages, mid-90s

		With means-tested benefits	Percentage of the beneficiaries' average disposable income	With private pensions	Percentage of the beneficiaries' average disposable income
Canada	60-64	17.6	29.6	38.8	46.1
	65-69	15.9	10.0	59.1	37.6
	70-74	18.7	7.8	57.3	37.9
	75+	29.4	6.9	47.5	35.2
Finland	60-64	18.3	12.4	4.1	2.0
	65-69	14.2	13.2	..	..
	70-74	15.7	12.7	..	..
	75+	20.7	11.7	..	..
Germany	60-64	10.1	16.0	11.8	15.1
	65-69	7.3	12.3	16.5	19.8
	70-74	..	..	16.7	15.3
	75+	..	..	11.1	20.2
Italy	60-64	..	..	3.5	33.6
	65-69	..	..	5.1	33.0
	70-74	..	..	..	..
	75+	..	..	..	..
Japan	60-64	..	..	8.4	13.6
	65-69	..	..	9.1	11.9
	70-74	..	..	..	..
	75+	..	..	..	..
Netherlands	60-64	11.6	45.1	54.8	97.5
	65-69	..	..	73.6	56.0
	70-74	..	..	77.4	50.3
	75+	12.9	9.3	66.4	43.9
Sweden	60-64	10.5	19.5	59.0	39.5
	65-69	15.7	14.2	89.4	27.5
	70-74	24.9	15.2	83.4	22.9
	75+	41.7	17.9	71.1	23.8
United Kingdom	60-64	20.3	37.9	62.5	45.1
	65-69	17.4	26.9	78.6	39.6
	70-74	26.7	26.1	72.7	38.7
	75+	38.4	29.1	60.7	37.8
United States	60-64	12.3	20.3	39.0	40.2
	65-69	10.9	22.3	49.5	35.9
	70-74	11.0	18.7	51.1	37.0
	75+	11.5	17.5	42.9	32.8

.. Data not available. The cell has samples (unweighted) of less than 50.
Sources: OECD calculations based mainly on data from the Luxembourg Income Study. See Yamada and Casey (2001).

Table A.9. **Percentage of individuals by household type**
Age 65-74 and 75 and over, mid-90s

	Single women living alone		Single persons living with others and the person is not household head		Persons living with spouse and at least one other and neither the person nor spouse is the household head	
	65-74	75+	65-74	75+	65-74	75+
Canada	17.5	31.5	4.7	9.3	1.7	2.0
Finland	26.1	43.4	3.0	8.5	3.7	4.1
Germany	26.8	53.9	1.0	4.7	0.2	0.4
Italy	15.8	28.1	7.0	22.7	2.2	2.9
Japan	9.1	10.6	10.3	35.2	6.6	10.0
Netherlands	24.1	40.4	0.3	1.5	0.0	0.2
United Kingdom	19.1	35.7	2.7	6.7	0.2	0.4
United States	17.8	33.3	4.8	9.2	0.7	1.1

Note: Since the numbers are obtained by income survey data, the numbers could be different from the National Census data.
Sources: OECD calculations based mainly on data from the Luxembourg Income Study. See Yamada and Casey (2001).

Table A.10. **Combination of private and public pension of early retirees and normal retirees**

	Male aged 55-59					Male aged 60-64					Male aged 65-69			
	Percent who are:		As a percentage of average disposable income of working age population		Percent who are:		As a percentage of average disposable income of working age population		Percent who are:		As a percentage of average disposable income of working age population	
	Beneficiaries of public pensions (own)	Beneficiaries of private pensions (own)	Own public pension	Own private pension	Beneficiaries of public pensions (own)	Beneficiaries of private pensions (own)	Own public pension	Own private pension	Beneficiaries of public pensions (own)	Beneficiaries of private pensions (own)	Own public pension	Own private pension
						Non-working pensioners								
Canada	41.5	73.3	11.3	56.5	85.6	63.2	19.2	46.3	99.8	60.7	41.0	30.6
Finland	100.0	1.8	86.3	0.0	100.0	4.1	89.0	0.0	100.0	3.3	95.2	0.0
Germany	97.4	6.0	63.4	6.2	99.3	19.2	66.8	2.1	100.0	16.4	79.3	4.6
Italy	97.7	2.3	93.7	3.2	98.6	4.2	86.3	2.1	97.5	5.2	75.0	4.2
Japan	..	..	..	..	99.4	15.1	56.8	4.1	99.3	12.8	65.2	2.5
Netherlands	..	..	..	..	7.6	95.2	7.3	176.3	95.0	82.7	50.2	52.5
Sweden	79.8	61.1	60.7	27.0	78.6	73.3	63.3	51.6	100.0	88.2	87.8	25.8
United Kingdom	47.0	70.1	0.2	51.3	41.9	80.1	0.2	47.8	99.0	80.7	27.2	36.6
United States	50.4	60.3	20.4	45.8	77.0	60.9	27.2	40.9	96.8	54.4	39.6	27.8
						Working pensioners								
Canada	14.7	85.9	2.3	54.8	75.2	43.5	13.1	32.9	100.0	37.4	33.1	
Finland	100.0	19.9	47.2	0.0	100.0	8.6	39.5	0.0	..	..	..	..
Germany	..	..	..	..	..	..	..	..	..	..	..	..
Italy	85.7	14.3	61.8	29.0	..	..	..	..	..	..	..	..
Japan	0.0	..	..	..	93.4	16.5	36.4	4.6	99.2	7.6	48.0	
Netherlands	..	..	..	..	..	..	..	..	..	..	..	..
Sweden	41.9	85.7	17.5	23.0	69.6	60.3	32.8	27.0	98.6	83.8	75.6	
United Kingdom	0.0	100.0	0.0	93.9	0.0	100.0	0.0	55.3	100.0	81.0	33.4	
United States	7.3	95.9	2.3	70.3	45.2	72.9	12.9	47.3	91.2	45.8	38.0	

Note: The "private" pension is not identifiable in Finnish data, and therefore the numbers are approximations based on household level private income.
.. Data not available. The cell has samples of less than 40.
Sources: OECD calculations based mainly on data from the Luxembourg Income Study. See Yamada and Casey (2001).

Table A.11. **Views on role of government in providing a decent standard of living for the old**
Age, gender and labour force status, 1996

Percentage indicating that it should definitely be the government's responsibility to provide a decent standard of living for the old

	By age group					By gender	
	Under 30	30-39	40-49	50-64	65+	Men	Women
Canada	38.4	47.2	51.0	54.0	62.7	42.0	55.8
Germany	45.6	47.0	46.2	53.7	56.7	46.3	53.3
Italy	69.3	77.9	73.4	78.1	80.4	73.5	77.5
Japan	40.5	42.9	45.9	47.3	48.5	44.6	45.7
Sweden	59.1	57.4	69.7	68.3	80.9	64.2	69.8
United Kingdom	57.9	70.0	71.6	71.7	80.3	66.6	73.1
United States	38.7	36.0	35.3	39.3	41.8	32.8	42.0

	By labour force status					
	Full-time employees	Part-time employees	Unemployed	Retired	Keeping house	Other
Canada	45.4	46.4	35.9	61.7	45.6	52.9
Germany	47.2	48.0	57.3	57.0	53.0	40.3
Italy	74.8	74.1	73.2	81.7	75.4	70.4
Japan	43.5	47.4	. .	51.5	51.8	37.1
Sweden	60.1	65.6	74.1	81.6	. .	70.5
United Kingdom	63.7	68.5	92.4	78.2	71.3	76.2
United States	34.2	36.0	. .	42.1	46.5	51.6

. . Data not available.
Source: ISSP.

Table A.12. **Views on more public retirement spending**
Age, gender and labour force status, 1996

Percentage indicating they would like to see more, or much more, government spending on retirement benefits (being asked to remember that if you say "much more", it might require a tax increase to pay for it)

	By age group					By gender	
	Under 30	30-39	40-49	50-64	65+	Men	Women
Canada	34.8	23.4	24.6	30.5	20.5	24.2	30.0
Germany	45.5	41.6	41.6	48.4	51.7	41.7	49.6
Italy	55.8	60.4	65.8	65.8	75.6	63.5	69.2
Japan	54.6	48.0	53.9	57.9	60.9	55.2	55.8
Sweden	41.7	51.3	51.9	59.8	66.8	45.7	65.2
United Kingdom	63.3	79.2	79.7	79.8	87.1	76.9	78.2
United States	55.0	51.0	45.7	48.9	45.2	46.3	52.0

	By labour force status					
	Full-time employees	Part-time employees	Unemployed	Retired	Keeping house	Other
Canada	24.6	28.6	41.3	22.9	25.7	41.4
Germany	40.2	41.8	61.1	56.3	48.4	42.0
Italy	63.0	65.6	70.3	72.8	68.7	62.9
Japan	53.7	62.9	. .	56.7	57.9	53.2
Sweden	46.3	60.7	59.5	68.2	. .	55.1
United Kingdom	73.6	71.9	76.9	86.9	82.5	78.6
United States	49.9	45.7	. .	42.6	52.6	57.4

. . Data not available.
Source: ISSP.

Table A.13. **Preferences for spending more time in a paid job, 1997**

Percentage that picked "Wanting to spend more time in a paid job" in answer to the question "Suppose you could change the way you spent your time"

	Canada	Germany	Italy	Japan	Netherlands	Sweden	United Kingdom	United States
By age								
Under 30	44.0	22.4	47.3	10.1	39.5	28.6	21.6	38.6
30-39	25.5	15.2	33.8	9.1	25.2	11.2	20.6	25.5
40-49	20.8	19.5	22.4	11.9	23.8	12.6	9.8	15.5
50-64	16.5	15.7	31.9	6.0	12.7	8.8	9.8	21.1
65+	5.5	9.3	21.4	2.6	2.6	8.3	3.0	11.1
By labour force status								
Full-time job	11.0	8.0	15.0	5.1	9.8	3.6	3.0	18.9
Part-time job	49.3	16.1	35.1	12.5	30.5	33.3	21.5	31.5
Unemployed	50.7	46.6	91.3	..	51.7	45.7	46.2	57.9
Retired	8.2	10.4	22.2	2.7	2.9	8.7	3.6	11.4
Keeping house	31.6	32.5	45.0	12.0	24.8	..	24.8	30.0

.. Data not available.
Source: ISSP 1997.

Table A.14. **Proportion of households reporting market wealth, mid-90s**
Couple households

Pre-retirement age

	Financial wealth						Housing wealth					
		Income quintile						Income quintile				
	All	1	2	3	4	5	All	1	2	3	4	5
Canada[a]	..	..	..	..	..	..	88	81	85	90	87	96
Finland	81	78	84	87	78	79	90	79	91	93	90	97
Germany	98	93	98	98	99	99	59	40	50	55	66	83
Italy	96	88	95	98	99	100	83	68	79	84	89	96
Japan	97	94	97	97	99	97	84	74	78	84	93	90
Netherlands	99	99	99	100	100	100	60	47	42	57	68	84
Sweden	100	98	100	100	100	100	84	74	82	85	88	92
United Kingdom	76	58	63	79	90	93	81	76	71	80	89	88
United States	95	83	95	97	99	99	90	75	90	94	95	95

Post-retirement age

	Financial wealth						Housing wealth					
		Income quintile						Income quintile				
	All	1	2	3	4	5	All	1	2	3	4	5
Canada[a]	..	..	..	..	..	..	85	80	81	82	87	93
Finland	83	81	81	86	84	83	92	93	90	85	92	99
Germany	97	93	96	99	99	99	58	46	48	49	63	82
Italy	93	79	91	95	100	100	82	70	79	83	85	95
Japan	99	99	100	99	99	99	92	82	91	94	95	97
Netherlands	99	100	100	98	100	98	41	40	20	31	44	69
Sweden	98	94	98	99	100	100	75	69	64	69	86	88
United Kingdom	81	66	71	83	90	96	78	74	67	79	79	93
United States	91	74	90	94	97	98	88	75	86	93	93	95

.. Data not available.
a) Numbers of households reporting housing wealth in Canada are obtained by the OECD calculations based on the data from the Luxembourg Income Study.
Source: OECD Wealth Data.

Table A.15. **Earnings of the average production worker, 1998**

	National currency	US dollars at PPP[a]
Canada	35 000	30 200
Finland	140 600	23 300
Germany	59 500	29 600
Italy	38 873 400	24 000
Japan	4 203 500	25 800
Netherlands	57 500	27 800
Sweden	215 500	22 400
United Kingdom	17 500	26 600
United States	29 100	29 100

Note: All values rounded to the nearest hundred.
a) Conversion to dollars uses OECD purchasing power parities, net of taxes and social security contributions.
Source: OECD (2000c).

Table A.16. **Maximum pensionable earnings and maximum pension benefits**

	Percentage of average earnings	
	Maximum earnings	Maximum benefits
Canada	107	44
Sweden	130	72
United Kingdom	144	44
Japan	167	75
Germany	171	50
United States	250	73
Italy	365	135
Finland	..	..
Netherlands	..	..

.. No ceiling.
Source: OECD Secretariat calculations.

Table A.17. **Concessions to the elderly in personal income tax systems**

Canada	Age credit	Credit of 17% to maximum of nearly $2 500. Withdrawn at 15% rate between approximately $26 000 and $49 000
	Private pension/annuity income	Tax relief on up to $1 000
	Guaranteed income supplement	No tax on this income-tested benefit
Finland	Age deduction: local income tax	Deduction of around FM 34 000 for a single person and around FM 29 000 for each partner in a couple
	Age deduction: central government income tax	Deduction of FM 23 000. Both allowance withdrawn at 70% by amount which pension exceeds the deduction
Germany	Private pension income	40% of benefit not taxable up to ceilings (DM 6 000 for occupational plans, DM 3 700 for personal schemes)
Italy	Private pension income	12.5% of occupational pension benefits not taxable; 40% with personal pension
Japan	Age deduction	If over 65 flat of ¥0.5 m plus ¥0.48 m for local tax up to total income ¥10 m. If dependent household member or spouse is above 70, ¥0.48 m plus ¥0.38 m for local tax.
	Pensioner deduction	Disability or survivors pension tax-free. Other pensions subject to flat rate plus varying rate tax, with level depending on age and income. No tax if below 65 and income below ¥0.7 m, or if above 65 and income below ¥1.4 m.
	Lump sum retirement benefit deduction	All lump sum retirement benefit eligible for tax relief. Amount depends on the length of service – if below 20 years, min. ¥0.4 m, if 20 or more years, min. ¥8.7 m.
Netherlands	Age deduction	Additional allowance of around NLG 500; increased to NLG 2 200 for incomes under NLG 57 000
	Pensioner deduction	Additional deduction for recipients of basic pension; worth NLG 500 or NLG 3 100 for low-income pensioners
Sweden	Age deduction	Varies between SKr 8 700 and SKr 56 000 depending on pension income
United Kingdom	Age deduction	Additional deduction between around £1 400 and £1 600 depending on age; withdrawn at 50% above *circa* £17 000
United States	Age deduction	Additional deduction of around $1 000 for a single person
	Tax credit	Up to $1 125; withdrawn once total income exceeds $17 500 or untaxed public pension exceeds $5 000
	Social security relief	Between 15% and 50% of social security is not taxed depending on total income

Note: Most values have been rounded for simplicity.
Source: OECD Secretariat.

Table A.18. **Defined-benefit occupational pensions in Canada, the United Kingdom and the United States**

	Canada	United Kingdom	United States
Earnings measure	Final salary (70%)	Final salary (95%)	Final salary (55%)
Vesting	2 to 5 years' service	2 years' service	5 years' service
Pension age	65	65	65 (47%)
Accrual rate	2% a year (70%)	1.25% a year (65%)	1.5% a year
Integration method	1.3% accrual up to public benefit ceiling	Deduct value of basic state pension (12%)	Lower accrual rate on earnings covered by public benefit
Pre-retirement indexation	None	Price inflation	None
Post-retirement indexation	Half price inflation	Price inflation	None

Source: OECD Secretariat.

Table A.19. **Data sources and definitions for Tables 4.3, 4.4 and 4.5**

Data source

Data source	Definition of size of challenge	
Table 4.3		
Percentage of total population that is employed from Table A.3 in the Statistical Annex. Current estimate – to avoid the unrepresentative high unemployment in some countries in the mid-1990s.	Relatively large challenge: Relatively moderate challenge: Relatively small challenge:	– under 40% employed – 40 to 49% – 50% and over
Ratio of retired people to employed people, current estimate from Table A.3 in the Statistical Annex. Retired people are defined as those aged 55 and over who are not employed.	Relatively large challenge: Relatively moderate challenge: Relatively small challenge:	– 0.45 or more – 0.40 to 0.44 – under 0.40
Public pension spending, current estimate from Table 4.1. Current old-age pension spending as a percentage of GDP	Relatively large challenge: Relatively moderate challenge: Relatively small challenge:	– 10% or more – 6 to 9% – under 6%
Public pension spending (future change), change from 2000 to peak spending on old-age pensions as a percentage of GDP from Table 4.1.	Relatively large challenge: Relatively moderate challenge: Relatively small challenge:	– 4% or more – 2 to 4% – under 2%
Duration of complete retirement, men, most recent year, from Table 5.1.	Relatively large challenge: Relatively moderate challenge: Relatively small challenge:	– durations of more than 18 years – of 15 to 18 years – under 15 years
Change in age of withdrawal from labour force in last several years from Chart 5.2.	Relatively large challenge: Relatively moderate challenge: Relatively small challenge:	– average age decreasing – average age steady – average age rising
Percentage of workforce aged 55 and over – change 2000 to 2030 (middle scenario) from Chart 5.4.	Relatively large challenge: Relatively moderate challenge: Relatively small challenge:	– more than 60% growth – 25 to 60% growth – under 25% growth
Percentage of total male population aged 65 and over that work part-time, from Table 5.4.	Relatively large challenge: Relatively moderate challenge: Relatively small challenge:	– under 2% – 2 to 4% growth – over 4%
Table 4.4		
Public social expenditure related to the retirement population in 1995, from Chart 6.1.	Relatively large challenge: Relatively moderate challenge: Relatively small challenge:	– over 13% of GDP – between 7 and 13% – under 7%
Size of largest component (among working income, capital income and public transfers, mid-1990s), from Chart 2.5.	Relatively large challenge: Relatively moderate challenge: Relatively small challenge:	– 75% and over – 50 to 74% – under 50%
Share of capital income in total retirement income, from Chart 2.5, mid-1990s. Excludes investment income from reserves within public plans.	Relatively large challenge: Relatively moderate challenge: Relatively small challenge:	– under 10% – 10 to 40% – over 40%
Table 4.5		
Quasi replacement rates from Table 2.1. Mean disposable income of people aged 65-74 as a percentage of those aged 51-64 in mid-1990s.	Relatively large challenge: Relatively moderate challenge: Relatively small challenge:	– under 70% – 70 to 79% – 80% and over
Percentage below low-income cut-off lines from Chart 2.2. People aged 65 and over in mid-1990s.	Relatively large challenge: Relatively moderate challenge: Relatively small challenge:	– 20% and over – 10 to 19% – under 10%
Situation of lowest quintile from Chart 2.1. Disposable income of lowest quintile of those aged 65 and over as a percentage of mean disposable income of the working-age population, mid-1990s.	Relatively large challenge: Relatively moderate challenge: Relatively small challenge:	– under 30% – 30 to 39% – 40% and over

Source: OECD Secretariat.

Ageing and Income

Chart A.1. **Retirees/employees ratio and social expenditure as a percentage of GDP**
1980, 1990 and 1995

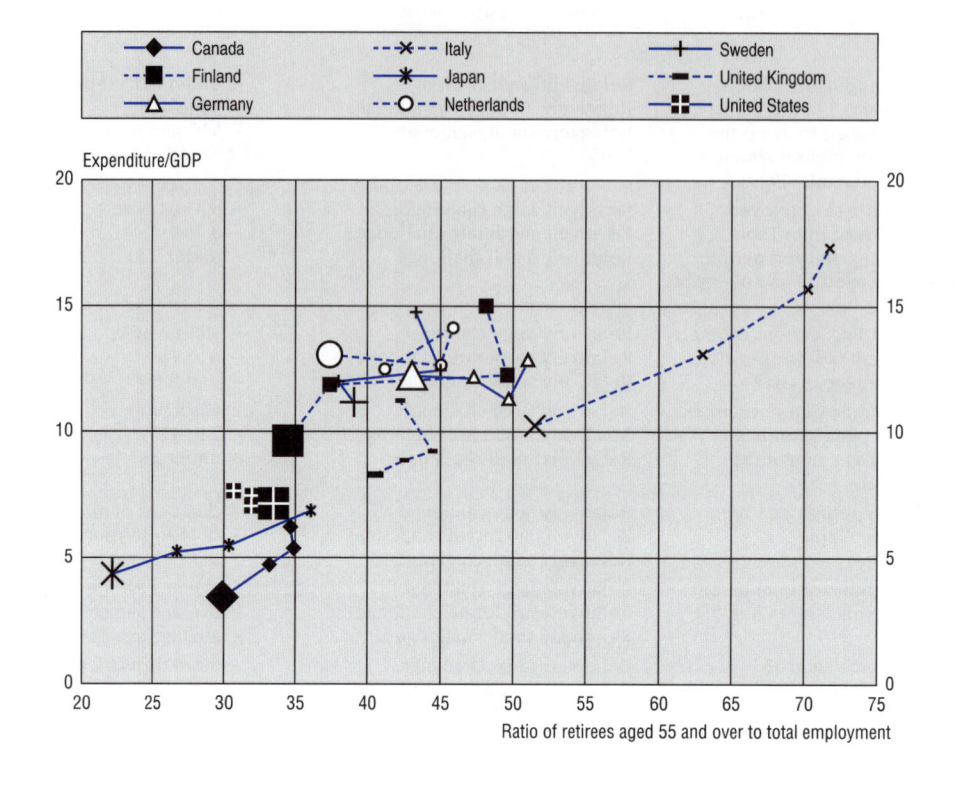

Note: 1980 is represented by a larger marker.
Sources: OECD Secretariat estimates and OECD social expenditure database.

Chart A.2. **Percentage of young adults living with parents**

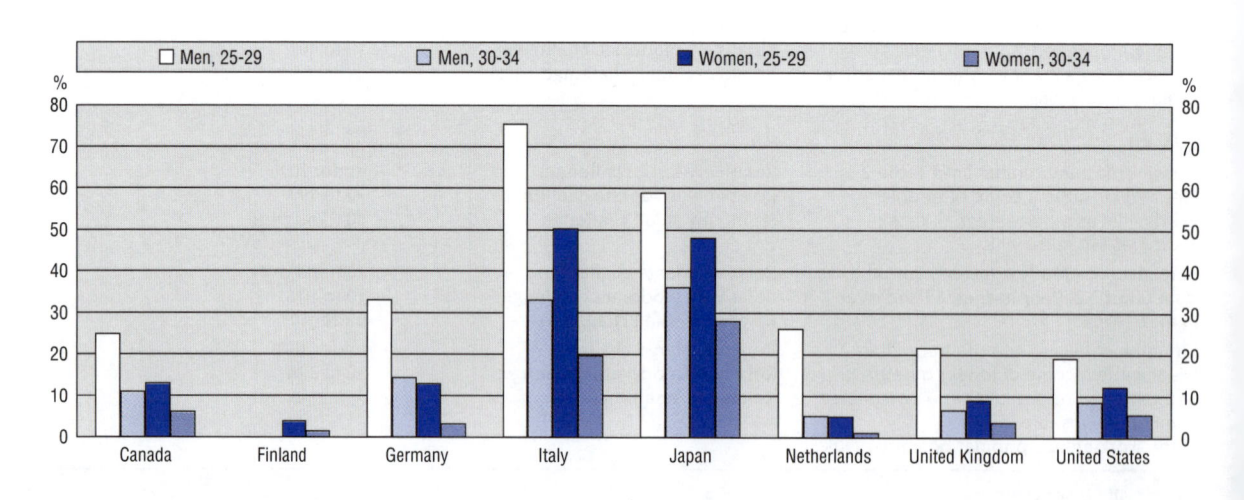

Note: The coding of the relationship to household head is based on an original definition of each country. Since the numbers are obtained by income survey data, the numbers could be different from the National Census data.
Sources: OECD calculations based mainly on data from the Luxembourg Income Study. See Yamada and Casey (2001).

© OECD 2001

Annex III

Chart A.3. **Percentage of workers (without a pension) and early retirees (not at work, with a pension), by income quintile**

Population of quintiles as a percentage of each category, mid-90s

Men, age 60-64

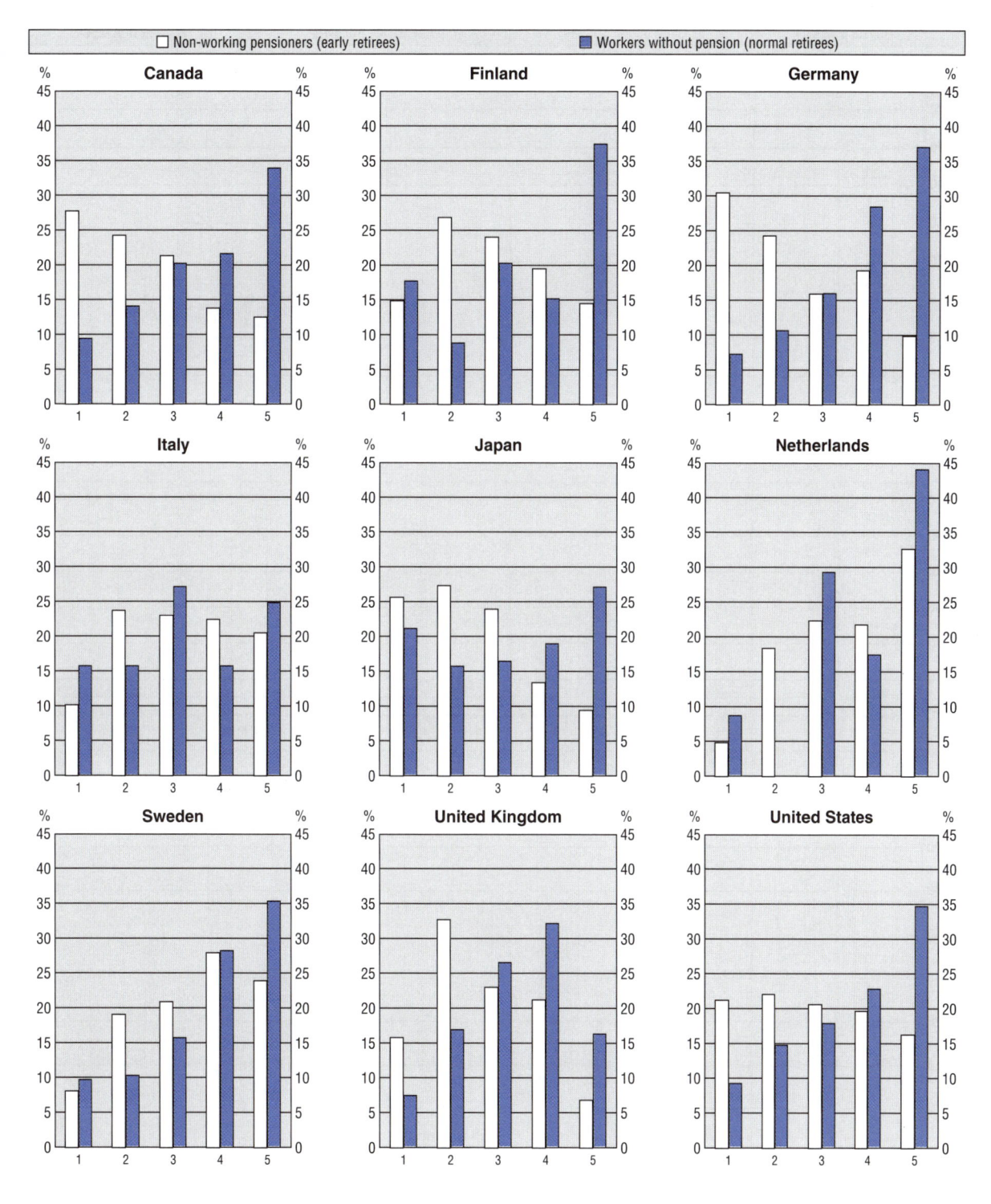

□ Non-working pensioners (early retirees) ■ Workers without pension (normal retirees)

Note: The sample size of "workers without pension" for the Netherlands is below 50.
Sources: OECD calculations based mainly on data from the Luxembourg Income Study. See Yamada and Casey (2001).

Chart A.4. **Income composition by quintile**
Age 65+, percentage of adjusted disposable income of each quintile, mid-90s

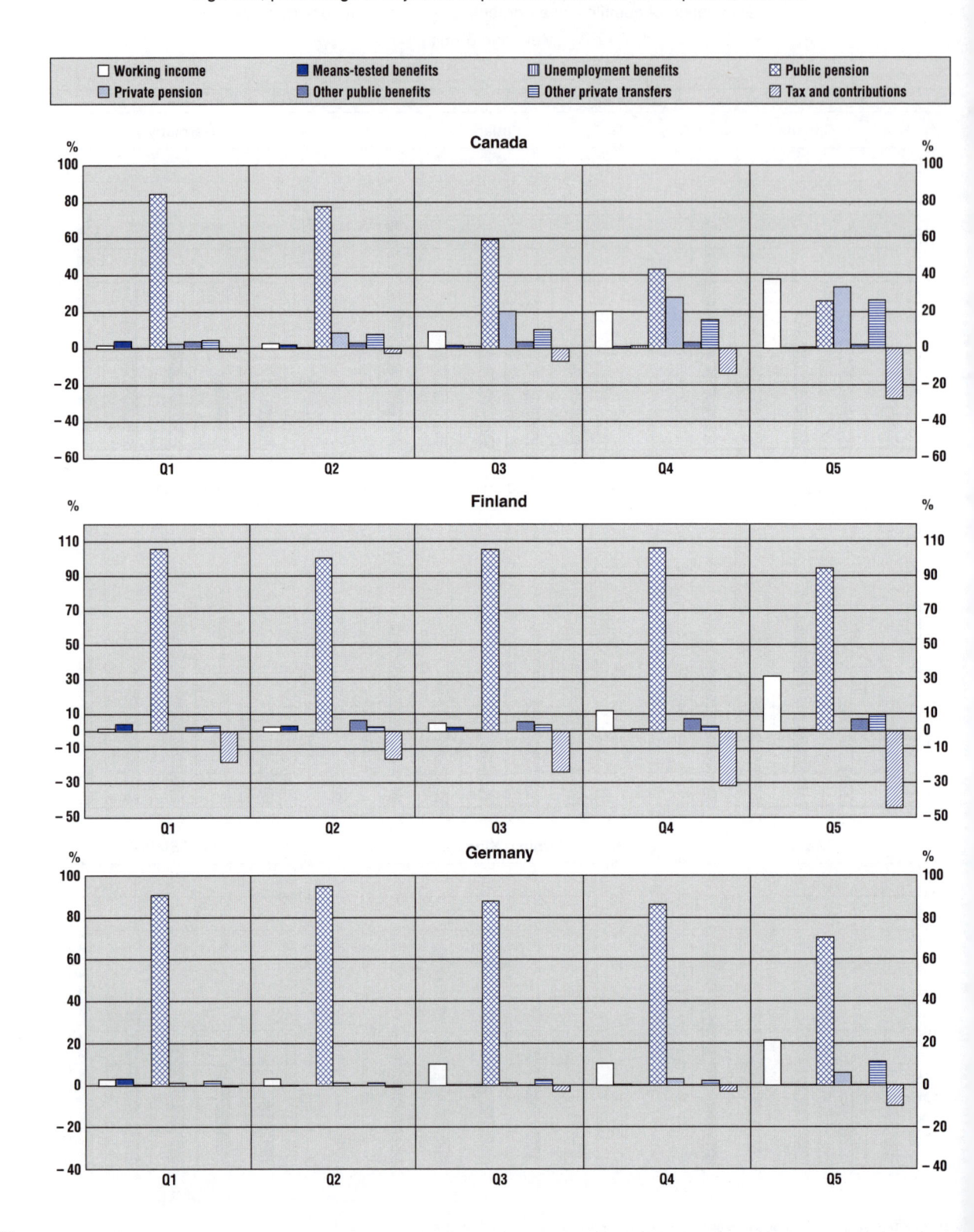

Legend: Working income | Means-tested benefits | Unemployment benefits | Public pension | Private pension | Other public benefits | Other private transfers | Tax and contributions

Canada

Finland

Germany

Sources: OECD calculations based mainly on data from the Luxembourg Income Study. See Yamada and Casey (2001).

Annex III

Chart A.4. **Income composition by quintile** *(cont.)*
Age 65+, percentage of adjusted disposable income of each quintile, mid-90s

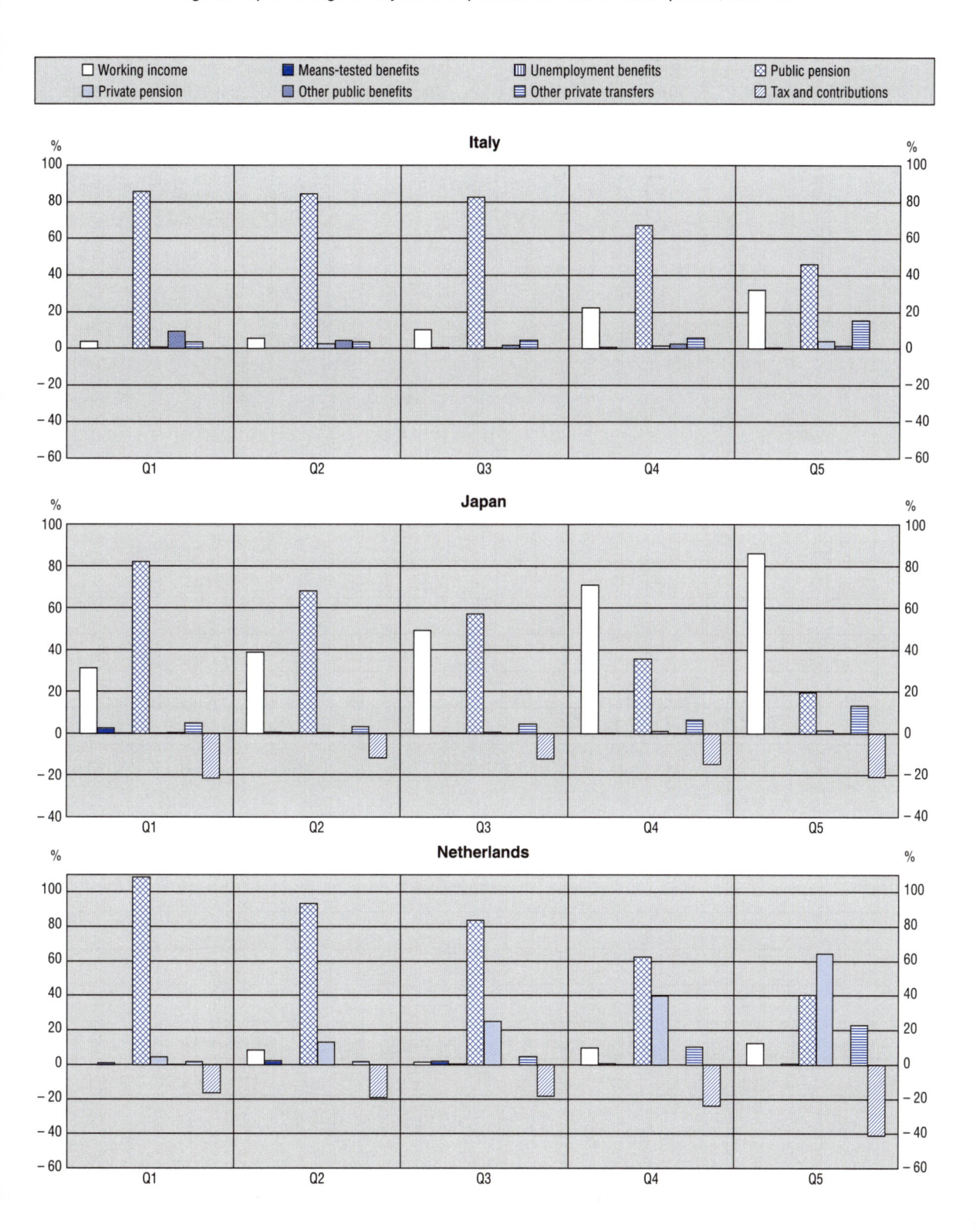

☐ Working income   ■ Means-tested benefits   ▥ Unemployment benefits   ▨ Public pension
☐ Private pension   ■ Other public benefits   ☰ Other private transfers   ▨ Tax and contributions

Italy

Japan

Netherlands

Sources: OECD calculations based mainly on data from the Luxembourg Income Study. See Yamada and Casey (2001).

Ageing and Income

Chart A.4. Income composition by quintile *(cont.)*
Age 65+, percentage of adjusted disposable income of each quintile, mid-90s

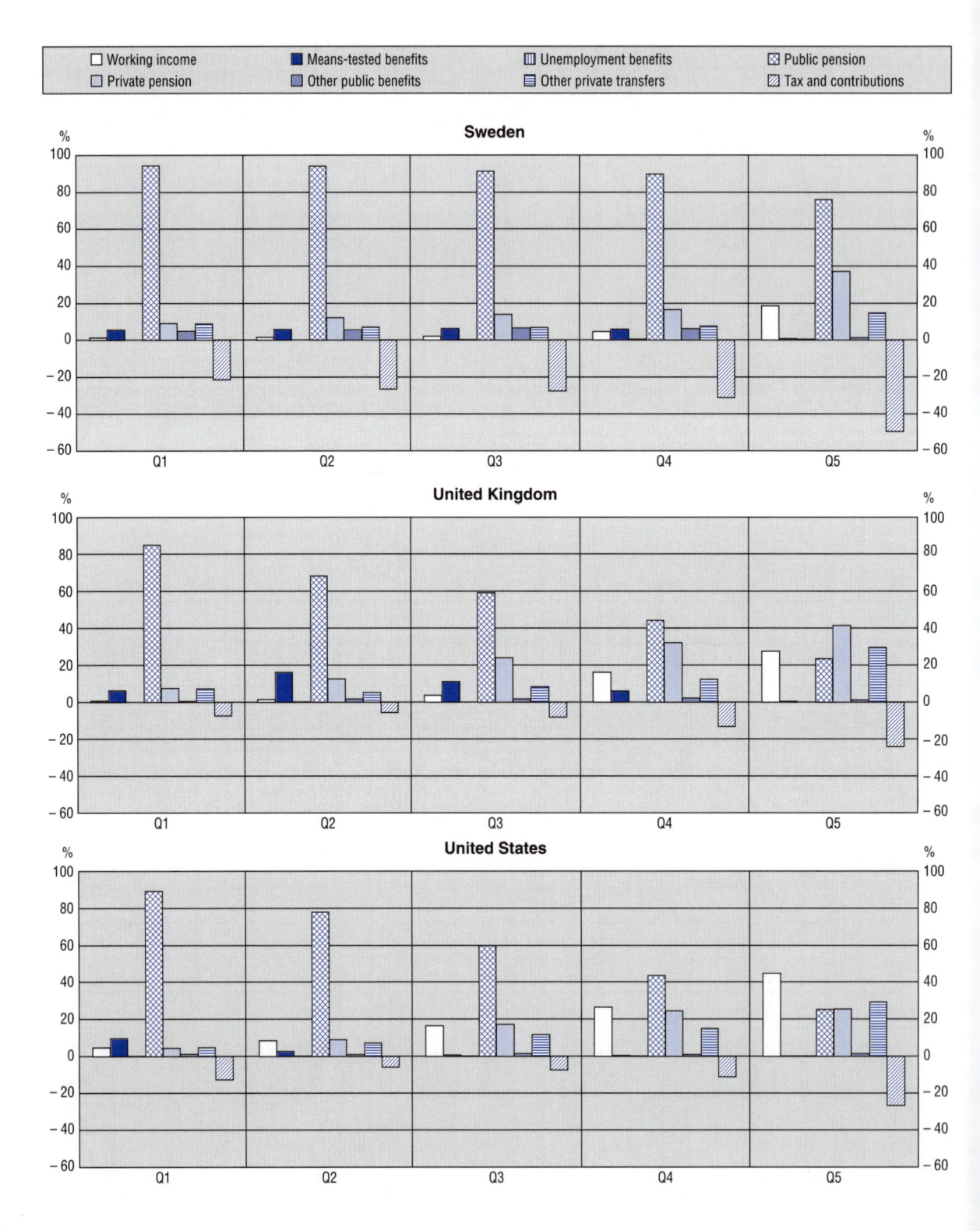

- ☐ Working income
- ■ Means-tested benefits
- ⊞ Unemployment benefits
- ⊠ Public pension
- ☐ Private pension
- ☐ Other public benefits
- ☰ Other private transfers
- ⧄ Tax and contributions

Sweden

United Kingdom

United States

Sources: OECD calculations based mainly on data from the Luxembourg Income Study. See Yamada and Casey (2001).

Annex III

Chart A.5. **Pensioners who work and who do not work by income quintile, age 60 to 64**
Population of quintiles as a percentage of each category, mid-90s

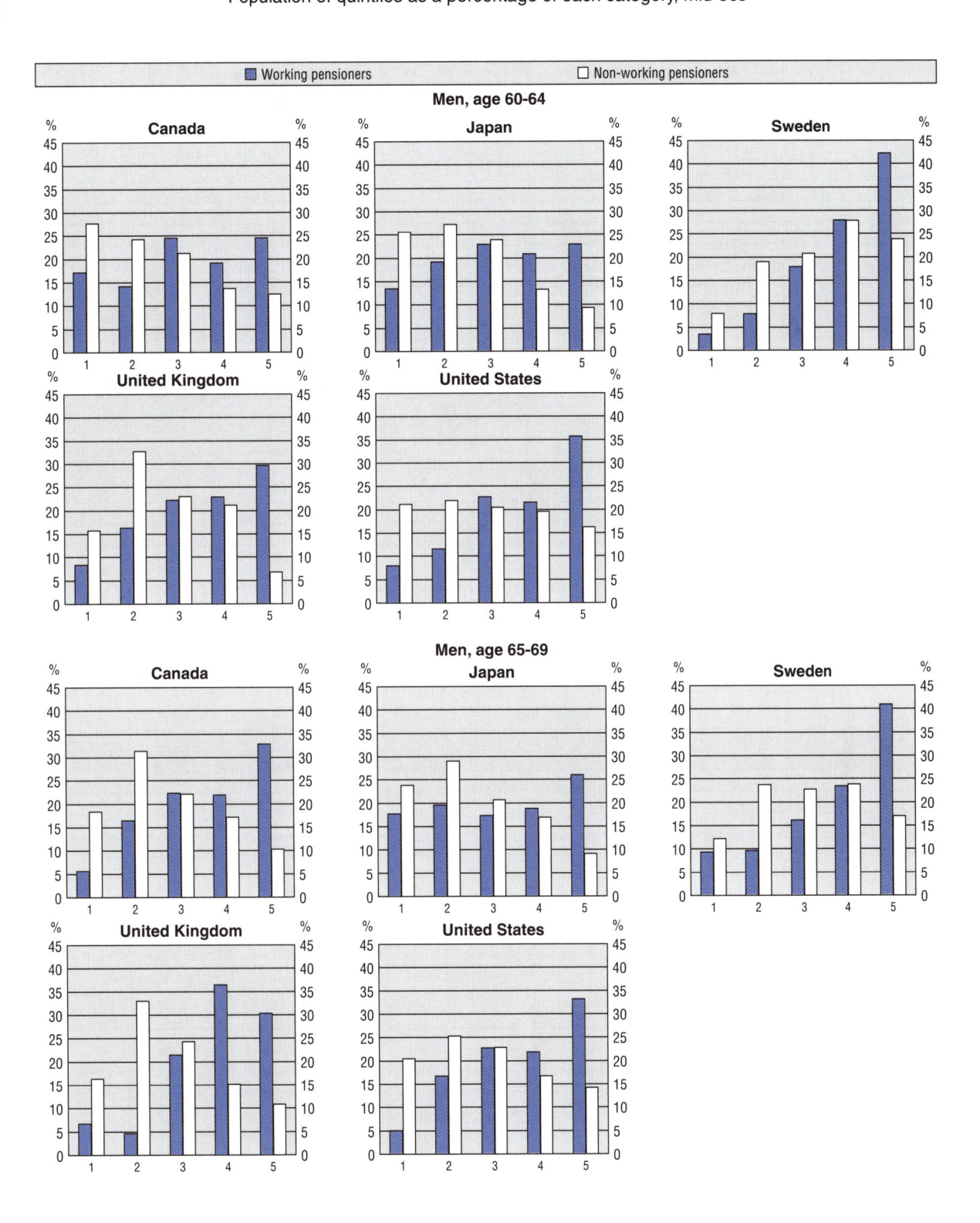

■ Working pensioners   □ Non-working pensioners

Men, age 60-64

Men, age 65-69

Note: The countries where the working pensioners are not important are excluded.
Sources: OECD calculations based mainly on data from the Luxembourg Income Study. See Yamada and Casey (2001).

Ageing and Income

Chart A.6. Recipients of private and public pensions, by income quintile
Population of quintiles as a percentage of each category, mid-90s

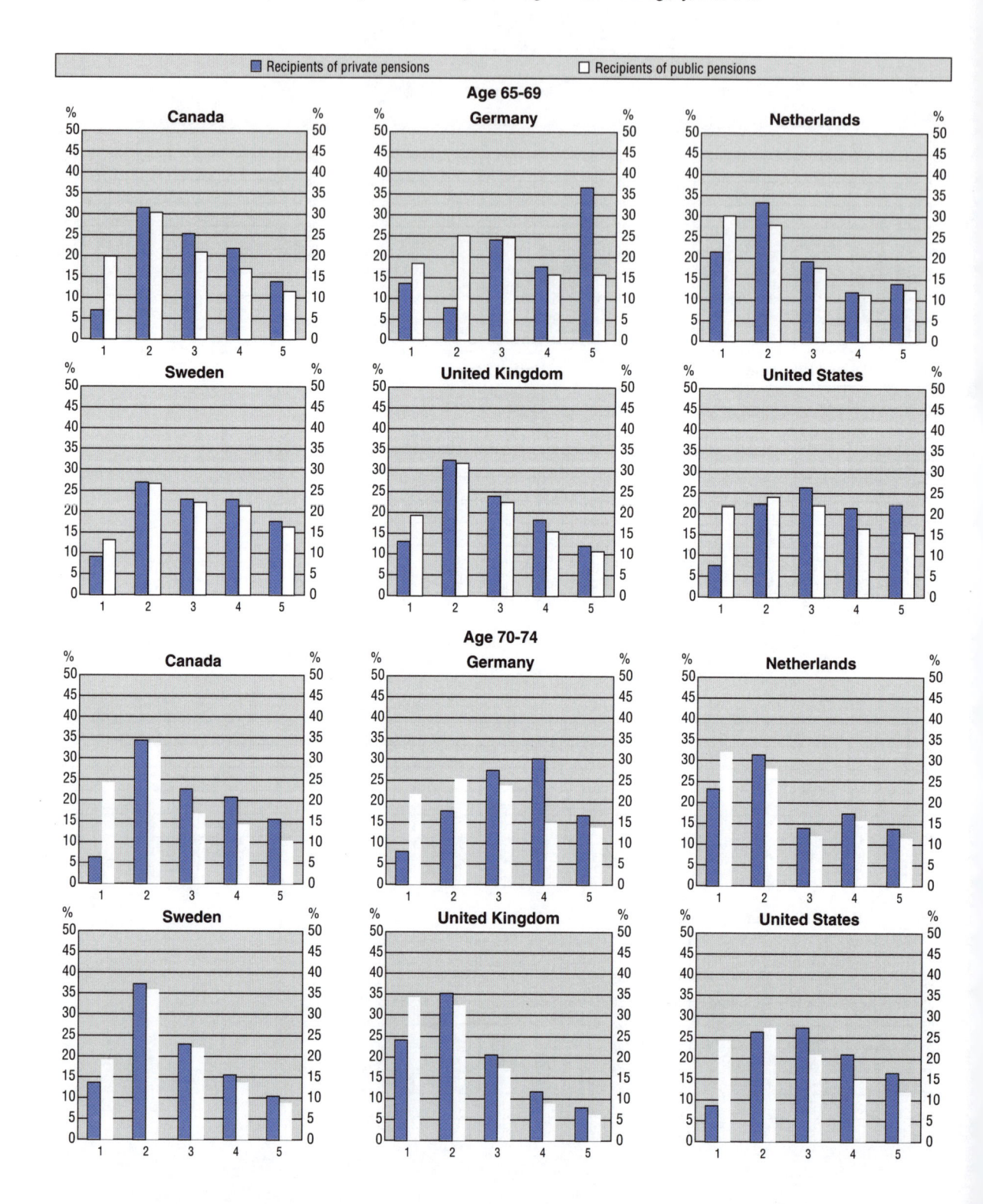

Note: The countries where the beneficiaries are below 10 per cent of the age category are excluded because of limited sample size.
Sources: OECD calculations based mainly on data from the Luxembourg Income Study. See Yamada and Casey (2001).

Annex III

Chart A.7. **Percentage of population that is above the middle-upper income cut-off line**[a]
Mid-90s

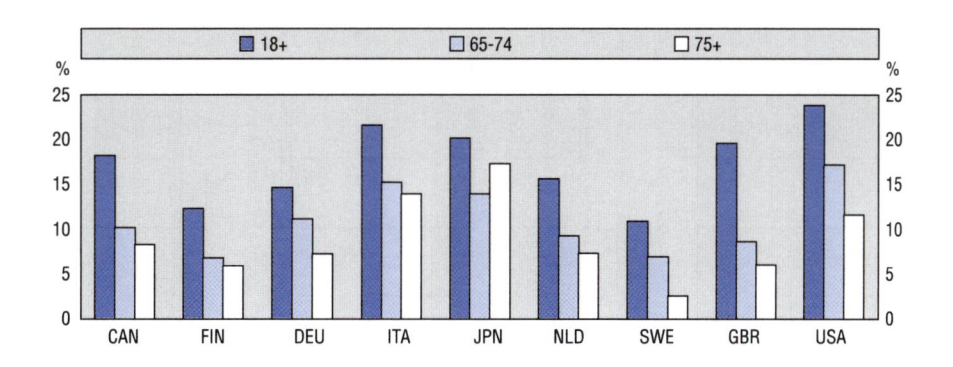

a) The middle-upper income cut-off line is 150% of the median disposable income of age 18-64.
Sources: OECD calculations based mainly on data from the Luxembourg Income Study. See Yamada and Casey (2001).

Ageing and Income

Chart A.8. Workers per retiree, 1970, 2000 and three scenarios in 2030
Retirees defined as people aged 55 and over who are not employed

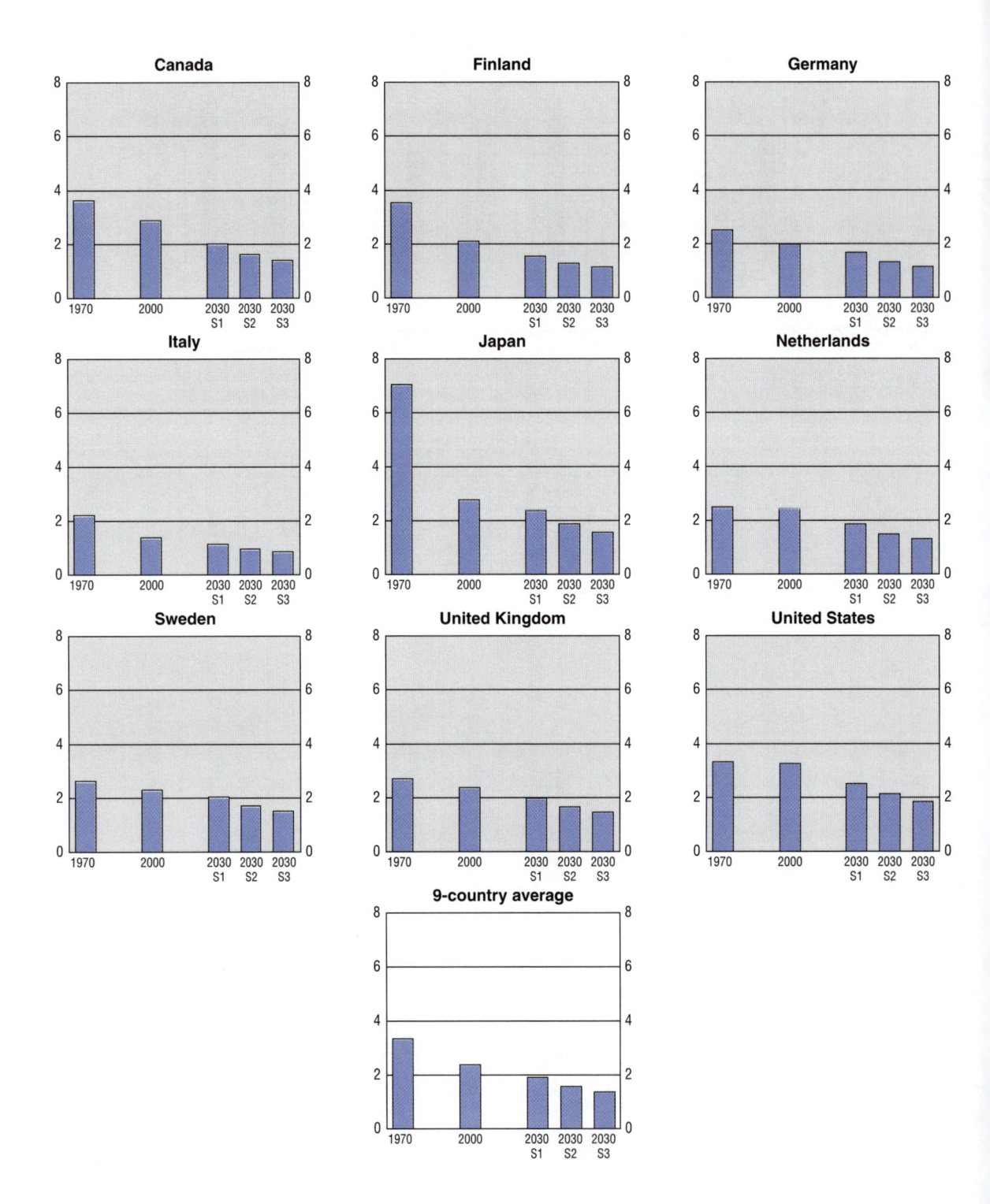

Note: The 9-country average is an unweighted average. For definitions of the 3 scenarios (S1, S2 and S3), see Section 5.2 in Chapter 5.
Source: OECD Secretariat estimates.

Annex III

Chart A.9. **Percentage of total population that is employed**
1970, 2000 and three scenarios in 2030

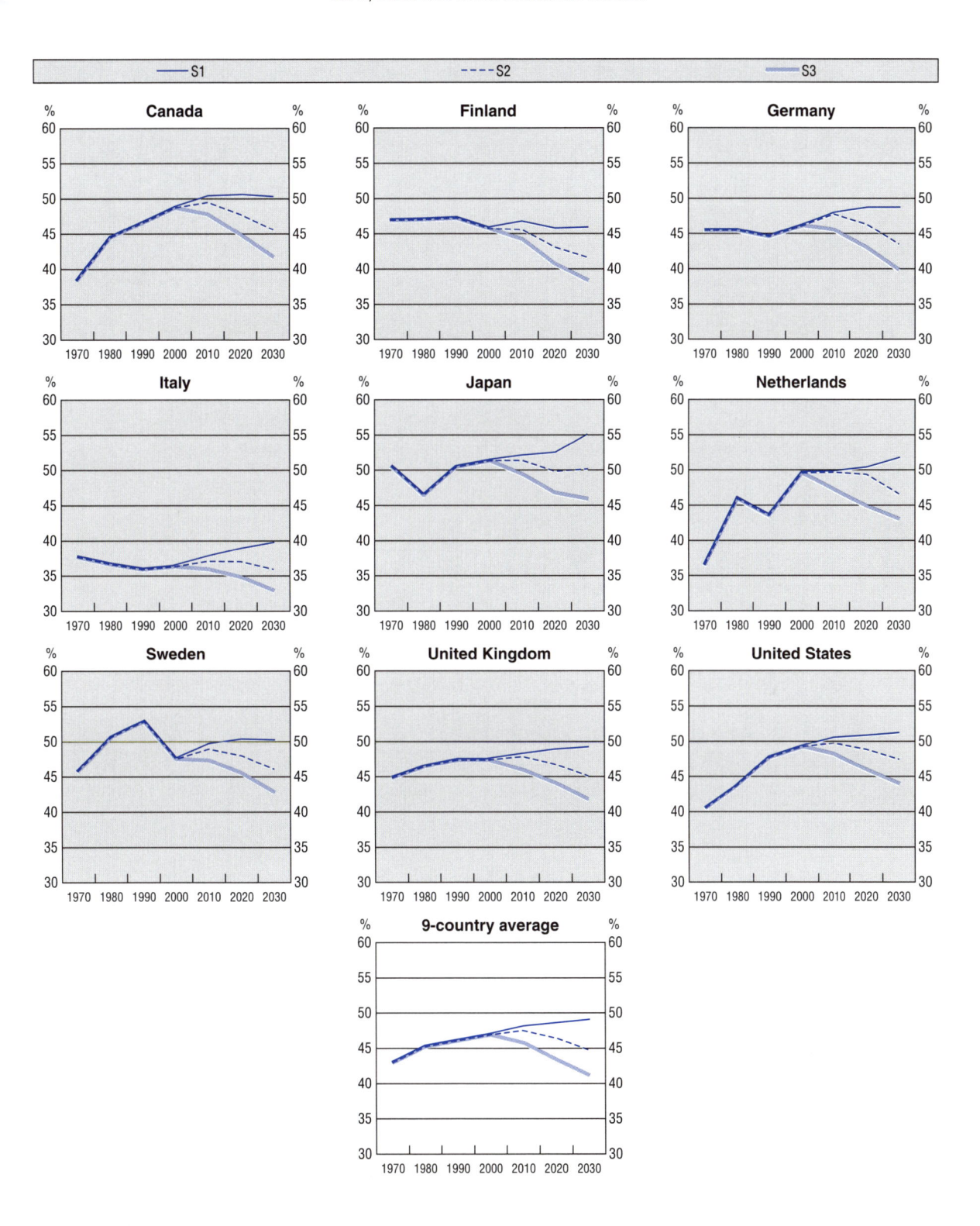

Note: The 9-country average is an unweighted average. For definition of the three scenarios (S1, S2 and S3), see Section 5.2. in Chapter 5.
Source: OECD Secretariat estimates.

OECD Online Services

PERIODICALS • STUDIES • STATISTICS

SourceOECD
www.SourceOECD.org

A single institutional subscription provides unlimited access to OECD books, periodicals and statistics online 24 hours a day, 7 days a week

OECD direct
www.oecd.org/OECDdirect

Stay informed with our free e-mail alerting services, personalised to your interests

OECD ONLINE BOOKSHOP
www.oecd.org/bookshop

Your gateway to our extensive catalogue of books, and statistics on CD-Rom – and now, pay-per-view

www.oecd.org

sales@oecd.org
sourceoecd@oecd.org

OECD

OECD PUBLICATIONS, 2, rue André-Pascal, 75775 PARIS CEDEX 16
PRINTED IN FRANCE
(81 2001 12 1 P) ISBN 92-64-19542-4 – No. 52145 2001